The ETHICS of DISCOURSE

THE SOCIAL PHILOSOPHY OF JOHN COURTNEY MURRAY

The ETHICS of DISCOURSE

THE SOCIAL PHILOSOPHY OF JOHN COURTNEY MURRAY

J. Leon Hooper, S.J.

Georgetown University Press

Bx
1753
.H63
1986

Library of Congress Cataloging-in-Publication Data

Hooper, J. Leon.
  The ethics of discourse.

  Bibliography: p.
  Includes index.
  1. Murray, John Courtney—Contributions in social
ethics.   2. Social ethics—History—20th century.
3. Sociology, Christian (Catholic)—History—20th
century.   I. Title.
BX1753.H63   1986   241'.042'0924   86-18362
ISBN 0-87840-438-4
ISBN 0-87840-416-3 (pbk.)

Contents

FOREWORD

In the years since the close of the Second Vatican Council in 1965, the Roman Catholic Church has played an increasingly vigorous role in the social ethical debates of our time. Numerous statements by the popes during their worldwide travels, the engagement of U.S. bishops in moral questions concerning strategic nuclear policy, human rights, abortion, and economic justice, and the writings of liberation theologians in developing countries are all highly visible examples of church efforts to contribute to the building of a society that supports the dignity of men and women everywhere. All this activity testifies to heightened Catholic participation in what Martin Marty has called "the public church"—"a family of apostolic churches with Jesus Christ at the center, churches which are especially sensitive to the *res publica*, the public order that surrounds and includes people of faith."

Both the history of Western Christianity and of nearly all other faith communities shows that the presence of religion and religious people in public affairs is nothing new. But history and contemporary political experience should alert us to the ambiguous nature of religious engagement in matters of great social import. Religious communities can be sources of great good or considerable harm for the commonweal when they "go public." Thus the emergence of communities of faith as high profile actors on the social stage is a source both of hope and of apprehension for many today.

Leon Hooper's excellent study, *The Ethics of Discourse*, provides a rich and sustained reflection on how the church can realize its potential as a positive force for justice and human dignity while avoiding moralistic oversimplification of public debates. *The Ethics of Discourse* is a probing analysis of the writings of John Courtney Murray, the preeminent practitioner of public theology and public moral discourse in the whole history of American Catholicism.

On one level, Hooper's study is an urgently needed reminder of the giant contribution Murray made to the Catholic Church's understanding of its religious and moral mission in a pluralistic society. The relation of church to state and the meaning of religious freedom were, of course, central to Murray's intellectual achievements. This achievement was affirmed in ringing tones by Vatican II's *Declaration on Religious Freedom*. In the present environment of confusion about the proper relation between religion and politics in the United States, nothing could be more salutary than for those unfamiliar with Murray's writings to be introduced to them. For those who read Murray in the 1950s and 1960s, Hooper's book is an important invitation to return to him once again.

On a second level, *The Ethics of Discourse* is a moving portrait of the growth and maturation of a great theological and ethical mind. Previous book-length studies of Murray have presented more or less objective and chronological accounts of the development of this thinking. Hooper moves our understanding of Murray to a deeper level. He takes us to the plane of Murray's understanding of his own task as a theologian both within the church and in the public life of the larger society. Hooper's attention to the influence exerted on Murray by his fellow Jesuit Bernard Lonergan is especially valuable. Lonergan's philosophical and theological method was marked by a "turn to the subject," a recognition that all knowledge is inseparable from the people who do the knowing. And since all "knowers" are immersed in the flow of history, coming to knowledge of the truth is always historically and socially situated. Hooper probes beneath the surface of Murray's writings to show us Murray the man engaged in such a quest for theological, social, and political truth. *The Ethics of Discourse* thus presents us with a model for pursuing the theological and ethical task in areas that reach far beyond the set of questions Murray dealt with in his lifetime. It reveals the work of the theologian as a high adventure of the mind and a deep affair of the heart.

Finally, Hooper distills from Murray's writings and personal example several conclusions about the *mode* of Christian engagement in public life that are of particular importance today. Chief among them is the central theme expressed in the title of this book. The church's participation in public debates must be governed by ethical criteria rooted in responsible love of *all* one's neighbors. The task of public discourse and public argument is first and foremost to meet and then support the moral agency of the citizens of the commonwealth. This means that persuasion, not coercion or manipulation, must be the hallmark of the Christian community's public style. In some circumstances, we must reluctantly rely on the coercive power of law, because of human sinfulness and frailty. Nevertheless, a truly theological understanding of Christian public engagement must begin with the conviction that God's presence and God's truth are not exclusively confined to the Catholic Church and its traditions and institutions. For this reason, efforts to shape public affairs that have not been tested by the rigors of intelligent public argument that presupposes the good will of one's neighbors risk degenerating into ideology or self-deception. We have seen more than enough of this sort of thing in recent years, and Hooper is right to call it immoral. John Courtney Murray lived out an ethic of public discourse in a self-conscious way, especially during and after Vatican II. In making this ethic explicit, Hooper's book will bring rich rewards to all who have been the beneficiaries of the great Murray legacy. It will help them shoulder the responsibility of carrying this inheritance forward in new historical and social contexts.

David Hollenbach, S.J.
Weston School of Theology.

Introduction

Finding the Social in Social Ethics

The Olympic relay runner who, at the starting blocks for a race, is currently debating between three untried methods of stride placement, will not likely help his team advance beyond the first qualifying rounds. The race is the time for concentration on intermediate and final goals—on covering the distance, on smooth baton passes, on crossing the finish line. The starting gun does not signal a time for experimenting with new technical methods. The public competitor must focus attention on specific, concrete ends.

Nevertheless, periods of extended attention to technical method are important. Unless our runner has come to know the three forms of stride placement, has tried them out and integrated them into his or her semiautomatic responses, the runner's full potential as a racer cannot be reached. Through such training, the runner comes to recognize his or her own physiological constitution and the most effective methods for harnessing its potential. Training helps the runner learn something new about oneself, and particularly about one's own body. Moreover, practice sessions can open up other necessary perspectives for the runner. Beyond knowledge of one's own makeup, concentration on technique further trains the runner to notice other relevant situational factors, such as the changing conditions of the track and the differing abilities of the other runners. Without an acquired ability to understand the people and the track, the runner's responses will be inadequate. Experimentation in method, then, helps the runner to develop a wisdom, an ability to read the field, to recognize the important changing elements that make up that field, and to react appropriately to them.

Yet, technical training and a growing ability at application do not exhaust the requirements for successful competition. No matter how single-minded the runner, he or she lives within a web of human interactions, all qualified by general, rather elusive attitudes toward surrounding peoples. There are attitudes toward the runner's own team members, and toward those of the competing teams. Actions must be taken prior to the qualifying rounds to build up a sense of the team in mutual support and challenge, or the team's collective response will be fragmented. And beyond the personal relations with team members and competitors swirl the complex human relations of

1

each racer with family and friends, sponsors and spectators. Most coaches at one time or another must act as counselors, recognizing the impact that attitudes toward individuals and groups have on concrete competitive performance. The coach or runner who ignores either technical training or the interpersonal attitudes that surround competitive performance operates at a disadvantage.

This book is a discussion of public ethical argument—the attempt to place in public consciousness an awareness of socially important values and, through that consciousness, to construct institutions that will support, not hinder, the development of those values. While both the ethical arguer and the competitive runner operate in social worlds, their worlds do significantly differ. First, the social arguer's world of action is broader than the runner's in that the former's range of conversational partners must include all who can have an impact on the setting of large-scale social directions. The difference here is one of the sheer numbers of participants. Second, that world is also more complex in that both the range of goals to be pursued and the differing attitudes of the multiple actors far exceeds the diversity of a group united around athletic competition. And third, the arguer's world is more conflict ridden, not only because of its scope and diversity, but also because membership in the arguer's social world and participation in burdens and benefits of that world are much closer to the nonvoluntary than are membership and participation in the runner's world. We can easily, with little personal cost, walk away from the world of athletic competition, as contestants or as spectators and supporters. But the cost of absenting ourselves from our social world impels most of us to fight when someone challenges our membership or adversely affects the proportion of our burdens and benefits.

Today, many social arguers are unaware of, or ignore, the technical factors and human attitudes that must enter into the pursuit of social goals. We more often concentrate on specific ends, and even more narrowly on single means for attaining those ends. In the process we miss the full range of ethically relevant elements that must enter into social ethical action—particularly the distinctly social realities that are intrinsic, not incidental, to the task of social ethics. Like the relay runner, we have to be trained into a wisdom that reads the field of our action. The following three examples of ethical arguments might outline the type of ethics and the social realities that I will study here.

A. Abortion Politics   Consistent with an old American custom, the leadership of several American religious communities ventured into the public discussions that accompanied the 1984 presidential elections. Specifically, some religious spokesmen targeted American

abortion practices and public abortion policies. Their primary professed goal was to stop or at least slow down the frequency of
abortion, for which they declared publicly their own evaluations of
abortion and quickly issued policy recommendations for those states-
men who would, or were forced to, listen to them.

However, among those religious leaders, one group positioned
their cause within the partisan polarities of that election by (1) simply
asserting, without discussion, their own evaluation of fetal life, and by
(2) calling for severe coercive restraint, while offering little or no
policy action beyond juridical restraint. In terms of *publicly perceived*
languages, those leaders did little to clarify our understanding of fetal
life. In fact, the narrow languages of civil law, situated as they were
within an already partisan setting, discouraged that needed ethical
discussion. The immediate threat of coercive penalties predictably
threw most public arguers into stances of sectarian defensiveness (or
allowed them to remain there). Only those who are cynically partisan,
or those who fear a public discussion of fetal life, could endorse this
collapse of ethical discourse into political slogans.

Beyond this deadening of public discussion, these exclusive
appeals to coercive restraint further ignored a wide range of social
methods that might have more accurately matched their professed
goals. Chief among these methods is the Christian way of the cross,
the practices of Christian self-sacrifice and the this-worldly wisdom
embodied in those practices. The cross calls the Christian to witness to
the values at stake in each particular issue, that is, to educate others
effectively concerning that which is harmed and that which is
developed through our actions. Moreover, the cross demands a
witness to the redeemed human person that is to emerge from our
public discussions. Concerning the issue, Christian self-sacrifice
recognizes the limited informative role of civil law. Attempts to force
someone into following one's own evaluation have little educational
potential; they merely focus attention on the brute strength of the
would-be enforcer, not on the claimed value itself. To convince others
that fetal life is worth preserving, one must publicly demonstrate a
willingness to subject oneself to financial and social risk for the sake of
fetal life. Alternative means (which would include a full range of
financial, psychological, and religious supports for the pregnant
woman) share in common a large personal and social cost, a cost which
when borne stands some chance of directing attention to that which is
being defended. Publicly visible self-sacrifice can change evaluations;
brute coercion seldom can.

Second, the methods of self-sacrifice witness to, that is, educate
to, a redeemed ethical maturity. At their core the methods of publicly
visible self-sacrifice attempt to evoke moral maturity in their hearers,

to evoke deeper reflection and the corresponding ability of the hearer for self-sacrifice, while they forgo the perpetual temptation to abandon one's opponents to the realm of the morally subhuman. And to advance beyond the means of simple coercion is to recognize the dignity, well-being, and maturity of the women who are considering abortion, certainly one of the many values that must be recognized and protected in policy approaches. Yet, to respect and call forth mature ethical reflection is to put one's own judgments at risk, to submit to the social processes of self-correction and to the need to reasonably defend one's own evaluations. Without those discussions beyond simple assertion, these leaders did little to evoke an awareness of the value of fetal life. And by threatening only civil restriction, they did little to evoke further mature human responses to the value they sought to defend, or to convince us that they wanted to deal with others as moral agents.

Several other religious leaders attempted to rescue the argument from immediate partisan identification and from narrow policy demands by publicly joining the abortion question with other life questions. But the public forum was dominated by the first group, with the result that, two years after the election, public perception of what we have in fetal life or of the socially effective ways to render abortion less acceptable or necessary remains equally clouded. By ignoring the limited ability of civil law to evoke moral maturity, and by further ignoring or, in fact, encouraging the partisan dynamics of the 1984 political forum, the first group boxed themselves into a sectarian corner, relinquishing whatever effective public leadership they might have offered. By not clearly putting themselves at risk in defense of the full range of values involved in abortion decisions, the second group did little more than partially neutralize the first.

In the analysis that follows, these responses will be seen to be inadequate to the social problems being addressed, since they naively ignore or obscure the social instruments and human forces that can hinder or can develop public moral growth. They can even be judged within the requirements for social ethical discourse to be immoral, independently of the specific ends that are being pursued.

B. South Africa and American Social Responses   In the spring of 1985, amid growing calls for institutional divestiture of South African portfolios, one university that had previously unloaded all but one South African stock publicly called into question the value of divestiture, that is, it challenged the value of divestiture as a means for positively affecting racial relations in South Africa. In contrast to the 1984 abortion debate, the university here clearly questioned the adequacy of one means to achieve a specific end, arguing publicly and with some evidence that divestiture would hinder rather than help the dismantling of South African apartheid policies.

Nevertheless, the publication of the university's statement evoked claims of racism and moral indifference, claims which stimulated outbreaks of moral indignation on all sides of the issue. It soon became apparent, however, that the basically negative tone of the statement, rejecting one response to apartheid while offering no constructive alternative, was perceived by many as hindering the rising American concern over United States support of that racist regime. When challenged that they were doing nothing to contribute toward the growing American consensus, some university officials dismissed such concerns as "public relations" problems, treating the public manner in which they addressed the apartheid issue as of secondary importance.

In what follows, it will be argued that the manner of public presentation is of primary social ethical concern. Every social ethical argument erupts into a specific historical environment, and each argument alters or preserves not only a policy response to a specific issue, but also alters or preserves publicly held attitudes. To ignore those publicly held attitudes and the effects of one's public statements on those attitudes, is to miss an essential ethical dimension of public statements. The dynamics and directions of developing social attitudes are an intrinsic ethical aspect of social argument.

C. *Poverty arguments*   In the context of a quarter-long institute on national and international poverty, I had the opportunity of again encountering arguments for and against the alleged ethical obligations of the rich for the poor. In a backhanded way, both proponents and opponents of such an obligation confirmed two intrinsic, necessary, unavoidable aspects to any social argument: (1) the manner that one deals with the actual human realities within which one lives, and (2) the general attitudes that one takes toward all that is human.

First, all those who maintained that the rich are obliged to help the poor tended to argue from concrete facts, from presentations of the sufferings of the actual poor. Here, appeals to the actual were advanced to engage the moral sympathies of the reader, as well as to shape the direction of policy recommendations. And, likewise, most arguments against such an obligation tended not to mention, to ignore, the sufferings of the actual poor, or to appeal only to the possible sufferings of the rich if they themselves fall into poverty. That is, most arguments in part based their public effectiveness on their treatment (or nontreatment) of actual human beings.

Second, anyone who argued for an obligation had to make or presume a universalist appeal, either to God, or to common rationality or common susceptibility to pain, that is, to a common humanity. They in fact needed the affirmation of positive attitudes toward all who are genetically human, if their appeals to actual sufferings were to be persuasive. And again, those who argued for no obligation avoided discussion of a common grounding for our humanity. An awareness of, or an appeal to, common humanity would weaken their claim of no obligation.

Third, I noticed an inherent tension within all explicitly Christian arguments. These arguments, based as they would be on the notion of one God, Creator of all, had to face in a special way the problem of common humanity. The thesis of one Creator of course helped the arguments of those endorsing not only a universal obligation, but even more the call to action on behalf of, or in union with, the poor. God saw that all that he made was good. And the inherent goodness of all he has created evokes a call for its preservation and development. Further, however, many of those who endorsed what would normally count as "uncaring" responses to the poor had to argue additionally that whatever action they took would actually benefit the poor. Even classic Malthus had to argue that we should allow the poor to starve for their own long-term well-being. There are arguments, within a Christian context, that avoid an obligation toward the poor—based, for example, on the claim that the poor stand outside the order of redemption. Yet even here the case has to be made that they are, in fact, excluded.

A survey of these obligation arguments suggests that at the hidden heart of each is an attitude toward the other. Sometimes those attitudes are crystallized in commands to love one's enemies, or in appeals to destroy the subhuman adversary. But more often they lurk beneath the surface of the public argument, effectively and sometimes fiercely masked under the device of unraised questions concerning the other's humanity. Even the supporters of an obligation toward the poor or the enemy often falter at raising the appropriate questions, for whatever reasons. But most of us peacefully allow our critical imaginations to sleep, not even dreaming that the other might be on this side of the wall that divides us from the less than human. Without the raised questions, we perceive no obligations incumbent on us. Any and every social ethical argument, for or against any social obligation, is an attempt to evoke or quell some type of general attitude toward humanity at large. And often those attitudes are maintained as ideologies, as unexamined premises for thought and action.

I will here argue, then, that a primary task of social argument is the unmasking of generalized ideological premises, making clear what is naively presumed by the arguer and/or the hearers of the argument. All social arguments either encourage prevailing social attitudes toward the other, or challenge those attitudes. Responsibility in argument demands an awareness of the humanity one is endorsing.

These peculiar problems in social argument (of social methods masking or negating the values we profess to advance; of the dynamics of consensus formation; of the turning of the heart to or from segments of human society) appear strange to most of us. We usually argue one on one, or among the few members of a family or in a classroom. And if we perchance are thrust into a public argument, we wander about with no clear conception of the different forces active in that forum, and are therefore absorbed by goals that constitute only part of the values that demand our responsible action. Like the relay runner, we can discover and develop the realities at play in our action, and work out methods for handling them, only in combination with reflective exercises between and in the midst of direct competitions. The following study suggests some of the equipment and methods for the arguer's reflection, as well as for action, taken from the life of one who learned of them over many years of public debate.

Some years ago, the academic powers that held my future coerced me into a short study of John Courtney Murray's religious freedom argument, justified by the claim that, fifteen years after the publication of the Second Vatican Council's *Declaration on Religious Freedom*, much of Murray's argument was being distorted. Immediately, I noticed that many Roman Catholics and Protestants made appeal to Murray, often in justification of contradictory social policy recommendations. These contradictory appeals further suggested either that Murray was inconsistent or that, as was claimed, some people were badly misinterpreting him. Yet they also suggested that there is something distinctly American about Murray, some aspect of his thought that serves at least as a totem around which many Americans rally when trying to advance a moral or religious argument in American society. Perhaps, I thought, Murray's work might serve as a source for a distinctly American Christian social and religious theory. Then, as I read Murray, I discovered that the suggestions that he was inconsistent and that some were misinterpreting him were both true. Murray was not simply a proponent of the timeless, socially naive natural law theory, as I had initially supposed. Although he did at one time argue in that style, he was also blessed by being good at both theoretical argument and popular argument, and he learned to socialize his theory from what he learned of social forces, mostly inadvertently, in his popular arguments. Murray learned from his practice of argument.

The following is a study of what he learned. First, he discovered that many of the definitions with which he initially worked were inadequate to the reality in which he lived: definitions of the state, the church, of human cognition (particularly of the social variety). He had to recast some of those definitions, and adopt terms and definitions that had earlier not even occurred to him or to the school out of which he developed. Second, he learned that any and every social argument unfolds within its own historical field. That is, Murray had to face the historicity of human factual and value judgments, a problem that he could resolve only during the Second Vatican Council, with the help of Bernard Lonergan. Third, Murray gradually noticed that all but the most totalitarian attempts at social improvement rested on an appeal to, and a faith in, the moral reasonableness of at least some people, if not all people. Whether the arguer admits it or not, every social ethical argument attempts to evoke moral responses; each implies an under-lying notion of moral reasonableness that is elicited in its assumption by the arguer. And Murray could then, and only then, question some ecclesiologies that discouraged the moral maturity on which he had come to rely in his civil society arguments, the maturity demanded in the taking up of social moral responsibilities. Finally, by learning that all public arguers are situated within their environments, and that the act of public argument is always interactive with actual historical persons, Murray could then come to the notion of a social arguer always in social interaction with a historical God. Only in the last years of his life could he consciously conceive the task of social argument as itself intrinsically theological, as the pursuit of a God who offers redemption to peoples as well as to persons. And he was forced into this perspective and profession by what he encountered in the act of public argument. He reflected on his stride and on his attitudes, and became a theological, social ethician, meeting a social God.

This study, then, is not simply a description of the developments in Murray's own social ethical theory, nor simply a description of the social realities that he encountered and attempted to define and shape. It is also meant to be an examination of the ethically normative aspects of social argument, an examination of what makes a social argument moral or immoral, independently of the specific issue or issues under discussion. The individual who is thrust into the public forum, or the institution that has public voice, can pursue moral or immoral specific ends. But also the very manner in which they advance those issues can be socially moral or immoral, distinctively and independently so.

Murray learned all this, yet the manner of that learning was historical; it was not spun out with the clean lines of mathematical derivation. He could shed definitions and methods only after he had discovered them to be morally inadequate, but also only after he could come up with alternatives. The following presentation is therefore itself historical. The first chapter spells out the cognitional, political, and ecclesiological premises that guided Murray's thought in the 1940s. That chapter presents his arguments in all their deadly abstraction, deadly not only due to their dryness (and, as one reader commented, their screaming for one concrete metaphor to relieve the otherwise stark landscape), but also deadly because those arguments allow and, in fact, force the arguer to ignore certain social realities and methods that are vital to public action. The second and third chapters follow the 1950s challenges thrown against Murray's initial premises and manners of public argument, and his theoretical and behavioral responses to those challenges. Chapter 4 concerns his recognition of the appeal to moral agency in all ethical arguments, while chapter 5 follows out the implications of that appeal in the church's own pastoral mission. And in chapter 6 Murray emerges as a theologian, pursuing his God in a pluralistic world.

I have presumed many others' studies of Murray's development, some of which are cited in the text, in notes, or at least in the accompanying bibliography. My debt to them runs deep. Here, however, I want to mention some of the people who directly helped in my own reflections—as team members, competitors, sponsors, and spectators. First, my thanks to Dr. Max Stackhouse for applying the initial coercion mentioned above, and then to Drs. Fred Lawrence and David Hollenbach, S.J., as well as again to Dr. Stackhouse, for following the project beyond its clumsy beginnings. Their faith that our four quite different perspectives might generate significant points of common understanding gave rise in me to a social hope similar to that which Murray himself had had to discover. Also my thanks to my Jesuit brothers, my colleagues and friends at Santa Clara University, and particularly to the directors of the Bannan Foundation for their encouragement and for the form that encouragement took, namely, funding. I also wish to mention John Dunlop of Santa Clara and John Breslin, S.J., of Georgetown University Press. Both tilled earlier versions of this manuscript, attempting to evoke growths that at least distantly resemble English prose. Mr. Dunlop watered that arid soil while holding reasonably in check his own distinctly different evaluations of many of the social phenomena described here.

Finally, I especially thank my mother Anne, my father Jim, and my sister Rosalie for early lessons in the dynamics of mutual understanding, and for the ongoing lesson and experience of love as a necessary requirement for that understanding. To them this work is dedicated, and particularly to Anne. During the long process of her dying, she the teacher deepened the lesson that loving and the understanding that rests in loving can break through even death itself.

Chapter One

TWO ARGUMENTS THAT FAILED

Murray's Initial Confrontations with
Social-Ethical Argument

In the space of some twenty years, Murray slowly and painfully arrived at two sets of concepts and judgments which, in the early 1940s, he did not affirm, nor even clearly recognize. The first set revolved around his understanding of moral authority for the Roman Catholic, and resulted in two distinct judgments: (1) that valid moral insights could and did arise outside of the church, and (2) that the church ought to be attentive to those insights. At issue, then, was his understanding of the structures and practices of moral authority within his own church. Murray's adoption and then use of the above two judgments or propositions did not mean that at one time he consciously held their opposites, then clearly changed his mind. Rather, his initial theories of church authority and moral reasoning precluded any serious consideration of these two propositions, much less of their implications for policy recommendations. The reasons for affirming these propositions would arise from sources other than his own theories, but his eventual clear affirmation of those judgments would serve as a basis for turning back to his own earlier theological and epistemological theories and revising them.

A second set of understandings and judgments concerned his evaluation of the epistemological factors which must be brought into social-ethical arguments. Initially, he had adopted a natural law notion of "conscience" as a sufficient epistemological category for social-ethical arguments, and had structured his own arguments on the premise that such a notion could adequately ground a socio-political obligation, and even a socio-political right. He later rejected such a narrow understanding of human social reasoning, and of the episte-mological factors which must be brought into discussions of rights and obligations. In the process, he had to develop clearer notions of the types of ethical languages to which a social ethician must appeal. Once again, theory had to be dialectically adjusted for the sake of moral concerns. Moreover, these fundamental shifts in Murray's concep-tions of the church and of social reasoning almost emerged as accidental corollaries while he was arguing more specific ethical issues.

In this chapter Murray argues for mutual forms of intercredal cooperation (section I), and then for civil religious freedom (section II). Both arguments failed to yield the conclusions he desired. Both collapsed under inadequate conceptions of (1) the relationship of practical, theoretical (theological), and evaluative (ethical) thought; of (2) the nature and location of moral authority in this historical world; and of (3) the necessary social categories for any social-ethical argument. Their collapse spurred Murray into developing political, social-ethical, and cognitional categories that would more adequately ground his ethical judgments. As such, these failures represent an integral factor in the maturation of his thought.

My claim that these two arguments failed must then be qualified. In his arguments for cooperation and religious liberty, Murray immersed himself in a social world of meaning, a world with both a past and a future. That world proceeded from presuppositions to judgments, from value claims to reflections on value commitments, by rules and processes that were not purely logical, but were nonetheless reasonable. And Murray learned of this world by participating in it. The failure of these arguments led him to examine consciously that world of social meaning, and then to formulate a distinctly social ethics based on the dynamics of social discourse.

The following two discussions are meant, therefore, as preparations for the developments that were to come. In each, I present a brief outline of the categories Murray inherited, his initial adjustment of those categories, and his methods of argument. The abstraction of both arguments makes for some deadly, mind numbing reading, both because of their ethereal terminology and the tightness of their logic. However, I ask the reader to attempt to put on the mind and adopt the methodologies of a 1940s natural law ethician, so as to more fully appreciate the fact that it was not the logic, but rather the conceptions of the church and of human cognition that led to the collapse of Murray's initial arguments. After tracing these arguments to their (inevitable) disintegrations, I will then conclude with a preview of the directions in which Murray was forced to move as he then reflected on his own social argumentation.

I. INTERCREDAL COOPERATION: THE CONFUSION OF THEORETICAL AND EVALUATIVE REASONING.   Murray's first public debate, undertaken in the mid-1940s, concerned possible Christian responses to the massive international chaos of World War II; it therefore centered on an issue that was at once social and ethical. The governing question of this debate was not the necessity of Catholic action for the reestablishment of a worldwide peace, for it was understood among most discussants that Catholics must work for world peace. Rather, the problem concerned the manner and degree to which Roman Catholics should cooperate with non-Catholic Christians in such activity. As Murray inherited this debate, he could presume a commitment for international social action, but he could not further presume an acceptance of intercredal cooperation.

Donald Pelotte has documented Murray's own participation in the American National Conference of Christian and Jews and his contribution to the Catholic portion of the 1943 "Catholic, Jewish, Protestant Declaration on World Peace" (Pelotte, 1976, 14–15).[1] His participation and the Declaration were forms of intercredal cooperation, and Murray found the basis for this cooperation in four Christmas allocutions of Pius XII (Murray 1944a, 6).[2] His activity and his understanding of Pius XII's call for international cooperation resulted in five articles dealing with intercredal cooperation and another two articles on the related topic of the theological education of Catholics. Before turning to these arguments, several initial observations should be made.

First, three distinct forms of cooperation were under discussion. The first envisaged separate, denominationally defined organizations, each autonomously having as its object the establishment of a just international order. These separate organizations, however, lacked any joint institution or committee (made up of mixed denominational members) by which their disparate activities could be coordinated. This first form was called "non-federated, parallel." The second form was also based on the premise of separate denominational organizations, but united by joint committees composed of members from the various denominations. This second form was designated "federated, parallel" or "cartel." The third form allowed for interdenominational organizations composed, throughout their various levels, of mixed-faith membership; this form was called "mixed" or "mutual." The two parallel forms of cooperation allowed for direct control by Catholic bishops over all members of the Catholic organizations and therefore over all aspects of the institutional and social action processes. Bishops had only indirect control over mutual organizations, through direct control over the partial Catholic membership.

Second, the primary resource for argument used by Roman Catholics was papal and episcopal responses to previous forms of cooperative organization. Murray repeatedly referred to two letters of Pius X, his 1912 *Singulari Quadam* (1943b, 263–69) and 1910 *Notre Charge* (1945b, 201–9), and to the allocutions of Pius XII. He also gave extended treatment to the English Sword of the Spirit Movement (1943b, 281–86) and to the previously mentioned American "Declaration on World Peace." *Singulari Quadam* was directed to the German church and permitted both mutual and federated forms of labor cooperation. *Notre Charge* was a condemnation of the Sillonist mutual and ecclesiologically independent movement. The Sword of the Spirit (1940–47) was a Roman Catholic social organization in federation with the Protestant Commission of the Churches for International Friendship and Social Responsibility. The "Declaration on World Peace" was a statement jointly issued by American denominational leaders (the Roman Catholic portion under the title of "The Pattern for Peace," see 1944a), presupposing cooperation between the leadership of different religious confessions.

Third, a difference obtains in societal scope between the "evidence" which Murray and others used and the initial state of the problem under consideration. Pius X's two letters, the "Pattern for Peace" statement, and the Sword of the Spirit Movement involved limited intranational movements. The question of cooperation addressed by Murray, however, was internationally defined: the reestablishment of a structure of peace between nations. The question, then, in some sense lacked historical precedent (1943b, 259). As will become obvious, this difference muddied the waters of the public argument.

Fourth, an apologia for cooperation was necessary in Catholic circles because of a longstanding fear of doctrinal indifferentism. Murray did not elaborate the sources of Roman Catholic fears concerning indifferentism, nor give a clear definition of it. But from his writings of the period, two varieties of indifferentism surface. Indifferentism is the belief that Catholic social and religious teaching is irrelevant to the constitution of society.[3] In its clearest social expression, it is a public belief held by an institutionally defined group of people that all religious denominations either hold in common the necessary beliefs for social health (therefore, they are all equal) or that none of their beliefs are necessary for social well-being (and again they are equal). Any institutionally defined group which would base itself on a belief that Catholic doctrine does not have a unique social import would be a potential creator of doctrinal indifferentism among Catholic participants. Or, again, Murray defined indifferentism as the destruction of the Roman Catholic sense of ecclesiastical uniqueness, the Catholic "difference," although it is clear in the context of his writings that this uniqueness is used in the sense more of conscious doctrinal commitment than of sociological self-awareness.[4] The awareness of unique social import and the sense of doctrinal singularity are both included in Murray's phrases "Catholic Unity of the Church" and "full Catholic integrity."

Of course, any cooperative institutionalization based on the doctrine of indifferentism had to be rejected by Roman Catholics. But the indifferentism that worried Murray's American theological interlocutors was of a more subtle variety. In Francis J. Connell's judgment,[5] Catholic participation in any organization in which there was no Catholic religious consensus (a group of people in a state of religious pluralism or religious war) would de facto weaken Catholic commitment to the unique elements of Catholic doctrine.

The problem, then, as shaped by Murray's American debate, became not only a question of the relative worth of cooperation and of particular forms of cooperation for the international common good. The problem was also one of relating measurements of the good and evil effects in two distinct orders of existence: the danger of disorder in the temporal political realm versus the dangers of indifferentism within the ecclesiastical realm. Connell did not deny that the church and Catholics in general had a responsibility for the temporal common good. But he did suggest that American Catholics had gone a sufficient, perhaps an excessive, distance toward cooperation. Now the danger of indifferentism outweighed the problems of the temporal common good.

Finally, behind Connell's argument was the expressed preference of Pius X for federated cooperation in the German labor movement. This preference was interpreted as a Catholic *ideal*, a valuation which Murray at this point shared (1943b, 167, 274). The notion of federated structuring as an ideal was then further understood to be an expression of the primacy of ecclesiological concern for the unity of Catholic faith. And finally, if Pius X's major concern was for the unity of Catholic faith, and if he preferred on that basis at most parallel cooperation, then all Catholic arguments for cooperation must proceed from that concern and that institutional preference. Both the principles and the conclusions of Pius' manner of argument were to hold authoritative force over the 1940s' debate. In effect, the two principles of Catholic concern, integrity and the common good, were situated in a lexical[6] relationship. Either the integrity principle must be absolutely guaranteed before mutual or federated cooperation could be allowed, or, at the very least, the burden of proving overriding danger rested on those who advocated mutual cooperation. This argument from a papal expression of preference was biased against full cooperation.

Against this backdrop, and relying on these concepts and sources, Murray argued for mixed intercredal cooperation, and then for both clerical and lay education to facilitate cooperation.

A. Murray's Argument for Mutual Cooperation: Principles as Directive of Ecclesiastical Concern.   The social problem under consideration was the establishment of an international order of peace. But Murray's understanding of the problem was shaped, as so much of his later concerns would be shaped, by papal understandings of the problem. At issue was not simply the destruction and atrocity of the war itself. The core of the problem, international in scope, was cultural, religious and moral disintegration (1943b, 267). Any resolution of the war would have to take account of such disintegration. A lasting peace could only be formed by addressing the question of international religious and moral reconstitution (1944a, 4–6, 9, 19).

Murray's basic argument for active Catholic participation in this reconstruction is at once an appeal to and a justification of Pius XII's own involvement. As a starting premise, he drew a sharp distinction between the natural and the supernatural or (according to his current terminology) the "temporal" and the "spiritual." To the objection that the Catholic spiritual leader's participation in social reconstruction constitutes an unjustified intrusion into the temporal sphere, Murray claimed a limit on papal intrusion into that sphere: "Were [the social reconstruction] not a spiritual objective, our Holy Father could not authoritatively summon the Church to its attainment" (1943b, 259); but he nevertheless allowed such intrusion on the grounds that the present crisis is at core "a spiritual crisis, but located at the heart of the temporal order" (1944a, 11). The resolution of this spiritual crisis is dependent on the promulgation of the moral notion of justice (as a requirement for the common good of the international community) and on an increase in charity (as an energizing will for peace). Since it is a spiritual crisis, the church can and must address itself to the content and the volitional elements necessary for its resolution. The temporal order, then, depends on conceptual and volitional "spiritual" elements which constitute a primary concern of the church. Since the problem is beyond the technical and pragmatic, Catholic action is demanded.

According to Murray, Pius XII recognized that, "whether we like it or not, we are living in a religiously pluralistic society at a time of spiritual crisis; and the alternatives are the discovery of social unity or destruction" (1943b, 274; also 1944a, 12). Further, since the spiritual crisis is in the temporal order, Pius' call for cooperation among "all men of good will" was an admission that the pattern for social reconstruction had to be something other than a full Catholic understanding of what is good and true. The Catholic must settle for another pattern to avert the immediate danger of deepening moral chaos. The well-being of the pluralistic international community demanded cooperation even though a full Catholic program could not be put into effect.

Finally, Murray claimed, Pius wanted the cooperation to be in some sense "institutionalized in an international organization, that will function as a sort of collective conscience and be able to enforce its imperatives" (1943b, 262). That is, Murray insisted, as he would continue to insist, that the creation of an ethical will for peace would be useless unless there were accompanying institutional structures to express and support such a will. This would rule out parallel, nonfederated structuring, with no institutional organs for coordinating the common task of establishing peace. The present danger necessitated such coordination, for the alternatives were, again, organization or destruction of the common good. Murray further implied that the cooperation should be as mutual as possible. An institutional response adequate to the present danger and to Pius XII's call would be "twice removed" from direct ecclesiological control. First, such organizations would be at the level of action, as distinct from the level of religious doctrine. Second, it would be further removed from an "organic relationship" with the bishops (1943b, 261).[7] And this latter "removal" was characteristic of mutual organizations.

These three arguments for (1) Catholic action, (2) intercredal cooperation, and (3) mutual structuring were consequentialist, or justified by the reasonably predicted outcomes of the various forms of institutionalization. Each of these arguments was based on judgments concerning the relative health of the common temporal order, and the effects each of these forms would have on the development of that good.

Murray countered Connell's objections to mutual cooperation with a somewhat different understanding of the manner in which papal decisions were reached. First, he tried to dispel some of the either/or, conflictual tone of Connell's presentation. Murray claimed that Pius X had made his judgments always within the dual principles of integrity and common good (1943b, 270–71), that is, both directive[8] principles were at work in Pius' evaluations. Murray was even bold enough to assert that Pius' preference for federated organization was based on the judgment that distinct Catholic organizations would best serve the temporal common good. "On this principle [of the church's contribution to the common good], his preferential recommendation of Catholic trade unions is based, rather more than on the practical dangers of interconfessional unions" (1943b, 270). In effect, Pius was understood to have been operating primarily under the common good, not the integrity principle, in his particular preference.

Second, if all papal decisions are made in light of the dual principles, and if the common good with its historical particularity is a factor in all those decisions, then an argument concerning cooperation cannot be historically bound to a past problem (German trade unions) and a past time (1912). Murray therefore asserted that "the cooperation that Pius X had permitted out of concern for the common good Pius XII has invited, urgently and on a far wider scale, out of what amounts to anguish lest it be almost too late to rescue the common good from destruction" (1943b, 272). Judgments in either case were, according to Murray, made out of the same two principles of ecclesiastical concern and differed because of changing social conditions. Pius XII's compassionate reading of the present situation and his lack of concern for the dangers of indifferentism should guide Catholic action toward cooperation. In fact, any clear reading of the present dangers will result in judgments concerning the value of mutual cooperation.

> We must, in a word, ruthlessly subject ourselves to the experience the piercing effects of which speak out in almost every line of Pius XII's utterances—an experience, wholly Christlike, of intimate self-identification with all the woe that war has brought upon the race of men, members of Christ and our brothers ... such an experience would compel us to reject, as intolerably selfcomplacent, any notion that our efforts have been at all adequate either to the desperateness of the situation or to the urgency of the Pope's pleas for action (1944a, 29).

B. A Christian "Intelligence" of Faith.   Murray, then, understood the judgments governing the necessity and the form of cooperation to be consequentialistic within a field of presumably permanent, yet not lexically related, principles. Further, he argued not so much *that* the world was in great danger, as *from* the papal evaluations of the immediate danger. This mixture of theoretical and authoritative appeals appears even more in his consideration of who should participate in intercredal cooperation. Murray argued that both laymen and priests should be involved in cooperative, social activity. But his principal concern seems to have been the establishment of the autonomy of the layman.

Murray presented three distinct arguments in support of the role and autonomy of the layman in Christian cooperation. The first was an authoritative appeal to Pius XI (1944b, 64–69). Again, cooperation hinged on the state of the temporal common good. Murray understood Pius XI to have removed priestly action from the temporal arena when he disallowed priest-controlled labor and political organizations. Pius' creation of the nonpolitical Catholic Action Movement restricted priestly action to a forum which was "purely spiritual." If Catholics were to participate in the reconstruction of the world through political and economic means, then the task was a lay responsibility, and theirs alone, for "only the laity, by reason of their particular situation, are in a position to solve [social problems]" (1944b, 70). Pius XI, then, has authorized this relative lay autonomy in practical, social action.

A second argument was based on a theology of priesthood. Murray distinguished clerical and lay priesthoods with respect to their functions and to their intended objects. Just as the clerical priest is "charged with official mediation between God and man," so the laity "is to mediate between the spiritual and the temporal" (1944b, 71). Just as the priest's object of concern is an order of divine truth and grace, so the layman's object of concern is an order of temporal justice and peace. Both participate directly and distinctly in the spiritual authority and power of the bishops. The layman does not derive his spiritual commission through his parish priest. They deal in different realms, derivatively participating in the dual concerns of the church, as these two concerns reside integrally in the magisterium.

Behind these authoritatively and theologically based arguments—and much more significant for Murray's present and future methods of argument—is a third basis for distinguishing between lay and clerical cooperative activity: the types of intellection proper to their different spheres. As noted earlier, Murray held that the realm of political and social action belonged to the layman, whose responsibility it is to create institutions which are supportive of a just temporal order. Even Pius X, according to Murray, recognized that the initiative and constructive intelligence for such institutions was the preserve of laymen, not of the clerics and the bishops.

> The Holy See was evidently reluctant to intervene officially in a practical matter [the German forms of cooperation], wherein it wished Catholics to enjoy liberty to adapt their action to the needs of specific situations, given that no Catholic principle was at stake. For our own times, this means that the practical initiatives in organizing intercredal co-operation must come from below, and simply be controlled from above. As a matter of fact, interconfessional organizations, insofar as they are interconfessional, are not ecclesiastical organizations; and hence ecclesiastical authority has no mandate to erect them . . . (1943b, 269).

Even the bishops in their pastoral role should exercise only the function of judging the value of such organizations. The action of the layman was conceived to be in some sense autonomous, centering on the notions of initiative and organizational formation.

At this time, Murray did not develop these notions of constructive, lay intelligence much further. The second term of the contrast between laymen and clerics is, however, the theological (theoretical) knowledge of the clerics. And this notion of theological knowledge or reason was somewhat more clearly developed. "The simple priest is under the necessity of being trained as a theologian because of his association in the magisterial office of the bishop" (1943b, 269). Pure

Scholastic theology as it should be taught to priests has its own autonomy and its distinctive object: the deepening of the theological understanding of the nature of God as manifest through Christian revelation. Murray held this notion of theological intelligence in contrast to the purely doctrinal, "positive" notion of theology which he considered prevalent at the time (1944b, 50). The goal of seminary training was to be the understanding, beyond mere assertion, of Catholic doctrines and of the interrelationships between the doctrines. It was to be systematic, intellectually holistic.

Priestly education, then, was thought to have as its immediate end the development of theoretical reason or intelligence. Scholastic theology attempts to bring to completion man's theoretical reason, as an aspect of "the intellect's native dynamism toward the assimilation of all that is real" (1944b, 51-52). By participation in Scholastic modes of thought about God, each priest is in effect to redeem human theoretical reason, to be nourished in his own life by insight into the restricted but important realm of theoretical questions. The term of such a pursuit is a *quoad se* theology, a theology which understands God insofar as possible "from the standpoint of God as God," finding its own unity by way of "an imitation of the unity of the divine knowledge, . . . of God's own vision of Himself and all things else" (1944c, 360).[9] The development of theoretical reason and the term of its use are the ecclesiastically defined vocation of the priest, "in defense of the faith against rationalistic incursions . . . as the price of survival of faith" (1944b, 51, 53).

The Scholastic theology of the priest is also theoretical in that it is general in relation to the temporal order of particular action. Murray repeatedly stated that the social import of theology is the motivational effect which Catholic doctrine has on Catholics in their participation in social concerns (1944c, 354, 356, 366). And the truths of Catholic doctrine are the most effective keys for unlocking the driving force of charity (1944c, 356). Such truths have, then, an indirect but essential relationship to the temporal order. They serve to motivate and, in a general sense, to inform the value commitments of the layman, whose task then is to determine the proper ways to construct the temporal order so that it reflects those general values and truths.

Murray's distinction between the priest and the layman with regard to theological knowledge and practical action effected a clear framework within which the problem of indifferentism could be handled. If the realm of doctrine was the province of the priest-theologian, and if the normative reason of the priest was theoretical, then the priest's separation and, in a sense, isolation from the realm of the practical established a forum in which doctrinal integrity could be maintained. And if the layman's role was understood by the layman as that of constructive action within the temporal, while at the same time admitting to, and submitting to, the doctrinal import and autonomy of the priest-theologian, then religious indifferentism could be avoided.

Murray then had two distinct orders of Catholic life, the temporal and the theological/spiritual, each clearly distinguished by different personnel and by the type of activity proper to each.[10] Such a clear-cut analytic argument, however, was still open to several objections. A practical problem was the general level of understanding within the Catholic community. Related to the practical problem was the further theoretical problem of the relationship between the knowledge of priests and the activity of laymen.

The practical problem was the possibility of encroachment beyond the arena of one's own competence. If one granted that the practical/theoretical distinction gave a basis for integral Catholic participation in intercredal cooperation, there still remained the problem of how such cooperation would be perceived by the majority of Catholics. Without an understanding of the relative autonomies of practical action and of doctrine, some might be scandalized into the false belief that cooperative action rested on mutual doctrinal confession. Such a belief by laymen would be an encroachment into the theological and would involve a heresy; for the priest, such a belief would simply be heresy. And, without a clear understanding of the temporal/spiritual orders, a priest might be tempted to "clericalism," and the layman to social inactivism or "angelism" (1944b, 70). The problem was, then, one of scandal.

Murray responded to the practical possibility of scandal by claiming that such a possibility could not eliminate the church's responsibility for the common good (1944a, 28; 1944b, 68–69). Rather, what was called for was an intensified effort at clerical and lay religious education (1943a, 109). Once again, the object of priestly education was a (partial) understanding of God as God knows himself. Such knowledge is at most general to the temporal order. Once the priest understands the nature of this knowledge, he will not interfere in the layman's realm of action.

> The priest's primary function is that exactly defined for him in the theory of Catholic Action; he is to be ecclesiastical assistant, or theological counsellor, whose action is essentially priestly, terminating at the enlightenment and direction of conscience. It is a function of cardinal importance, which makes the priest the soul, in a sense, of the enterprise. Success depends on his confining himself to it (1943b, 279).

Lay religious education, however, presented a special problem. If he were running an exact parallel between seminary and lay education, Murray could call for an increased training for laymen in the area of practical, technical determination, that is, at the level of temporal action. And he did indeed call for the training of an elite among laymen who could then prudently establish orders of law and institutions which would work toward a more Christian society (1944a, 20–21; 1944c, 343). This technical elite would then form agendas which less technically trained Catholic laymen could support in the public arena.

There remained, however, the question of the type of religious knowledge which would motivate both elite and ordinary laymen in their work for social justice and peace. Just as Murray had endorsed with Pius XII a "rising will among all people for justice," so in this more limited context Murray looked to the generation of a socially dynamic charity which would issue in a rechristianization of society (1944b, 67–68). And just as he did not accept a simple assertive, positive theology for priests, nor did he settle for a lay theology which was "the mere handing on of hereditary formulas" (1944c, 350). The goal of lay religious education, however, was a type of knowledge which constituted a second type of theology, distinct from both Scholastic theology and from practical/temporal competence. It was an "intelligence of faith," a system of beliefs which both could be rationally presented and further serve as a basis for charity or will for justice (1944c, 354). Other names which he used for this type of knowledge were "spirituality," "piety," "*mystique*," and "vision."

Lay theological training was not to be simply a watered down version of the clerical course, "the *Summa Theologica* with the hard parts left out" (1944b, 46). Since laymen had as their direct goal the rechristianization of society, not the intelligibility of God in himself, their training was to be sensitive to the world situation. It was to result in a total vision, since the forces which the layman confronted in the world were themselves guided by a total vision, a *mystique* with an agenda for all aspects of society.

> Against an all-devouring *mystique* one must turn the full force of another *mystique*, whose inner dynamism is still more triumphant and whose engagement of the whole man is still more imperious (1944c, 352).

This vision was to be total also in the sense that the full range of Catholic doctrine was to form that vision, "for only through its organic relations with every other truth will the full and vital meaning of any single truth appear" (1944c, 355). It was not to be only a partial, perhaps deistic, view of reality. However, the interconnections of the

Catholic truths were to be psychologically, not systematically, related. "Doctrinal instruction will be religiously formative only if the manner of its organization and exposition is adapted to the psychology of the student and to his existent state of mental and spiritual development" (1944c, 347-48). This manner of presentation and assimilation Murray called "pre-Thomistic," "Augustinian." It was the manner of *quoad nos* theology, the manner of God's revelation to humanity as witnessed in the Scriptures. Whereas Scholastic theology began with the notion of God, lay theology should begin, as did the historical order of discovery, with Christ (1944c, 366-69).

Murray, then, described the role of the priest as mediating the realities of the spirit, grace and truth to the Christian community, and the role of the layman as mediating the values of the Christian vision to the temporal order. His notion of lay spirituality in effect mediated between the arena of theoretical reason and that of practical action. Murray did assert that even priest-theologians should have a total spiritual vision (1944b, 55-56). But, even though priests are the teachers of *quoad nos*, lay-orientated theology, they will in those courses only present "general conclusions" of Catholic faith concerning the temporal order. And, although lay spirituality contains generalities of Catholic faith, the layman's expertise is not Catholic dogmatic truth. Concerning such truths, laymen are subject to the spiritual direction of the priest-theologians. In this respect, once again, the problem of indifferentism was to be avoided. "[O]nly when Catholicism is thus as a *mystique* set apart from other religious or quasi-religious systems will the ground be cut completely from under the secularist and indifferentist temptation" (1944c, 354). The lay religious vision remained on the side of the magisterium both in its generality vis-à-vis the temporal order and in its uniqueness as formed by the full, specifically Catholic doctrine.[11]

C. The Necessary and Sufficient "Intelligence" for Intercredal Cooperation.   So far, Murray has justified, consequentially and in part epistemologically, the possibility of mutual cooperation at the religiously pluralistic international level. He also outlined a Catholic spiritual vision which he considered a necessary condition for motivated Catholic action. Now, it would seem, Catholic laymen could operate in the pluralistic temporal order, motivated by a hidden, clearly Catholic spirituality. And, indeed, Murray hoped that they would so operate in an integral Catholic manner (1943a, 102).

Yet, there still remained the question of the sufficient grounds for intercredal cooperation. Do the separate, mutually antagonistic creeds which motivate different Christians provide a sufficient basis for mutual action, if the religious bases for their action are kept out of the public forum? Or is there a need for or possibility of a common basis for cooperation, around which both Catholics and Protestants can rally? The discussion over cooperation, as Murray had inherited it, was already immersed in a debate concerning such a common basis. Murray's first two articles on cooperation were for the most part reviews of European discussions of a common ground.[12] Three basic positions, with variations within each, presented themselves.

The first position sought a common point of intercredal action in the structured goals or products of action. By mutual but differently motivated commitments to preserving social institutions, it was suggested, different religious groups could find sufficient grounds to spur and direct cooperative action. Two such goals were proposed: either the institutions of natural justice that already existed or needed to be developed, or "a remnant of the Christian tradition . . Christian ideas, Christian institutions . . . a common orientation to Christ," that is, cultural forms in the West that still expressed Christian beliefs (1942b, 418). Although Murray insisted that any work for the common good must entail the (re)construction of institutions, he judged that simply concentrating on the technical structures of institutions would be inadequate for the task ahead. More general, value-ladened considerations must also enter into public consciousness. And Murray gave no attention to the preservation of explicitly Christian institutions and values (for reasons that will surface presently).

A second group sought the common basis for intercredal action in the volitional springs of human behavior. Murray cited, with mild approval, the suggestion of Maritain that there are two possible levels of fellowship (1942b, 423). Both are, in Murray's sense, at the spiritual level, a unity of heart and love, but not of intellect. The first, however, is the theological virtue of charity, most fully manifest in the Christian community. The second level of fellowship can derive from the first (but also from other sources), and is situated in the temporal order; it is the natural virtue of civic friendship. For the Christian, the realm of charity can and must flow over into the temporal order, while remaining distinct from it. But Murray pulled back from Maritain's suggestion that, since true Christian love can arise among non-Catholics (despite nonculpable doctrinal differences), this religious virtue of charity could serve as a basis for common cooperation, even in the temporal sphere, much less in the religious.

However, just as Murray questioned the sufficiency of commonly desired institutions for guiding pluralistic action, he likewise questioned the sufficiency of a common volitional basis. He placed himself among a third group, who insisted that, prior to the volitional, there must be a shared conceptual content at the basis of cooperative action—a content consisting in either a "common Christian set of beliefs" or the statutes of a purely natural law. As common Christian grounding there was further suggested the existence of "common true baptism and some content" (1942b, 420), or, as with Maritain, an analogical community of specifically Christian beliefs. Murray, however, gave the discussion of common Christian beliefs little credence. Echoing Max Pribilla, he admitted that there might be some common Christian collective consciousness left in Western society; but that this consciousness is too "thin" for a common Christian grounding (1943b, 104). It is too weak to operate as a motivating key which would be strong enough or complete enough for the task before the postwar world. Further, the search for such a grounding leads only to confusion (1943b, 104). In this, Murray was consistent with his early 1933 article on Catholic and Protestant dogmatics (1933), where he had suggested that there did not exist a basis for even analogical communication between them. And he would remain consistent with this judgment until the early 1960s. In 1943, again echoing Pribilla, he advised a "methodological avoidance" of dogmatic (read: theological) questions in any cooperative activity. So, a historical, religious heritage could not form a common content for social action.

In part consistent with Pribilla, the content grounding Murray did accept was "purely within the sphere of the natural law," the promotion of "a more perfect observance of the law" (1943b, 106). The realm of natural law is the temporal, and as such can offer a grounding for peace in arenas of religious pluralism. All Christians should be able to agree to the principles of the natural law, even if they do not and cannot reach any consensus on dogmatic issues (1943a, 190).[13]

In 1944, Murray spelled out what he considered the four essential principles of natural law which all men of good will could accept. They were

> 1) a religious conviction as to the sovereignty of God over nations as well as over individuals; (2) a right conscience as to the essential demands of the moral law in social life; (3) a religious respect for human dignity in oneself and in others—the dignity with which man is invested inasmuch as he is the image of God; and (4) a religious conviction as to the essential unity of the human race (1944a, 11).

There was, then, both a moral and a religious content to the discovery/product of purely natural reason. Murray did not consider the moral and religious tenets of natural law to be a least common denominator derived from examination of various denominational creeds. Such would be a "common Christian basis." Rather, these dictates had as their object the human person as examined independently from revelation.

Reason, then, could discover a moral and religious content which was common to all peoples, despite their revelational beliefs. For Murray, the only sufficient base for cooperation could be a spirituality which rises out of a reasoned view of the natural order. He could then claim a spiritual response to the "spiritual crisis at the heart of the temporal order" which was formed independently of any religious creeds but which did not prescind from the moral and religious elements of human nature. The basis for Christian cooperation should be a "natural spiritual unity of the human race, whose effective bond is belief in God and obedience to the universal moral law" (1943b, 260).

Such a spiritual vision was admittedly only partially true to the world in which God had definitively manifested himself in Christ and in his church (1943a, 111). Neither the action arising out of the natural law consensus nor the consensus itself is a "milieu of grace" (1943b, 259); neither have in Murray's sense a theological object. Their object is merely a social unity, an aspect of the common good, the temporal happiness of persons and nations. However, a natural law spirituality, although not complete to the present economy of salvation, is a valid place to begin the necessary postwar spiritual reconstruction. And, just as natural reason and grace are in principle complementary, so natural law spirituality and Catholic spirituality are compatible. Natural law "is Christian ground, indeed, but only because it is common human ground" (1943a, 106).[14] A Catholic can accept cooperation on a natural law basis without endangering any of his doctrinal commitment.

This social unity in a natural law spirituality must exclude any belief system which rejects a natural law understanding of God. I have already noted the "four natural truths" which, according to Murray, served as the bases for Pius' call for cooperation. Murray continued:

> It is clear to whom the invitation to co-operate was issued, namely, to all men who believe in God; for belief in God necessarily entails acceptance of the moral law and of human dignity and equality (1944a, 12).

In a word, any system of public belief which is at core atheistic is an enemy of the only workable grounds for cooperation in modern pluralistic society.

What, then, is the relationship between clerical and lay theology, lay Catholic spirituality and natural law spirituality, on the one hand, and human action, on the other? That is, what is the relationship between these various "intelligences" and ethical action, as conceived by Murray during this period? He appears to have viewed human behavior as something of a continuum between the stirrings of charity (or human civic love) and action. A spirituality has a publicly discussable and teachable content. It engages the energies of charity or love for the task of social action, and explicitly motivates such action. Depending on the context, the action can be prayer, systematic reflection, liturgy, or the creation of a just social order. The engagement of spiritual action requires an encounter with religious doctrine, the most complete and true being that of the Catholic Church. For the priest, the religious doctrine is the traditional, *quoad se* theology in the Scholastic mode; for the layman, the doctrine is a spirituality formed out of *quoad nos* theology. Both Catholic Scholastic theology and *quoad nos* theology engage the charity in the hearts of Catholics.

Lay theology unlocks Christian charity for the sake of the social reconstruction of the world. Given, however, the pluralistic composition of modern society, this lay theology is not sufficient in appeal to meet the massive task of postwar reconstitution. What is needed is another "intelligence of faith," but a faith[15] which is not antithetical to Catholic doctrine. It is the product of reason's penetration of the natural order. At this point Murray did not spell out the manner in which this reason operates. He only enumerated several of its dictates. It should be noted, however, that natural law reason as described by Murray is already a social form of knowledge. Unlike even Pribilla, Murray more clearly insisted that between charity and social action there must intervene a form of reason which was not simply practical judgment; it was something prior to practical judgment, involving generalized value commitments that form and direct practical judgment, while being distinct from it. Only if there exists a consensus on this common intelligibility can collective drives be engaged and the spiritual reconstitution of Western society proceed. A common intelligible content is necessary for social well-being and social action.

D. Confusion of Evaluative and Theoretical Reason.   A final exchange between Murray and Paul Hanley Furfey deserves some attention. Furfey had argued that "what we need to do is become more aggressively Catholic and reclaim *our* social doctrine in parallel organizations" (Furfey, 1943, 471). Murray understood Furfey to be against even parallel organizations federated through a common committee at the top level of each (1943d, 474). Furfey also argued that Murray was invalidly extending Pius X's particular permission for mutual organized cooperation to a general, church-wide recommendation, that *"an* organization" should be formed between Catholics and Protestants which would govern mutual action nationally and internationally.

Murray argued, as he had previously, that Catholic judgments concerning the "expediency" of parallel vs. mutual structures must be formed within the two principles of Catholic integrity of faith and the common social good. Particular judgments concerning the form of organization must therefore be conditioned by particular circumstances. In actuality, papal judgments were so conditioned.

But, in this final exchange, there has surfaced what at first appears to be an insignificant retrenchment. In the face of Furfey's criticism, Murray particularized the forum in which the decisions concerning cooperation are to be made. He did not want to be understood as "raising a small rebellious fist" against the hierarchy (1945b, 212). Furfey's preferred nonfederated structuring had been rejected by Pius XII. But the question of federated vs. mutual organizational structure must be left up to the local ordinary. It is the role of the ordinary to decide whether his control over local cooperative institutions should be direct (as in a federated structure) or indirect (as in a mutual structure). Murray claimed that his own argument had not endorsed mutual organization in the United States, that his entire argument had "been more general than that" (1945b, 197–98).

Under pressure from the American Catholic theological community, several problems appear in Murray's own manner of argument. He had earlier argued from a crisis at the international level to the need for organized cooperation to address the crisis. Yet under the accusation that he was endorsing large organizations perhaps as wide in scope as the World Council of Churches or the National Conference of Christians and Jews,[16] Murray quickly retreated under a subsidiarity principle to the diocesan level. Each bishop would presumably make his determinations within the dual directive principles of religious integrity and of common good. But in this last argument Murray had lost two features from which he initially began his argument and on which he based his conclusions,[17] namely, the element of internationalism and his further insistence on adequate institutional tools to deal with large-scale social-ethical issues. The theme of internationalism will reemerge in his thought and become an important element of his 1950s discussion of religious liberty. In the present debate, strict adherence to his subsidiarity principle would at most mean international organization of a nonfederated variety, which he had claimed Pius XII had found inadequate.

A second problem is evident in Murray's somewhat clumsy handling of the church authority problem, and, behind that, in his rather ad hoc epistemological appeals to theoretical and practical reasoning, by which he attempted to differentiate clerical and lay social roles. That he had not yet found a theory of knowledge that would be adequate to church life is also suggested by a curious omission in his response to Furfey. In 1943 Murray had posed as his three directing questions:

(1) Should the co-operation be organized? (2) What should be the
organizational form? (3) What should be the co-operating personnel?
(1943b, 262).

This last item, of course, encompassed the role of laymen and the
epistemological theory by which he had tried to grant them relative
autonomy, while preserving the "unity of Catholic faith." But it is
precisely this last question that he eliminated in the Furfey article
(1945a, 195–96). Why this omission?

The justification of lay Catholic autonomy appears to have been a
primary concern throughout these discussions. Murray's appeal to the
practical action/theoretical reason distinction tended to keep the priest
out of the formation of particular laws. But his distinction also kept
the layman from an active role within the theological realm. Murray
never explicitly stated that the lay role in intra-ecclesiastical, theological discourse was purely passive, but the logic of his argument seems
permeated by such a notion, and his practical/theoretical distinction
did nothing to challenge such a presupposition. Against the background problem of possible lay Catholic religious indifference, the
question of an active lay role in that field of knowledge which is
particular to the church never had a chance to develop. Murray had
already ruled out the possibility and advisability of theological
discourse in that temporal order proper to the layman.

Now, all of this worked fairly well as long as the actors in the
drama were only the layman and the priest, and as long as the content
was theological. Practical judgments and theoretical or theological
judgments are kept distinct both in a sociological sense (according to
visible positions within the church) and in an epistemological sense
(practical determination and motivational generality). But a problem
entered at the level of episcopal action within the church. The bishop is
not simply a determiner of theological or motivational content. The
bishops and the pope actively judge particular forms of social action
and the moral health of the temporal common good. Through the
bishops' concern for the temporal common good as well as for the
integrity of Christian faith, Murray preserved the affirmation that the
church (and Pius) could and should address social value questions. But
these judgments of value have been seemingly reserved to the bishops.
This notion of evaluation reunited the temporal and the theological (or
politics and faith) in the common sphere of the ethical, but had also
denied to the layman any autonomous, evaluative judgment. Practical
reason defined solely as construction of organizations and of laws was
not sufficient for a conception of lay involvement in particular moral
determination. In a sense, then, what Murray differentiated according

to matters of intentionality (the natural order and the divine), he dissolved in a consideration of matters of value.

Nor does Murray's notion of a natural law "spirituality" appear to break the purely technical notion of practical judgment that he ascribes to laymen. Granted lay "spirituality" as a general field of motivational truths directing laymen toward common, interfaith cooperation, Murray had not yet considered these natural law truths as in some sense informative of lay, constructive judgments. Between motivating theory and practical action Murray would have to discover and situate a full set of ethical valuations which, although general in relation to specific determinations, are specific enough to indicate the primary values that must be maintained by large social realities. In time, he will identify the necessary natural law principles not simply as symbols or propositions that engage human civic friendship, but more fully as judgments that direct the social agent's attention to the valued aspects of social organization. The principles will be at once value laden, but also specific to questions of social justice.

Here Murray has in effect equated the theoretical and the evaluative, at least concerning the social location of theological reflection and ethical evaluation for the Catholic. The church in its clerical differentiations is the proper forum for theological reflection, either of the *quoad nos* or the *quoad se* variety. And the episcopacy is the proper and final forum for the consideration of matters of social-ethical value. It is one thing, however, to claim that the church has a right and ability to address all social questions of religious and moral value. It is another to claim that the hierarchy is always and immediately accurate in its perceptions of the values at stake in the social arena, that it is always correct in its judgments concerning those values and their proper institutionalizations, and that, therefore, lay Catholics must always remain submissive and passive in the face of hierarchical, ethical evaluations.

Although the force of Murray's argument dissipated amid his epistemological and ecclesiastical confusions, two key advances over his opponents should be noted. First, Murray broke with the notion that the principles which govern moral choices are in a strong sense lexically ordered. The relationship between principles differs from one age to another, varying with the relative internal and external health of surrounding social realities, including the church itself. Second, because of his fairly rationalistic theory of human knowing, Murray was led to formulate the need for a (natural law) spirituality. Between internal human drives and social action there must intervene some type of knowledge that is socially communicable and socially affirmed. Murray's notion of a spirituality will soon evolve into that of social consensus.

These two advances opened the way for Murray to develop his notions of historical prudential judgment, general social value commitments, and society as the forum for social ethical determination. But prior to defining these social-ethical realities, he would have to confront and face down the individualistic limitations of his own epistemological theory. This confrontation and eventual rejection took place in his first attempt to justify civil religious liberty.

II. RELIGIOUS LIBERTY: AN ARGUMENT FROM ESSENTIAL DEFINITIONS.

While Murray's debate over intercredal cooperation was primarily framed, at least in its final phases, with Catholics in mind, his first advance into the religious liberty debate was shaped by a concern for Protestant misunderstandings of "the Catholic position."[18] He sought to correct such misunderstandings for the familiar reason that secularism and totalitarianism present grave dangers to modern society (1945e, 241). In light of these dangers, Catholics, Protestants, and Jews must come to some common understanding on the religious liberty issue, thereby establishing an atmosphere of mutual trust in the face of those socially destructive forces. Murray's first argument, then, was an attempt to ground a common, mutually acceptable understanding of religious liberty.

He divided the general religious liberty question into three distinct, but related aspects: "the ethical question, the theological question, and the political question" (1945e, 244–45). As many have commented, Murray's first Catholic religious liberty argument collapsed (Love, 1965a, 46–48; Sebott, 1977, 22). Only the ethical expression of his argument managed to get into print, before Murray himself abandoned the method that directed the project. We do have, however, an outline of all three arguments in a preliminary draft that Murray had sent to Archbishop Edward Mooney in April 1945 (1945d). The draft will be of some help in understanding the general structure of his argument and the reasons why he himself considered it a failure.

A. The Three Arguments and Their Interrelationship.   Just as the post-World War II international order would be condemned to chaos without a consensus concerning the moral basis of society, likewise all Christian attempts at shaping a just society would be sabotaged without a properly ethical, mutually acceptable grounding for the affirmation of religious liberty. Catholics and Protestants must then begin their argument in the realm of ethical theory. Any attempts to begin with historical analysis or an analysis of contemporary facts (such as Spain) perforce included the importation of unexamined ethical and theological judgments which added confusion to the debate.[19] An ethical argument was necessary for a clarification of the bases of such judgments. Murray's call for a specifically ethical discussion was both a reflection of the natural law insistence on the necessary moral basis for social living and an assertion on Murray's part of the necessary (and sufficient) conditions for Protestant and Catholic mutual understanding.

The initial ethical discussion, as Murray conceived it, was abstract in two respects. First, it had to be detached from the fact and content of divine revelation in the person of Jesus Christ. Murray had a clearly formulated notion as to the center of the Protestant-Catholic theological maelstrom. "Catholic and Protestant theologies of the Church are radically divergent and irreconcilable" (1945e, 241). Since Protestants and Catholics were in a state of theological war, the ethical grounding had to prescind from the theological/revelational principles of the particular faiths.

> In reason, we cannot be asked to accept a solution to the problem of religious liberty that is conceived in terms of Protestant ecclesiology. In turn, we cannot demand that the solution of the problem be postponed until Protestants shall have accepted our ecclesiology (1945e, 241).

A public discussion of religious liberty must rest "initially and fundamentally, not on the dogmatic assertion of a theology . . . , but on a philosophical explanation of the structure of human conscience and of the State, for whose validity reason stands sufficient guarantee" (1945e, 234). That is, a mutually acceptable discussion of religious liberty must begin in the natural law. Second, the ethical argument must also be abstracted from the problem of applications in the concrete world. The argument was in the realm of theory, not involving prudential or practical judgment. One could form an ethical argument which would be ideal in the realm of theory, but was not immediately applicable to the political arena.

The theological argument must also be abstract in that it must be separated from practical or political reasoning (1945d, 16; 1945e, 235). Just as the ethical argument would result in an ideal conception of religious liberty, likewise would the theological argument; but neither was immediately applicable to the real world. The theological argument differed from the ethical in that it took account of the fact and the content of divine revelation.

As with his cooperation argument, Murray contended that the political institutionalization of religious liberty (the "political argument") must proceed out of a consensus in the realm of theory (1945d, 17). And, it might ideally be possible to form an understanding and institutionalization of religious liberty out of both an ethical and a theological understanding, but Murray's discussion was conditioned again by a judgment of the impossibility of theological consensus between Catholics and Protestants.

> Briefly, I would put the possibilities thus: (1) we can reach an important measure of agreement on the ethical plane; (2) we must agree to disagree on the theological plane; (3) but we can reach harmony of action and mutual confidence on the political plane, in virtue of the agreement previously established on the ethical plane (1945e, 239–40).

Murray then had three arenas of understanding—the ethical, the theological, the political. The first two were within the theoretical pole of his theoretical/practical distinction, with the first being the only practicable basis for the last. Two further presuppositions of this general argument are important here.

First, Murray argued that whatever conclusions resulted from the ethical, purely natural, argument would not be contradicted by conclusions derived from the theological argument. Just as grace brought nature to a higher fulfillment without contradicting nature, so "the [religious] rights of conscience as determined by the natural law remain in their full validity under the Christian law" (1945e, 277–78).[20] Judgments made from a purely natural law perspective would not, and could not, be reversed from a theological/revelational perspective, for the presupposition in principle of such a reversal would infer a contradiction between God the creator and God the redeemer. That there might be theoretical problems with this quick theistic grounding did not draw Murray back from his conclusions. By claiming an essential harmony between his two theoretical arguments, and by his positioning of the ethical argument, he granted to the ethical argument its own relative autonomy and further granted to that argument some control over the premises and conclusions of the theological argument. This procedure did (and later would) allow Murray some maneuvering room that a traditional canonical argument did not.

Second, it should be noted that even a natural law basis for religious liberty was again judged to contain a socially necessary, religious content. Murray insisted that the first order of business for each question was the establishment of "essential" definitions, i.e., of the terms necessary to capture the moral world under consideration. For the ethical argument, one needed the terms "God," the "moral law," "human conscience," and the "state." At the theological plane, the terms "Christ," the "law of the Gospel," and the "Church" must be added to those terms of the ethical argument. The final argument needed the additional terms "political prudence" and, perhaps, "political constitutions" (1945e, 235), with an always necessary consideration of "the religious aspects of civil liberty" (1945d, 12). Some terms for the natural law, ethical argument are, of course, religious. And Murray insisted that, whether the political argument be spun out of the ethical and/or theological arguments, a discussion of the "religious aspects of civil liberty" as collectively maintained religious content guide political deliberations. A religious understanding of liberty was necessary, although this understanding could not, in certain circumstances, be revelationally based. Once again, only those who could reach consensus, at the very least, over these natural law, religious principles could hope to enter into fruitful public discussion.[21]

With these general comments, I may now turn to the content and dynamics of each of his three arguments: the ethical, the theological, and the political. For the ethical argument, I must present, in rather extended form, Murray's notion of conscience and the world in which conscience is situated, before I can outline his argument for religious liberty as based in natural law. The theological argument and the revealed universe as Murray defined it can then be presented more briefly. For both ethical and theological arguments, I will present schematic "maps" that Murray himself drew to organize the essential elements of a natural and a revealed universe, respectively. For the ethical argument, we have both a preliminary "map" from Murray's memorandum to Mooney (1945d) and a redrawn "map" of that same natural law universe as presented in his published article, "Ethical Problem" (1945e). (The differences between these two versions will help point out, in my conclusion, some movements in Murray's own thinking between the preliminary and the published forms.) However, I will be able to present only a preliminary map of the theological universe, since Murray never brought his theological argument to print. After outlining these two theoretical arguments, brief mention will be made of Murray's "Political Argument." And, finally, I will conclude this section with a discussion of some of the tensions within these arguments and between them. This entire consideration is important for understanding Murray's later rejection of all conscience-based arguments.

B. The Ethical Argument.   Murray attempted, first, to establish a natural law grounding for the concept of religious liberty, a grounding which is augmented but not negated by the new order of revelation. "We are supposing that the problem is posited in what Catholic thought calls 'the order of pure nature'; we are moving in the universe of discourse characteristic of Scholastic ethics, the natural science of morals, whose single architect is human reason" (1945e, 242).[22] A reasonable inspection of the natural order exposes both a keystone for the religious liberty argument and the moral universe within which that keystone is situated.

1. Conscience and Two Versions of the Natural Universe.   Murray chose conscience as the keystone or pivotal concept of his natural law argument because conscience is that faculty of the human person which is the most divine (1945e, 232). Conscience is the "voice of God," the manner by which the will of God is "mediated to the human order." Following from these metaphors of voice and mediation, Murray's definition of conscience is clear at its center and somewhat vague at its peripheries. In keeping with the conception of Thomas Aquinas, conscience is, in its narrowest definition, the ability to judge the moral worth of specific acts, "a practical judgment of reason, whereby in the light of the known law a man judges of the morality of a concrete act, whether it is licit, or prescribed, or prohibited" (1945e, 254). Within even this narrow definition, the reasonable functioning of conscience establishes the individual human person as an autonomous source of moral agency with immunities from external coercion. It is the basis and practice of freedom which is a participation in the freedom and power of God, even though the free determination of conscience concerns only specific acts. Murray, however, also sometimes extended the notion of conscience to include the orders of law or moral demand under which the human person operates.[23] In this broader notion, conscience is also the perception and internalization of those orders of law. As I will note, it is within this extended notion of conscience that Murray defines freedom as correlated with law. At any rate, the keystone of his argument for religious liberty is the dignity of conscience as demonstrated in the power of particular determination, in its freedom, and in the human perception of the dictates or principles of general natural law.

Murray insisted that any discussion of the rights of conscience must be situated within the moral universe as this latter is also discovered by reason. In this argument, his "principles" are both intentional and definitional: they point to elements of the ethical universe that must be included in an ethical argument, and they define those elements. The easiest way to get at the shape of his ethical universes, I believe, is by a consideration of two different natural mappings that he himself drew—the earlier form as part of the first outline presented to Mooney, the second form in the published, ethical argument. Since the following discussion relies heavily on the two different versions of the natural universe schematics, both are duplicated here for reference purposes[24] (the Mooney version of the theological universe will be presented shortly).

The general structures of these two versions of the natural moral universe are, of course, similar. Conscience is a mediating reality between general laws and principles, on the one hand, and particular

Preliminary (Mooney) Ethical Universe:

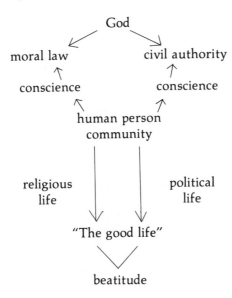

actions and beliefs, on the other (1945e, 258–59).[25] And both versions are composed of two branches which correspond roughly to the sphere of private, individual moral action and that of public action.[26] The polemical background for the positioning of conscience and for there being two sides to the universe deserves some attention.

Murray's positioning of "conscience" is determined within a discussion of freedom. According to Murray, liberty or freedom can become a morally intelligible concept only in correspondence to law. To substantiate this point he situated the freedom-law polarity against the background of the rational psychological relationship of will and reason. Will and reason are to the "physical" order what freedom and law are to the moral order. Will does not operate as a blind drive independently of reason, as some modern theories would have it. Will always proceeds to act in response to a conceived good.[27] And the conceived goods are presented by reason. "Every free act is an obedience to a judgment of reason" (1945e, 245). The only way in which human will can be turned from attainment of a good is by corrupting the understanding of that good.

Similarly, in the moral universe, freedom or "moral liberty is the power deliberately to obey the dictates of reason, i.e., of law" (1945e, 245). To claim no restrictions on human moral freedom is a contradiction of the dynamics of human rationality. The assertion of the

Final ("Ethical Problem") Ethical Universe:

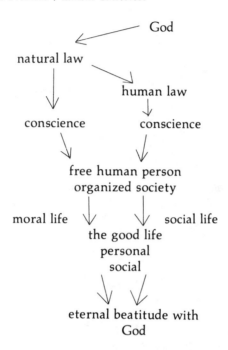

absolutely autonomous conscience, the conscience as outside of law (*conscientia exlex*), is a psychological absurdity. The human person may falsely understand the law and thereby end up with an erroneous judgment concerning the moral worth of an act, but such a possibility does not contradict the general structure of the moral, psychological reality within which human choices are made. Therefore, any discussion of the rights and powers of conscience must be situated within the appropriate orders of law.

The question then becomes, what are the appropriate sources of law? Just as Murray's general positioning of conscience within the moral universe was guided in part by a polemical concern with *conscientia exlex*, so the dual branches of that universe are shaped by other polemical concerns. A slight difference in polemical emphasis accounts for the differences between the preliminary and the final natural schemata. The preliminary schema suggests that it was generated primarily with the problem of laissez-faire theories of government in mind. In an earlier introductory article on religious liberty, Murray noted approvingly F. Ernest Johnson's condemnation (Johnson 1944) of the "entire laissez-faire conception of life and enterprise" (1945b, 106). Against the individualistic, absolute rights claims that ground such conceptions, Murray wrote:

> The old individualistic argument ("My mind is free—so therefore should be my tongue") does not work. As soon as one begins to spread ideas, one moves into a new ethical dimension—that of the social good; and one comes under a new ethical principle of control—the interests of the common good (1945b, 96–97).

This "new ethical dimension" creates another arena of ethical concern, which is not simply the aggregate collection of individual goods. Further on, Murray will spell out this distinction more clearly. But now his characteristic manner of describing this two-sided form of the moral universe is in terms of authorities or powers. "In the natural order, the human person is subject to two powers, the power of God (the natural law) and the power of the state" (1945d, 14). And the state itself is under "direct mandate" to "care for the common good." Thus the first schema emphasizes the divine authorization of both the moral law and the moral action of the state for the common good, the "directive" role of both authorities on the individual, and the obligation of the individual to respond to both. Divine authorization, law, and obedience to God and civil authority were, for Murray, intimately involved. He wrote that the "will of God is brought to bear on man (a) through the natural law [in what will be found to be a fairly private sense] . . . , and (c) through the civil authority in political society," with the state being, in the natural order, the "sole external moral authority over man."[28] It would appear, then, that in his first schema Murray's concerns were primarily theistic and concentrated on the individual agent in the latter's recognition of the authority of moral law and the moral authority of the state concerning social goods. Here his notion of the state might rightly be called "uncritical."

In the second published natural schema, Murray's polemical concerns appear to be just as theistic and obedience-orientated, but there has been a shift toward a concern with totalitarian regimes. The dropping of the state from this schema will be discussed further on, but it is obvious that Murray is attempting to situate more clearly the state and the agency for the common social good within the general moral law. Although government exists by divine command, the manner and the shape of its laws are dependent on the general natural law. Murray has absorbed some of the European church's awareness of the drive toward nationalistic claims to absolute moral autonomy. As will be discussed later, this raised some problems concerning the concrete moral authorities in the real world, in the realms of both private and social ethical behavior. But, between these two schematics, Murray was moving from concentration on the individual toward at least an awareness of the institutional and historical reality of the state.

For later consideration, three further aspects of these moral universes should be noted. First, even within the preliminary schema, Murray offered a control over state law in the imperative that the state is under a divine obligation to adjust its laws to maintain a harmonious relationship with the natural (personal) law. The state has a responsibility to pose its own laws in such a way that the internal peace of the individual is maintained. The two authorities (God and the moral law, on the one hand, and the state, on the other) cannot make contradictory demands on the individual. There seems here a presumption that private and public morality can and ought to be harmoniously related, much as nature and grace are related, but also as equally distinct (1945d, 9).[29]

Second, Murray's use of the term "law" is somewhat ambiguous. The problem lies in his use of metaphor and in a failure to distinguish between the kinds of forces which back up the various laws. In its closest connection with conscience, a law is a particular judgment concerning a particular act (1945e, 246). The judgment whether or not to perform this specific act at this time is the "mediated" will of God. One is obliged under divine law to follow the dictates of conscience since they are the "voice of God." These uses of the terms "mediation" and "voice" situate the individual act within the general human obligation to conform one's action and life to the specific will of God, but also endow specific judgments with the obligatory force of coercive law.

At a more general level (and more proper to the use of the term in the expression "natural law"), the term "law" is applied to general directives and definitions which serve as the theoretical principles out of which specific determinations are made (1945e, 246). True to his Aristotelian/Thomistic background, Murray maintained that human consciousness discovers these principles through the experience of living. The most general of these principles or precepts, "Do good and avoid evil," requires little more than breath and life for its discovery (1945e, 246). Secondary and tertiary principles, however, are found through increasing amounts of experience and examination (1945e, 256).[30] And as one's examination of human behavior moves through the further levels of natural law, the principles so derived become more specific, less universally applicable.

Now, specific acts of conscience carry the force of divine sanctions, since in Murray's version of the natural order there is a life-after-death accounting for faults. General laws understood as principles, however, while authoritative because mandated by God, transcend the order of punishment and reward. To be brought into the divine order of ethical sanction, these principles must be mediated to the order of the particular by the individual (through the judgments of conscience) or by a divine authority that directly enlightens the individual concerning each specific application. The individual has the obligation to allow the general formation of his understanding by authoritative sources, but the principles as such do not constitute an immediate legal order.[31]

This generalized use of the term "law" in "natural law" stands in contrast to its usage in the expression "human law." Human law is concrete, specific, and backed by direct coercive sanctions. The laws of the state are immediately juridical, at their best when clearly specifying the boundaries of coercive restraint and punishment, or reward. The more logical correlative of human law in Murray's framework is the specific dictates of conscience, not the general principles of natural law (unless one is a strict legalist). Both the specific dictates of conscience and human laws create an immediate situation of specific moral obligation for the individual, the first pertaining primarily to the private arena and the second to the realm of the common good, in Murray's present understanding of the state.

Finally, we should note an uneasy correspondence between Murray's twin law source theory and his social theory. He maintained that within a natural universe "there [are] only two natural, and therefore obligatory, societies—domestic society and civil society." Both are commanded by God, and are necessary for human development and formation of the conscience. The family, however, appears to have no points of contact with the common good or the concerns of the state. It is defined solely in terms of immunities from state interference.[32] It does not enter into the public arena as a source of law applicable to public order, except again as a field of immunity. All other subsidiary organizations in the natural order, including religious, are voluntary organizations.[33] And since they are not commanded by God, they do not appear to be sources of public moral norms or of public moral awareness, even though helpful to personal living. Voluntary organizations are to be granted liberties solely as "extensions of individual rights and obligations under conscience" (1945e, 257). Murray therefore had one intermediate institution (the family) which existed in its own right, but had no social role for the common good; all other intermediate institutions were extensions of one pole of the moral universe, the individual. For the problem of religious liberty, then, the only relevant sources of ethical guidance are the conscience and the state, even though there is at least one other necessary social unit.

2. *The Argument.*   Within this conception of the moral universe, Murray developed his argument for religious liberty as follows. Given his basic natural law assertion that all human liberty falls within a pregiven structure of law, Murray argued that obligations exist prior to rights at the levels of both the individual and the state.[34] Since God is absolute law giver, neither the individual nor the state can claim rights against God. But since they both have fundamental obligations toward God, they have obligations but also rights toward each other.[35] These obligations toward God establish both the individual and the state in positions of relative autonomy vis-à-vis one another. And they are further distinguished by the individual preoccupation with the individual good, whereas the state is concerned solely with the common good. Both have moral functions within their respective spheres of concern.

The individual, then, has no claim to rights against God (1945e, 263). He has only the obligation to follow the will of God as expressed through the natural law. The individual also has the obligation to submit to the common good dictates of human law or the state, but he possesses as well the immunities which follow from the nature of conscience: the right not to be coerced in matters of opinion (1945e, 261-62). The state has the obligation to follow God's law in its social aspect, and no rights to deviate from that law (1945e, 266, 273). It has further the right to claim the social, moral participation of citizens in the achievement of the common good, but it also falls under the obligation to harmonize natural and human law for the integrity of the citizen (1945e, 267).

The religious obligations of the individual and of the state toward God are quite similar. Both have an obligation to recognize the existence of God and the fact that God makes ethical demands on each in its own proper order (1945e, 267). Both are obliged to worship God, again each in its own order (1945e, 263, 267). And both, within the hypothetical possibility that God would reveal himself in some way other than pure nature, have an obligation "of accepting a higher belief, law, and mode of worship, if God reveals them as His will" (1945e, 264). There is, then, in Murray's conception of the moral natures of the individual and the state a near one-to-one correspondence between the obligations of both (achieved by a personification of the state).

The question of religious liberty arises between the individual and the state. While both have the obligation to worship God (as God chooses to be worshipped), the individual has an obligation to believe and act according to his conscience (1945e, 259). The principles and precepts which inform conscience may be adequate or inadequate, and may or may not be perceived by the individual to be inadequate. In the case where the individual is aware that his grasp of precepts is not adequate, he stands under the obligation to seek out direction from the moral authorities of society (1945e, 258–59).[36] He cannot in his present situation act reasonably, that is, he cannot arrive at particular, correct, moral and religious judgments, and, therefore, "action must be held in abeyance."

The problem of the erroneous conscience establishes the limits of social coercion over the individual. The person of erroneous conscience is not aware that his perception of fundamental principles is incomplete or wrong. Such an individual can then act reasonably (and is under obligation so to act), but objectively he will judge immoral acts to be moral.[37] In such a situation, the state has no right to force the individual to act in a subjectively unreasonable manner. But because conscience is an individual faculty, the immunities of conscience remain within the individual. The state, with its semiautonomous concern for the public good, cannot and must not allow an attack by the individual on that public good. Therefore, "conscience is a valid principle of liberty only in the internal forum of private morality, where the law is simply that conscience must be obeyed" (1945e, 262). From all this one can, of course, easily conclude to the suppression of atheistic or immoral public expression, as Murray did (1945e, 267). The state has an obligation to "exhibit a positive patronage of religion and morality," and a right "to restrict . . . the spread of opinions, and to prohibit external actions, that tend to destroy the community belief in God and fidelity to moral standards," wherever possible. "[The state] is, therefore, morally obliged to assume the position that atheism and actions contrary to the natural law have no rights in the social order, and that they can claim no freedom of public advocacy or practice" (1945e, 269). The internal forum as he has defined it is quite private.

Such are the general outlines of Murray's first attempt at a natural law argument for religious liberty.

C. The Theological Argument.   The fact of divine revelation alters the list of terms proper to a religious liberty argument. To the list of necessary governing concepts must be added an essential definition of "Christ," of the "law of the Gospel," and of the "Church." And it is the definition of the church which divides Catholic and Protestant theological arguments. According to Murray, Protestants insist on "the equality of all the Churches, and of the synagogue, in all matters of right and privilege" as a theological principle (1945d, 13). That is, they deny that the institutional carrier of the new revealed order is the Roman Church.[38] Rather, they claim that all religious institutions advance the new order of salvific grace. The Catholic theological argument proceeds from an assertion of the necessity of the Roman Catholic Church for salvation. Murray's sketch of the theological argument traced out only the Catholic position.

The fact of divine revelation fundamentally alters the shape of the moral universe as the latter is discovered through natural reason, but this alteration is primarily in the form of an addition. Revelation introduces a third necessary institution into society: the church as the necessary source of eternal beatitude ("all who are saved are saved through the Church" (1945d, 13). In his memorandum to Mooney, Murray proposed the following schema, parallel to the "natural" schema, to outline the Catholic view of the shape of the new, revealed universe. It is again presented here for the purpose of comparison (1945d, 15).

Whereas in the natural universe man had only his own conscience and the moral state as sources of enlightenment, in the redeemed universe the individual now also has the institutional, authoritative church.[39] Although the powers and concerns of the church are purely spiritual, "the state is indirectly subordinate to the Church, *ratione finis*" (1945d, 15). This subordination is not simply one of honor. In those matters of the spiritual in the temporal sphere, "the competence of the Church is primary." And, whereas in the natural universe the state stood under obligation to establish harmony between human law and natural law, now the state must facilitate harmony between its own human law and both the natural and the ecclesiastical or revealed laws (1945d, 14). The Christian who is both citizen and church member has a right to such harmony.

In the natural universe, the state was the only perfect society, the forum in which humanity could reach its perfection. In the revealed universe, the church is also a perfect society. And since the supernatural does not negate the natural, the Christian lives within two perfect societies with two compatible but distinct ideals of perfection. The church as a necessary social institution must stand in a juridical relationship with the state, since the institutional church has an independent right to its own freedom.[40] Further, Murray claimed, a purely theological argument (taking account of the philosophical argument, but prescinding from the "political argument") would conclude to "the juridical union of the Church and State [as] the natural and necessary consequence of the vital union of Christian and citizen in the one man" (1945d, 14). This he called an "ideal solution" to the relationship of church and state. Such an ideal juridical solution

Preliminary (Mooney) Theological Universe:

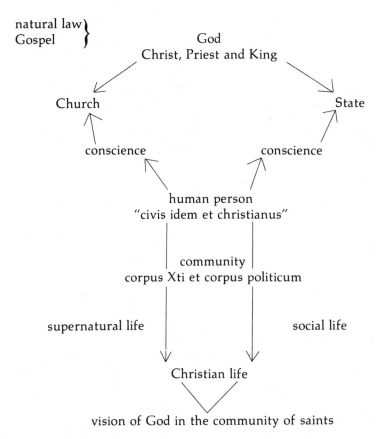

natural law ⎱
Gospel   ⎰

God
Christ, Priest and King

Church

State

conscience

conscience

human person
"civis idem et christianus"

community
corpus Xti et corpus politicum

supernatural life

social life

Christian life

vision of God in the community of saints

would respect the autonomy of the church as a perfect society and preserve "an inner peace and order which constitutes true freedom of religion" (1945d, 14).

Revelation therefore changes the governing concepts (principles) of argument and the moral universe in which the problem of religious liberty arises. It also establishes the necessity of an ordered (i.e., legal) relationship between church and state, but Murray refused to draw out from this an immediate conclusion for the political order. The reasons for his refusal rest in the nature of the political problem.

D. The Political Problem: Religious Establishment, Freedom, and Tolerance.
The political problem concerns the form of the "ordered" relationship between church and state. Reflecting his own insistence on the concrete institutional aspects of social realities, Murray offered as

possible forms for this ordered relationship only clearly juridical alternatives. This ordering could take the forms of union, concordat, or separation (1945d, 16-17). In arriving at a mutually acceptable juridical form, the governing criterion on the church's side is the freedom of the church (with its corollary of the internal harmony of the Catholic and citizen). From the state's side, the criterion is the common good, the collective health of the entire body politic. This common good is also expressed, at least in part, in the interior harmony of the Christian and citizen.

Murray asserted that none of these three forms can claim to be valid for all times and in all places.[41] However, he could only get to this assertion by avoiding any question of international institutionalization. Such political determinations are tied to the specific national conditions under consideration. And the common order of good for each nation will differ. Any generalized rejection of the Roman Catholic establishment in certain specific national contexts could only be based on a principle of "Protestant, abstract egalitarianism" (1945d, 18). The "political problem" is the evaluation of the particular common orders of good and the exercise of prudential determination for the care of those orders. The political order, in contrast to the ethical and theological orders, is practical judgment operating on specific, historical social objects, with primary attention given to the type of religious consensus available in each specific state.

Murray did, of course, want to present a Catholic view of religious liberty which would be acceptable to Protestants and would reduce Protestant suspicions of long-term Catholic political intentions, yet he did not want to deny that a state informed by a full Catholic theological doctrine would be more ethical and lead to a more fully realized common good than would a state informed only by natural law doctrine. There is such a thing as an objective order of common goods. His use of the particularity of political judgment could be understood to imply that the United States, in its apparent state of never-ending religious diversity, would be safe from attempted establishment. But there seems to be a deeper reason why he thought Protestants should rest easy—a distinction between Roman Catholic and the natural law states, on the one hand, and the atheistic and immoral states, on the other. It was on this basis that he distinguished between religious freedom and religious tolerance.

The mediating element in Catholic evaluations of specific forms of church/state relations is the character of a national group's specific religious attitudes. If only a natural law religious and moral consensus has been achieved, then society can be healthily if incompletely maintained without privilege for the church. If a Roman Catholic consensus has been achieved, then a position of privilege for the church will be a greater good for the society. But both of these determinations are good; they have positive moral bases for social construction.

The goodness of both the natural law and Catholic forms of moral consensus, however, stands in contrast to the state's allowing atheistic or immoral public expression. Such allowance for the sake of public peace must be understood as the acceptance of a lesser evil, the need for which arises out of a lack of moral fiber within society (1945e, 271). A morally degenerate people may destroy their minimal order of peace if their vices are suppressed.

This particularizing of the common good by linking it to consensus was only haltingly advanced by Murray at this time. The obviously different sympathies which he expressed toward religious pluralism and atheism, however, can be traced through the moral nature of consensus back to the principle of harmony. Given the alternatives of religious freedom or toleration, the governing index of the goodness of the first is the harmony which exists between the natural and the supernatural. That which is incomplete is not evil. However, any tolerance of common immorality or atheism, while perhaps being temporarily unavoidable, stands at variance with natural law ethics and, therefore, with Catholic theological thought. That is, toleration implies a lack of harmony between the public consensus and church teaching. This theological and moral contradiction can only be allowed for the sake of a lower order of harmony, the public peace in a physical sense (1945d, 16). Catholics could comfortably live with the lesser of two goods; but they must remain in an antagonistic tension with a lesser of two evils. The indices governing Catholic attitudes toward both situations are different. It was this difference in Catholic evaluation that Murray apparently hoped would lessen tensions between Catholic and Protestant Americans.

E. The Unresolved Problems.   Why did Murray's first religious liberty argument (even in his own judgment) "fail"? I suggest here six problem areas: the first two revolved around Murray's undeveloped notions of the social realities with which he dealt; the last four as possible ways out of his bifurcated individual/social universe that he was not yet able to appropriate.

One immediate problem can be noticed in a comparison of the preliminary and final schematics as shown on pages 35, 36 and 43. Both the preliminary ethical and theological models were, of course, institutionally specific. The state as a moral personality was empowered directly by God as the agent of, and the intelligence of, the common good. In the theological universe, the institutional church replaced the individual conscience as the source of personal moral understanding, adding also a revelational content. In the published ethical map, however, the state has been replaced by the "human law," and that has been situated under the natural law. There is an abstraction or deinstitutionalization here between the preliminary and final arguments, a shift from institutional carriers of meaning to the nature of the meaning by which the state and the individual are constituted. Murray's argument is shifting toward cognitive theory considerations (which will be further traced in chapter 3), and also moving away from a personalized notion of the state. (He will have to develop a notion of "society" to re-situate the social location of these laws.) Why this move?

If, in the final natural schema, the state was left in the place of human law and was situated under natural law, then the theological map with the church as custodian of natural and divine law would leave the state clearly dominated by the church. With Murray's yet confused notions of law and principle, such a schema would vacate any conception of the state's relative autonomy vis-à-vis the church. However, if a final theological model was similarly deinstitutionalized, then, although the schema might help in a discussion of the relationship of those various laws, much clarification of the relation of these laws to the institutions of church and state would be in order before the juridical question could be addressed. Such a legal theological universe would be too abstract for the notion of political judgment with which Murray was working. Several other social elements of that universe would have to be sketched before a political argument could advance, not the least of which are consensus and the juridical and social.

Second, Murray's argument was bound to fail in the American public forum because of the practical conclusions which seem to derive from it. Although Murray appears to have evaluated the grounding for religious freedom and for toleration differently, at a final glance the resultant differences in social position of the Protestant and the atheist dissolve. While he does seem to distinguish the bases of these two sets of choices, his theory of rights leaves Protestants (in the situation of union) and atheists (in a naturally moral, intolerant society) in about the same public position. In either case, the Protestant and atheist have the natural rights in public expression as these rights arise from the nature of conscience. That is, both groups are immune from coercion in the private forum (1945a, 103). And Murray avoids discussion of the fate of voluntary intermediate institutions in societies in which union and intolerance have been achieved. It will be recalled that the rights of voluntary institutions were merely extensions of individual rights in a natural universe. In a theologically ideal universe, Protestant churches seem to share no more than the rights of their individual members vis-à-vis the public order. In a natural ideal universe, atheistic or secularistic organizations fare no better, nor worse.[42] Publicly, then, this argument would not be deemed acceptable.

The four remaining problems revolve around Murray's inability to bridge the individual/social bifurcation of his moral universe. The third is the just mentioned grounding of a social right. Within a field of natural discourse, Murray has attempted to found the concept of religious liberty on conscience as an aspect of human reason. As he shaped his argument, however, two limitations should be noticed. First, the immediate moral universe is bifurcated between the arena of individual moral responsibility and that of social responsibility, and conscience as defined resides solely within the individual side of that bifurcation. In all his schematics of the moral and theological universe, Murray included "conscience" on both sides of the map, as operative in the personal and in the social/political realms. However, although he readily transferred an analogous, perhaps even univocal, concept of moral personality from the individual to the state, he did not similarly transfer the concept of conscience. Rights are based on a purely personal notion of conscience. Murray here lacked a notion of public rationality. And, further, he established the rights of conscience (to act according to reason) within the limited notion of conscience as particular ethical judgment. Although he at times wrote of *conscience* as a perception of principles, the rights of the individual arise solely out of the imperative to act in accordance with particular determination, not out of any activity in recognizing or developing an awareness of those principles.[43] Murray, then, left the individual and the state (society) within two disconnected moral universes, and even within the individual wing, based the right to religious liberty on only one aspect of individual moral cognition. Only after he connects the individual and the social through a theory of social reasoning (in the formation of specific determinations *and* general commitments), and extends the active obligations as well as rights of the individual beyond the limited rational function of particular determination, will Murray develop a grounding for religious liberty which bridges the gap between the internal and external forums.

A fourth problem, and a further reason for his inability to bridge his bifurcated universe, rested in his notion of "necessary" institutions. A partial way out of Murray's inherent individualism might have been through an appeal to other institutions formative of human conscience. One might argue that these institutions have their own proper autonomy, and therefore have claims of immunity vis-à-vis political power. Then the individual, through affiliation with said institutions, would have a claim of public expression, at least within those institutions. Such a possible extension of rights, however, appears to have been ruled invalid by Murray's conception of "necessary" institutions.

Throughout this argument Murray insisted that there are two sources of moral authority within the natural universe: the dictates of natural law as perceived by each reasonable person and the dictates of the morally concerned state. This assertion was directly counter to the outlaw conscience and the laissez-faire state. However, these are considered to be the only sources of ethical enlightenment in such a universe. The family, while dictated by natural law and therefore a "necessary" institution, has no determinative moral input into the collective moral awareness of society. The state is the only "necessary" (read: "authoritative") social institution for the larger social arena. And, it would appear, since all other institutions (including religions) are voluntary, they also have no collective moral import or input. They are not necessary for the collective moral life. They have their rights and also their focus only on the individual. No institutions, therefore, break open or mediate the bifurcated moral universe. And there exist only two "necessary" moral "authorities" even in the new order of revelation.

Another partial way of bridging the bifurcation might be recognition of the "political argument" as a social form of conscience, and therefore as a possible base for a social right. The specific judgments of conscience and specific political judgments are both defined as prudential. Why did Murray not yet recognize and utilize such an argument? The fifth problem appears to be with the contingent, historical nature of the social forum. As Murray had correctly identified, political judgments are always situated within the historical consensus of society, and that consensus could be degenerate. The prudential judgments of individual conscience are situated within a presumably permanent set of moral principles, and those principles are presumably open to enlightened inquiry, regardless of social context. The permanence of the moral universe and the relativity of the public consensus appear to have kept Murray from viewing conscience and political judgment as analogously similar, and so his theory of rights remained individualistic. He would need to recognize the social and therefore contingent nature of even private moral principles before he would be able to accept social processes of moral determination as grounding social rights.

Finally, a sixth problem is evident in Murray's tendency to equate evaluative reasoning and religious reasoning, ethics and theology. While this equation poses difficulties in its own right, here, by equating religion and ethics and visualizing ethics as primarily and exclusively an act of conscience or individual prudential determination, Murray has likewise thereby privatized his religion. There is no place here for a public religion and a public faith as a reasoning activity of the community. Murray is, of course, concerned with an institutional church, a material social reality, but he has yet to discover the forces by which that church is held together—forces defined primarily in terms of common meaning and the actions of coming to common meaning. In effect, then, Murray's ethical theory has betrayed the social dimensions of his faith, a betrayal that Gregory Baum has described as an "ideological captivity" of the church that masks the social dimensions of the Scriptures and of the church's own activities (Baum 1975, esp. 193–223). That such an ideological captivity can also be untrue to the social dimensions of the church's ethical universe will be the main impulse behind Murray's eventual abandonment of theories of privatized ethical judgment.

However one might judge Murray's notion of the compatibility of pure nature and graced nature, it is obvious that within his own presuppositions the difficulty with his argument resides in the narrowness of his grounding for religious liberty, even more so perhaps than in its abstractness. To found a social right on a demand for individual reasonableness between principles and particular judgments proved impossible.

III. CONCLUSION.   Two distinct aspects of the cooperation and religious freedom arguments suggest possible directions for Murray's further development. First, Murray based both arguments on a notion of ethical judgment made within a field of conceptually formulable principles. But there is a difference between those two sets of principles. In the cooperation debate, the principles of integrity and common good are directive in a very general sense of the church's apostolic mission; that is, they direct the moral intention of the church toward two social realities, church and temporal society. In the religious liberty debate, however, the principles under consideration are definitions of the distinct social realities within which the church operates, and as such both define and more importantly (if held to be timeless) limit the range of concepts within which the church can formulate justifications for specific types of actions. Yet, even here, both these directive and definitional principles in part assured that the universe of discourse in which Murray was arguing was conceived as essentially social, even if he did not yet have the conceptual tools for handling the processes by which ethical judgments and commitments are made within that social world. Murray's understanding of the directive principles will not substantially change, but primarily through a deeper understanding of those definitional principles, he will be able to escape the confusions of these two arguments. Changing defini- tional principles will facilitate changes in his conception of social ethical justification.

Second, throughout the following discussions, the role of the church in the ethical determinations and directions of civil society will present a constant problem for Murray. However, we should be apprised early of two blessings which the problem will confer on Murray's notion of social ethics. First, Murray's preoccupation with the actual, concrete reality of the Roman Church maintained for him a notion of society as basically pluralistic (a notion that was not at times clearly recognized). Neither the church nor civil society should be reduced one to the other, yet they must exist together. Murray increasingly envisaged, then, the need for mutual communications and intelligibility as foundational to social-ethical development within a differentiated public forum. As his conception of social pluralism expanded, so did his evaluation of the importance of discourse. Second, the notion of the church's role in reaching judgments of value (concerning all that Christian life touches) likewise preserved the large-scale nature of the social situation with which he dealt, thereby never allowing him to resolve social problems down to a level that would appear soluble simply by an appeal to, say, intersubjective feelings. The very complexity of the problems that an international church faces, their solution through difficult processes of public discernment and judgment, and the necessity for such a church of clear judgment, cast Murray's social ethics at a level distinct from what is normally appealed to even under the notion of "social solidarity." The love that is the core of human living is at the social level only analogous to the love typical of familial and smaller levels of social organization. This will remain true for Murray in his dealings with civil society as well as with the church.

The next five chapters, then, will attempt to show the develop- ments that the social theory of one American Catholic social ethician underwent during the mid-twentieth century. Again, my thesis is that Murray's own critical abilities (in the sense of reflective examination on his and other's arguments and arguing) and his growing awareness of the forces that constitute modern society led him, first of all, to an "ethics of discourse" and then, through a notion of society as a field of meaning, to the incorporation of even confessional languages as an integral aspect of social ethical discourse.

Chapter Two

RELIGIOUS LIBERTY:

The Historical Argument

In 1945 Murray had two choices: accede to the logic, defining terms, and methods of his previous arguments (along with their "inadequate" conclusions), or reflectively examine all three. He chose the latter, and the first to shift was his method. After his rejection of a Protestant historical methodology in the first church-state debate, his next move might have come as a surprise. In the first of fourteen articles (from 1948 to 1955)[1] he wrote:

> The discussion of the church's power in the temporal order must proceed from an historical point of view. Nothing is more unhelpful than an abstract starting point (1948f, 33).

A guiding maxim of this extended argument appears to have been *ab esse ad posse valet illatio*,[2] a whimsical twist on a debated Scholastic principle. If the church's arguments for and against various forms of juridical church-state relations have in the past changed, they can so change in the future. In order to account for and justify these changes, Murray had to develop a clearer notion of the church's ongoing evaluation of juridical forms.

In terms of his earlier distinction between natural law and theological manners of justifying religious liberty, these articles represent a seven-year examination and extension of the theological or ecclesiological argument. The argument is theological in that it takes account of principles which are revelationally based, and also in that natural and revealed principles are considered to be a permanent possession of the church. It is ecclesiological in that it arises out of the history or tradition of the universal church as that church adjusted to changing political and social forms. The turn to history or tradition was an attempt to reclaim both supernatural and natural principles which could then guide the present debate (1948f, 34). As in his 1945 argument, Murray contended that a theological argument for church-state relations must take account of both natural and supernatural premises. Any argument which proceeded out of purely theological premises could not adequately fulfill the church's obligations to the natural or temporal order.

The present argument was, then, an attempt to retrieve the set of principles which had guided the church's reflections on its relationship with the state, principles that Murray initially maintained to be a permanent possession of the church.[3] But when he turned to the history of ecclesiastical judgments, he found that more elements of the argument were involved in historical development than simply the relative degree of civil, religious consensus, and prudential judgments in response to that consensus. As he studied the past complex judgments that the church had made, he eventually had to admit that some natural law, definitional principles, which he had previously treated as timeless, are open to changing definition. That is, at least a "philosophical" argument is as much caught in historical contingent realities as is the "political" or prudential argument. And since the "theological" argument relies on the philosophical, the theological argument is at least indirectly open to historical changes in (some) "essential" defining principles.

Now, if the definitional principles that the church had used had changed (and could change), then it is certainly possible that other concepts might not have been used in past arguments, but might now be relevant to the present argument. Murray was thus able to make room in his thought for a sharp distinction between "society" and the "state." In the first argument, the state was defined as the custodian of the common good—this in reaction to excessively individualistic social theories (or nontheories). It was also defined as paternalistic. If that extended definition of the state has in fact changed, then the locus of moral concern for the common good might have to be relocated. Murray needed, at this point, the notion of "society" as a locus of such moral will and as the forum for moral deliberation. In the context of this religious liberty argument, he did not much develop this notion of society as a field of common meaning. He would have to turn to a study of American society to advance further toward such a notion (to be seen in the next chapter).

This eight-year study, then, yielded a wider notion of historical, contingent evaluations than did the first religious liberty argument. Murray took up an historical analysis, noticed changes in the meaning of the social realities that he encountered, and found the central importance of realities that he had previously only dimly recognized. With his argument now strengthened and deepened, Rome retired Murray to the sidelines of the debate, for a time.

In the following three sections, I will examine Murray's argument toward what he considered a more adequate understanding of ecclesiastical judgments concerning religious freedom. The first section turns on his study of indirect power, a study which exposed changing definitions of the state. The second section centers on Murray's confrontation with the conservative Catholic argument, a confrontation which somewhat ironically moved him toward the society-state distinction and toward a stronger argument. The final section follows his move into a study of the Leonine recommendations for civil intolerance, and Murray's transformation of that argument by incorporating the society-state distinction and his revised notion of social evaluation.

I. ACCIDENTAL AND ESSENTIAL SPIRITUAL MEANS.   When Murray considered the state under the single aspect of its dependence on the law(s) of God, his argument dissolved into the ambiguities of the notion of law with which he was working. Murray began his new argument in terms of "power," the power which the church exercises over the temporal order. The question concerned the means proper to the church in all times and in all social and political situations, not whether the church has a right to power over the temporal order. It is understood throughout his argument that the church has a divinely established right to direct, correct and judge particular institutions within the temporal order insofar as they relate to the supernatural end of the human person. Both social and private morality (as in the first argument) stand in essential relationship to the attainment of the human person's supernatural end.

What powers could the church claim by right? Murray began his argument with a consideration of the indirect power theory of Robert Bellarmine. He strategically established the basis of his critique of Bellarmine in a comparison of the Bellarminian theory to the direct power theory of what he called the "hierocrats" or the "political Augustinians" (1948f, 39–44; 1948g, 497, 503). Both Bellarmine and the hierocrats argued that the pope could depose a monarch on moral grounds and could call for the use of state civil coercion against heretics on religious grounds (1948g, 498). But Bellarmine's different grounding or justification for that right nearly led to his condemnation by the Roman curia and papacy.

The hierocratic or direct power position was based on the theory of one, sole source of moral authority within the redeemed universe. While these hierocrats agreed that the present moral universe was composed of two distinct moral powers—the temporal coercive and the spiritual of the two swords metaphor—the two powers were thought to have a unity in the person of Christ the King and Priest, with the two powers translated directly to the sovereign Roman Pontiff. It was then the right of the pope to confer the temporal power on the civil ruler. And if the pope could directly confer that power, he could also by divine right revoke it. Likewise, he had the right to direct the temporal sword toward the preservation of religious unity. Where possible within the limits of civil peace, the secular ruler had a duty (corresponding to the pope's right) to persecute erroneous religious opinions. Ultimately, the problem with the theory is a confusion of powers: "In a word, in this theory, the prince has a direct religious power, as the Church has a direct temporal power" (1948f, 39–42).

Murray contended that the theoretical underpinnings of Bellarmine's own theory rested in the mainline Catholic tradition of social thought (1948g, 502–3, 532). The first expression of that theory arose in the context of the caesaropapist attempts of Emperor Anastasius to take over control of the church (1948g, 523; 1948f, 53). Against this attempt to subjugate the church to political ends, Pope Gelasius I posed his claim that "two there are...," two powers of independent origins and distinct ends, two institutions which derive their rightful powers independently from God. Thomas Aquinas further refined the tradition by situating the ground for civil society in the natural law, a law which was again not negated by revealed law. Civil society has its origins and its ends in the natural social perfection of man. The church has its origin in the positive divine law of the revealed order in Christ, a law directing man to his supernatural end. State and church constitute two distinct societies, and the term "society" is defined at this point solely with respect to their independent origins and ends.

While Bellarmine's theological and natural social principles were, according to Murray, consistent with the mainline tradition of Catholic thought, Murray still had to explain why Bellarmine's thought resulted in the judgment that the church (pope) ought to intervene coercively in the political order (deposition of the king) and call for the use of coercive force in the realm of the spiritual (persecution of heretics). Murray discovered the ground for Bellarmine's conclusions ultimately in a political fact of the medieval life (1948f, 43–44). In the political chaos which introduced and accompanied the development of the Middle Ages, all institutions which controlled and governed the use of physical coercion (primarily the institution of law) had decayed. It was a time of "temporal disorder, ... a relative, contingent, time conditioned thing," a "disorder proper to immaturity" (1948g, 526). The breakdown of those political, legal, and social institutions necessary for the attainment of the temporal common good left the church as the only concrete institution available to check an unrestrained use of force.

> Actually, what the Church did was to step into a political vacuum, created by the absence of a political institution able to constrain the monarch to obedience to law. She found a vague and chaotic Germanic right of

popular resistance to unjust authority that was insufficient for its own purposes, and she transformed it into a new system of regular juridical procedure for the restraint, deposition, and punishment of Kings (1948g, 528).

In response to the political chaos, the church deposed several despotic rulers; the duty of the church toward the (now immature) temporal order was rightfully expressed by taking up some tools of that order. The fault of Bellarmine's conclusions was their basis: the now defunct medieval fact of political immaturity in the temporal order.[4] Unlike the hierocrats, however, he did not try to construct a unitary social theory to justify the assumption of coercive force by the medieval church. His theory, if not his conclusions, remained within the premises of dual origins and ends.

Although the medieval political fact of immaturity did not affect Bellarmine's theory, the image of society which resulted from the action of the medieval church did confuse a third essential distinction between church and state. Besides differing in origin and ends, they likewise differ in the means proper to the attainment of those ends. These means are correlated to those ends: the temporal order uses civil law with its coercive sanctions for the attainment of the temporal common good; the church properly uses noncoercive, spiritual means for the preservation and development of the faith of its members. The different means are the bases for the permanent rights by which the two orders affect one another. Any assumption by the church of properly political means can only be a temporary right[5] which disappears with the cessation of political immaturity. This state of immaturity is solved by

> ... the creation of institutions within the political order that will serve to insure the supremacy of law and its due processes against the encroachment of force, wielded either by the ruler or by other agencies. This is an exigence of rationality itself, a demand of the autonomy of the political order when developed to maturity, that it should be 'directed and corrected' from within itself, by the operation of its own political institutions (1948g, 527).

In his search for a purer expression of the Catholic dualistic social tradition, Murray then turned his attention to the work of John of Paris. John also held, as did Bellarmine, the Thomistic notion of the separate origin and end of the temporal, political order (1948f, 54–55). John, who in Murray's view wrote more as a "theologian than as a partisan," followed through the political consequences of this dualism, that is, he clarified the further distinction of means that are permanently possessed by the two powers or societies. The historical backdrop of John's exposition was the conflict between Pope Boniface VIII and Philip the Fair. Against the hierocratic claims of Boniface and Giles of Rome, John maintained the dualism of powers and the independent basis of political power. Against "regalism" (Philip's attempt to reduce ultimate societal meaning to the political) John posed the principle of the primacy of the spiritual. The church properly has the final word in matters of religion and morals, but the power it exercises in the temporal order must be moral or spiritual, not temporal and physically coercive.

As presented by Murray, John held that the church possessed six spiritual powers:

> His [John's] concern is to show that this power is singly and solely spiritual in character; and he does this by an analysis of it into its five component powers. These are (1) the consecration of the sacramental matter by the power of orders; (2) the administration of the sacraments, especially of penance—the absolution from sin in the forum of conscience by the power of the keys; (3) the preaching of the gospel by "the authority of the apostolate"; (4) the imposition of penalties in the external forum by "the juridical power" or coercive power; and (5) the distribution of ecclesiastical offices and faculties by the power of jurisdiction. To these is added a sixth power, (6) that of requiring from the faithful what is necessary for the support of the spiritual ministers of the Church (1949e, 204; the numeration is my own).

The first two powers (of consecration and absolution) are obviously spiritual in that they are sacramental. Even if the granting or withholding of absolution involves sanctions, those sanctions concern eternal, not temporal life. The fifth and sixth powers do not immediately concern the problem of physical coercion (1949e, 204–11).[6] The third, magisterial power of the church is directed not immediately to the political, legal order of political office, but rather at the conscience of the king concerning matters of faith, not politics. The fourth power of judgment concerning the external forum remains spiritual insofar as the church can only call on those sanctions which properly belong to the church, ultimately its power of excommunication from church membership. The church can excommunicate a king for ethical and religious crimes (sins), but this excommunication does not touch directly the king's right to his office. The church can further excommunicate the subjects of the king who follow him in his religious or moral crimes, and thereby set conditions for the deposition of the king. But such deposition must arise from sources other than the church. The this-worldly sanctions of the church only affect right of membership in the church, not title to temporal, political office (1948g, 534–35).

Now, if the church cannot by permanent right directly exercise coercive power in the temporal order, can it call on the use of coercive, political power in preserving or advancing purely spiritual ends? Or inversely, can the state allow its powers to be used for the maintenance of the spiritual society? At this point, Murray has some difficulty answering either perspective of the problem. He has not sufficiently developed a clear notion of society (outside of origins and ends) and a notion of limited government. But this argument seems to proceed somewhat as follows. If there has been a development from early medieval times to the rise of Philip the Fair's nation-state, and if this development has been from a condition of immaturity to maturity, then the nation-state must be allowed the necessary autonomy to pursue its own goals as these are dictated by natural reason. Murray, in fact, calls the rise of the nation-state a "dictate of reason" or an "intention of nature" (1949e, 181, 230). Now, if the church was forced in the early medieval period to assume direct care for the common good in the form of feudal relationships with immature governmental institutions, and if the necessity of this assumed direct control over temporal affairs disappeared with the rise of the mature state, then the state as sole custodian of coercive power can reassume its natural responsibilities for the temporal common good, including the means proper to the temporal order. Further,

> ...the state itself is a perfect society, with its own finality, outside of which it cannot act (any more than the Church can act outside of hers), and with its own autonomy, that forbids the use of its powers as instruments to ends that are not its own (analogously, the powers of the Church cannot be used to ends that are not her own) (1948f, 97).
> The Church has no right to demand of the state what the state is not required by nature to give (1948f, 75).

The state may not use its coercive means for religious ends, nor may the church demand such means. The rejection of a direct power theory with its confusion of the two orders must lead to a rejection of the use of state coercive means for spiritual ends. And inversely, the advocacy of coercive force for spiritual ends (as a permanent right) can be accepted only within an image of a unitary, nondualistic society, an image which is not true to modern political and social facts, nor to the theological truths of creation and redemption.

If all of this sounds rather tortuous, it was. Murray further complicated his argument by admitting that, even within the principle of social dualism, the state could in the medieval period advance religious unity by police means, but only for the sake of the temporal common good. At such a time, baptism was the entry sign to both the temporal and the spiritual orders (1948f, 41f). But the state, if it were true to its nature, would only inflict punishment on the heretic for the temporal effects of that heresy, a treasonous betrayal of the political unity necessary for social living. A state's punishment of the heretic for the religious aspects of his belief would be an encroachment by the civil power on the supernatural; such was beyond the competence of the state.

Further, this phase of a religiously based, temporal unity appears to have passed. For Murray, "the progressive differentiation of the political community from the religious community, and its consequent growth in autonomy through the perfection of its own institutions for its own self-direction" has made religious faith an invalid means for political unity (1948f, 72, 50). Murray implies that the real-world autonomy of the mature state means that the principle of national unity can and must be indigenous to the temporal, not the spiritual, order. "Political unity is now a particular order of unity in its own right" (1948f, 64). What that indigenous center of mature temporal unity might be is unclear in the present article.

So far I have traced only the effect that the direct/indirect question had in shifting into central focus the notion of Christian social dualism. If little has been said about the shapes and natures of the two societies, it is because Murray had not advanced a definition of them beyond the question of origins and ends. But, the abiding significance of the powers argument for Murray's later work was its redefinition of the theological or ecclesiological argument. The timeless theological argument of 1945 has been replaced by an ongoing historical argument which follows (it does not precede) forms of political institutionalization.

> In this matter [of church-state relations] fact has always held the primacy over theory. Political rulers acted, Popes acted; and then came the theologians—often politically partisan in their sympathies—to think out a theory. But their theories inevitably reflected the relativities of the time-conditioned problem that prompted the action about which they theorized (1948f, 35f).

Even a "political theology" will never reach a final, closed content (1948g, 491f), because one range of its theoretical starting points shifts with the temporal order.

Murray has extended the matters which are open to practical or political judgment, as the terms were used in the 1945 argument. Practical judgment is sensitive not only to the relative degree of religious consensus within a society but also to the maturity of the political institutions which govern that society. With these two concrete, historical elements (consensus and state), Murray could then assert that even with a return of Christendom (as a universal religious consensus), one need not conclude to juridical establishment of Catholicism.

> If there were a Christendom tomorrow—a Christian world government in a society whose every member was baptized—the Pope, for all the fullness of his apostolic authority, would not have the slightest shadow of a right to 'crown' so much as a third-class postmaster (1948g, 534f).

The autonomy and maturity of the state also enter into judgments concerning juridical forms of church-state relations, at least potentially ruling establishment invalid.

The theological argument of 1945 has become more an ongoing ecclesiological argument, tied both to the reality of the temporal order and to the church's understanding of that order. And reality and that understanding need not correspond. That which the church constantly pursues is its own freedom within the political order (a directive principle), but popes and theologians have misunderstood the rightful autonomy of the state. The afterglow of the medieval church's contingent exercise of coercive power, and the heat of particular encounters between king and pope, have clouded the understanding of the independent foundations of those two orders. Murray then must fall back on the "tradition" as the main carrier of the principle of social dualism, claiming it to be correlative or parallel to the perennial theology of nature and grace (1948f, 57), without, however, developing the correlation or relationship between a pure dogma such as nature-grace and a social "dogma" such as dualism.

The present debate has, of course, bypassed the notion of an ideal regime; the only significant political categories were "immature" and "mature," as determined by the state's effective ability to constrain and direct the uses of coercive power. However, Murray has here implied, within the natural universe, a source of ethical legitimization and limitation that is external to the state. (What other grounds could authenticate the church's temporary assumption of coercive force?) What, then, is that reality, other than the church, which foundationally so limits the state and the powers within the state? Murray's contrast of politically immature, barbarous feudalism with self-sufficient mature nationalism will not be his final word on the demands of nature.

II. THE DANGERS POSED BY AN IDENTIFICATION OF STATE AND SOCIETY.

If what Murray has said about "proper means" is true, then all one needs to affirm the correctness of the American disestablishment of religion is the judgment that the American political system is mature, i.e., that it effectively controls coercive force for the attainment of the common good. However, the problem which bothered most Protestants was not the somewhat abstract issue of power, but the rather impenetrable logic of those whom Murray called the "American Catholic Right." According to the latter's argument, establishment was considered an "ideal" solution to the church-state problem—although most likely unrealizable, at least in pluralistic America (Shea 1950). Murray's next series of articles were a response to challenges from the Catholic "Right," challenges which forced him to examine more closely the "mature" state of his first argument and to clarify in some aspects the societies which gave birth to modern forms of the state. I will first of all present Murray's understanding of the rise of legal religious establishment, then his growing notion of "society."

What is the source of the church's approval of and, in recent times, insistence on the establishment of Catholicism as the religion of the state? Against those who would claim establishment to be a pure and immediate deduction from the premise of the church's primacy, Murray found in the historical course of the rise of establishment both political and theological premises and concrete facts at work. Although the rise of the nation-state was a legitimate growth in state maturity, the fractioning of Western Christendom by the Reformation forced establishment on the church as a means of preserving its own unity. As Murray reconstructed the tradition, the church of the Middle Ages claimed and practiced a universality which transcended the territorial range of any prince or king. The church was understood to be the "true Church, which is one (i.e., universal)" (1951c, 344). With the treaty of Westphalia and its principle of *cujus regio, eius religio,* the church shifted into the defensive posture of maintaining the integrity of Catholic faith in limited territories. Its governing principle became defensive: the church as "the one (i.e., only) Church that is true." The church initially only grudgingly accepted this state of affairs, a de facto recognition of the destruction of its actual, although not theoretical, universalism. Establishment within still Catholic societies was both an expression of the collective faith of those societies and a means of preserving that faith.

If the church only grudgingly accepted establishment with the fractioning of Western religious unity, it clung to and positively endorsed it against the *laïque* religious claims of French democracy (1951c, 344). Totalitarian democracy asserted in a novel way that religion in any form had no social import, that God was irrelevant to the functioning of the state and of temporal society. Against this claim, the church asserted its right to "correct, judge, and direct" the public life of man. But, given the only available historical forms which it knew, it tied this demand for freedom to the monarchical political form and to establishment as a means of preserving its own freedom. Murray, then, understood the church's recent calls for establishment to be dependent on a type of inertia within the political thought of the church.

Murray wanted establishment to be understood as initially a fall-back of the church from a social condition of universality to that of religious diversity, a manner of preserving partially the freedom of the church in an age when the faith of the king did indeed determine the faith of the people. He developed this argument in a rather mild if assertive exchange with George Shea. Pivotal to Shea's argument was the notion of a "Catholic society," and the importance of that concept forced Murray to develop his notion of society in contrast to state or nation.[7] To Shea's undefined use of the term society, Murray, in an extended footnote, advanced four distinct but related terms: "civil society," "political society," "state," and "government" (1951c, 344). Civil society "designates the total complex of organized human relationships on the temporal plane, which arise either by necessity of nature or by free choice of will, in view of the co-operative achievement of partial human goods by particular associations or institutions." Their goal may be the attainment of either collective or private goods. For this largest temporal institution or collection of institutions, the "first structural principle of its organization is that of subsidiarity." As a subset of civil society, political society is the civil society as organized for the common good, in distinction from private goods. As mentioned before, Murray contended that the common good is not simply the sum total of individual goods, and political society is the pursuit of, in metaphorical terms, the "good of the body as such." The state is the functional agency of the body politic, directed toward social control and public service. It is "only one, although the highest, subsidiary function of society." But as subsidiary, the axiom of its operation is: "As much state as necessary, as much freedom as possible." The state is "in a privileged sense an order of law; law itself ... " Government is primarily a relational term within the structure offered by the state as an order of law; it is the ruler in relation to the ruled and the ruled in relation to the ruler, the action of "the power on the people and of the people on the power."

The term "people" served as Murray's challenge to Shea's "Catholic society." The "people" are for Murray political society or the body politic, that is, civil society organized through various institutions and beliefs for the attainment of the common good. A people never exists as some type of abstract essence, rather they are the product of historical growth and decay.

A people grows out of the moral soil of the country's history. "We the people" is a human thing, of flesh and blood, ensouled by a community of ideas and purposes; it has a common life, organized into myriad interlocking institutions, slowly built up in time, which impart to this life a structure and a form (1951c, 351).

A people is not a simple statistical majority, a conglomerate of individuals united only by territorial boundaries, nor even united by adherence to a common religious creed. Faith is the bond of ecclesiastical unity, but not of temporal unity (1951c, 350).

If a civil and political society share a common faith such as Catholicism, must that faith take expression as establishment? Murray's conclusion now is that it need not. Establishment as a legal form of church-state relations is in the order of positive law, "an act of reason, not of faith" (1951c, 345). As an act by and in the state, establishment is merely the recognition in the public legal order of the social fact of the people's faith; it is certainly not a dogmatic faith decree similar to the faith expressions by the church, nor an act of faith "on the part of the state—least of all on the part of Citizen Bonaparte," as in the 1803 Concordat. One need not demand establishment under the theological norm of worship, since civil law is a temporal, not a spiritual, instrument.

Murray even further suggested that the use of coercion against the religious beliefs of a societal minority betrays a lack of religious consensus (1951c, 346–47, note 17), the pivotal point of the conservative argument. Just as an increased exercise of coercion in matters of justice indicates a breakdown in a social sense of justice, so the use of coercion against heterodox religious opinions increases only in an environment of religious conflict and diversity.

These notions of the people, the temporality of juridical forms, and the inverse relationship of coercion and consensus were all brought to bear against the Catholic "ideal" argument—the central notion of which, a Catholic majority, Murray found unintelligible. Even the proponents of the theory, he maintained, did not clarify whether the majority necessary for establishment be a "simple majority," a "moral majority," or an "absolute majority" (1951c, 349f). In effect, any statistical notion of Catholic society reduces down to a power calculus (1952a, 39f), missing the only valid grounds for establishment, namely, a spiritual consensus which Murray described much along the lines of the lay spirituality notion of 1943, with added overtones of the necessary freedom of human conscience from coercion in his 1945 argument. That which constitutes a nation as Catholic is not related to the order of coercive force; it is in that sense spiritual. Underlying his present argument, then, is a distinction of the means which are appropriate to a supernatural reality. The two necessary components for his argument are the historical cause for previous allowances of establishment (no longer applicable) and the notion of people or society.

So far, Murray's argument against establishment has rested on a judgment that establishment was at best a sixteenth century compromise with nationally defined, religious diversity and that it does not make much sense with subsequent institutionalized distinctions between society and state. Francis J. Connell next offered Murray an opportunity to demonstrate his vitriolic skills and to situate a present endorsement of establishment within the earlier dual societies notion (Connell, 1950). Connell had argued that, in the new economy of salvation, the state was subject to Christ the King and that, therefore, the rulers as representatives of society must examine the truth claims of the Catholic Church and, finding them to be true, establish Catholicism as the religion of the state. Murray almost gleefully latched onto the claim that the state must "permit" the preaching of the gospel and must examine the truths of various preachers, restricting those who did not indeed preach the true gospel (1952a, 28–30). Again at issue was the state as a religious personality capable of an act of faith. Murray argued that, first of all, any claim that the state must examine and judge religious truth entails a commitment to a monarchical or dictatorial form of government, the tying of the church to a particular contingent political form of organization (1952a, 37–38), for only a monarchy or dictatorship allows the personification of the state. This itself is a denial of the independence of the church from the temporal order. More importantly, the claim that the state or ruler *in function of his political office* must permit and judge matters of religious truth is a submission of the religious order to that of the political. Murray concluded that "Fr. Connell's effort to exalt the Kingship of Christ over civil rulers results in an exaltation of the civil ruler over Christ the King, whose doctrine is made subject to judgment by the civil power" (1952a, 32). Both the church's independence from political forms and the primacy of the spiritual are compromised by Connell's establishment argument.

As he had done in his previous article, Murray also criticized the notion of a Catholic majority as the index of establishment. Western forms of religious establishment might have made some sense when one ruler both represented and dominated the body politic, the people. One can speak of a ruler making an act of faith, in the sense that any individual makes such acts. But in the modern, diversified forms of democratic organization, where does one locate those who are to make the act of faith which underlies the claim that the state must worship God, and worship him in the form that he chooses? (1952a, 34–36).

The problem which democratic structures pose to moral theory is that the state, as purely a form of law or arena of action, has been separated from the body politic. Modern democratic states are analogously personal only in that they are attempts to organize human, temporal society by means of reason and will, but no component of the democratic state speaks for the faith of the people. Only the people, who have limited the state to the order of civil law, can make such common faith acts.

If a political, religious personality can only be located within the political form of absolute monarchy, and if political establishment implies state control over the church, then contemporary forms of political organization which strip the state of any powers to judge religious truth offer the church "as good a hope of freedom as she has ever had" (1951c, 336). The essential responsibility of a Catholic people, a Catholic majority, or a Catholic minority is always the formation of the state according to the three general principles of social dualism, concordia, and harmony (1951c, 349). The question then becomes the prudential problem of what best protects the church's freedom to preach the gospel and a Catholic people's freedom to hear that gospel. And establishment in fact has been and can be a hindrance to those freedoms, although Murray did not discuss in these exchanges how it would be such a hindrance.[8]

This heated exchange with the *American Ecclesiastical Review*, then, allowed or forced Murray to develop a notion of political society which stands opposed to the state and constitutes and limits the state. The "mature" state of the first powers argument has now become the "absolutist" state of enlightened despotism with the latter's Gallican tendencies. Further, any confusion of the rights and duties in the fabric of the revealed universe, even if conducted by church members, leads to a denial of social dualism. Much of this was developed with little systematic clarity on Murray's part. But having at least initially distinguished society and state, Murray then moved to the work of Leo XIII to identify the perpetual opposition of the church to unitary absolutism, no matter what form that absolutism takes.

III. THE LEONINE SERIES: THE IMPLICATIONS OF SOCIETY AS MORAL CONSENSUS.   Before presenting Murray's argument for religious liberty as it weaved its course through the Leonine articles, I should make several preliminary comments. Leo XIII presented a special problem for Murray. Not only did Leo initiate a revival of Thomistic philosophy, with its natural law notion of the state and the principle of Gelasian dualism. He also resoundingly called for coercive restraints of democratic primary institutions, such as freedom of speech and assembly, and also for religious establishment along with the twin institution of intolerance. (In this, Leo argued much as did Bellarmine.) Through five or six articles and nearly three hundred pages of text, Murray attempted to understand the basis for Leo's condemnation of democratic institutions and his encouragement of establishment, again separating out the permanent in Leo's argument from that which was historically conditioned.

To understand Leo's conclusions and the manner in which he arrived at them, one must again delve into the political and social history of his times. Murray began laying the groundwork for such an analysis in a 1946 article "How Liberal was Liberalism?" (1946c) in which the liberalism under discussion was isolated to the continental French democratic variety, particularly that of the Third Republic. In the present series of articles, "The Church and Totalitarian Democracy" (1952b) and "Leo XIII: Separation of Church and State" (1953c) attempt to outline the nature of the political power which confronted the Leonine church, and to separate that understanding of democratic power from the Anglo-American versions of democracy. In "The General Structure of the Controversy" (1953a), Murray pushed the analysis further into Leo's conspiratorial theory of the forces which vied for control of Catholic peoples, a reading of society as well as of politics along clear-cut battle lines. Murray's fourth and fifth articles (1953e, 1954c) follow Leo's predominant concern with society (as opposed to the state) into an analysis of two forms of governmental action toward social institutions (economy and general culture). The last of the Leonine articles (1955a), the publication of which was stopped by Roman censors (Pelotte 1970, 44–54), was an analysis of Leo's argument for governmental care of religion, with a further analysis of the changing social, political, and theological factors which have altered the mid-twentieth century problem of religion and society, and with it, church and state. The last article which I will consider, the 1954 "On the Structure of the Church-State Problem" (1954b), is Murray's final recasting of the entire church-state tradition in terms of social dualism. It is the product of seven years of historical analysis.

Finally, the working papers structuring of these articles betrays the exploratory character of Murray's argument—an argument that gropes and tests, rather than one that relentlessly marches in systematic form, in a clearly, confidently defined direction. Titles of subsequent articles which were promised in earlier articles were replaced by other topics and orientations.[9] And there is much duplication of materials between the first and last. The following presentation, however, will follow what appears to be the eventual cornerstone of Murray's contrast of the nineteenth century statement of the problem with that of his own time: the changing notion of society and the relationship of political forms to differing societies.[10] The first part of my own presentation will take up Murray's analysis of the Leonine shift in governing principles from that of church integrity to the principle of social dualism. Next, I will consider his study of the "historical" factors which, in light of his prudential theory of ecclesiastical judgments, Murray judged to have determined Leo's recommendation for intolerance. Third, Murray will reinterpret Leo's principles of the relationship of the temporal and spiritual orders within a "church"-"society" framework, rather than in their original "church"-"state" setting. And finally this study will come upon some rather startling evaluations that eventually called down his silencing. Murray will reestablish his own premises, reinterpret the tradition in terms of those new premises, and then return to the realm of policy recommendations with a vengeance.

Leo XIII assumed the papacy after the dissolution of the papal territorial states; like Pius IX, he maintained himself as a prisoner of the Vatican. But unlike Pius, Leo shifted the question of church-state relations to the "level of principle," claiming the freedom of the church as a necessary aspect of social dualism in the tradition of Gelasius and Thomas, not as solely and pragmatically an instrumental requirement for the maintenance of Catholic religious integrity (1953c, 187). Within the tradition of dualism, Leo led the French hierarchy away from support for monarchical forms of political organization, and also forcibly restrained excessive support and participation of younger French clergy in the democratic forms of the Third Republic. "Two there are . . ." and a distinction of means and the relative autonomy of both was a necessary requirement for any form of church-state institutionalization (1953c, 206–08).

But the Third Republic, as understood by Leo, made claims that extended beyond the political and temporal. Consistent with the First Republic, the Third Republic understood itself as absolutely free from laws or principles of behavior outside of its own will.[11] Based on a socialized form of the ethical theory of absolute individual autonomy, France was, in its ethical and legal determinations, answerable neither to the church, nor to God, nor even to subsidiary social organizations. And within the tradition of royal absolutism, those who held governmental power were the sole representatives of France, or in the Rousseauistic variation, the Jacobin political party represented the people, even if the people did not agree with the party's orientations (1952b, 557). The Third Democratic Republic was at best a totalitarianism of the majority, at its worst a totalitarianism of an atheistic elite. Even in its somewhat mitigated grant of significance for religion in the domain of private belief, the base premise of totalitarian democracy was the social irrelevance of the church, and of God. And, against these ethical and ecclesiological claims, Leo countered with the tradition of social dualism and the primacy of the church in all spiritual matters of private or social scope. The church has a divine right to address the *res sacra*[12] of human society.

Within the monistic social principle of the Third Republic, disestablishment or separation of church and state could only be understood as a political institutionalization of a theological claim (1952b, 553f; 1953c, 186). The church must be separated from all cultural and political arenas of collective life. The Jacobin elite wanted to instill its own faith (social atheism) and have it as the exclusive faith of the realm (1952b, 530). Within the tradition of dualism, Leo understood this separation as the subjection of the spiritual to the temporal, an attempt to destroy the very reality of God's redemptive intervention. As he understood the present human economy, monisms of any form could only lead to anarchy or to slavery. Christian dualism is an essential element in the preservation of true human freedom; and in this sense (and other senses also) the Christian religion is essential to society.

While the Leonine-French battle was at root theological and ethical, Leo's further political and social recommendations were mediated by other historical factors, particularly by a notion of the state's role vis-à-vis society at large and the distribution of culturally significant forces within society. Behind the secularistic leadership of France or Italy, Leo saw a vast, well organized conspiracy to drive the church out of the public forum (1953a, 1). The church was opposed by "Sects," a new organized political religion made up of "Masons, anarchists and communists" (1953a, 2).[13] There existed, then, two Spains, two Italies, two Frances: Christian and secularistic powers and organizations which claimed to represent the particular nations. And "both sides seem to have been long agreed that the way to victory is the same for each of them, namely control of the government" (1953a, 10). Therefore, both were still operating under the political premises of the age of absolute monarchy. While still adhering to the concept of Christian dualism, Leo could call, because of his notion of the role of government, for the expulsion of the Sects from the Christian state. He viewed the battle primarily in terms of power, and power was the province of the political order.[14] The church would not and could not consistently take on political power directly as in the hierocratic theory of power. But, because of the dominant theory of effective cultural influence, Leo addressed all his appeals for the preservation of Catholicism to governmental personnel.

Although Leo's theory of coercive power and the role of power in shaping and protecting the cultural sphere was a residue of four hundred years of state absolutism, Gelasian social dualism directed his major concern beyond the state to the people who were controlled and directed by the state (1953a, 12, note 40). In Leo's view, the people of France and Spain and Italy were still truly Catholic. What the church required of political power was the freedom to touch the *res sacrae* of human life, those aspects of man which are related to eternal life. Ultimately, the *res sacrae* reduce to one reality, the human person orientated to both temporal and eternal ends (1953c, 208). To preserve this orientational dualism of the individual and the social dualism of the present redemptive economy, the state must suppress any Sects which would by force confine man and society to purely temporal concerns. The person who is both citizen and Catholic has an inherent right to harmony between the two sources of moral authority under which God has placed him (1953a, 19). The political order must not impose a monistic, temporal vision of human life.

If the principles of dualism and primacy are what is correct and traditional in Leo's argument, what are time-limited and historical? Murray fished around a bit for an answer to this question. An obvious candidate is the framing of societal relations in terms of "power," which he considered a hangover from the age of absolutism. But the very term *power* indicates a lack on Leo's part of a clear notion of what a state is and the range of a state's abilities (1953a, 20f). Although civil law must be in accord with divine law, it is in actuality a form of positive law with a minimal range of application and effectiveness. Coercive power which is the correlative of civil law can never induce an internal transformation of the human spirit (1953a, 23); civil law only maintains a social state of public peace by restraining external expressions of evil. Leo does not appear to have recognized the limits of civil law in the promotion of virtuous and Christian living. And therefore he misunderstood the role of the state in matters of morality and religion.

But the problem with Leo's conception of the state runs deeper than a lack of clarity concerning the limits of civil law. If Leo had been able to visualize the state in terms of the Thomistic theory of civil law, then, Murray claimed, he might have been able to "rise" from that notion of law to the question of moral authority within civil society. If civil law is minimalistic in application and guidance of society, then where does moral authority reside in the temporal order? The traditional medieval, Scholastic answer was that the authority of the king was mediated to him by the people, that their abiding and developing sense of social justice validated and at times negated the actions of the king (1953a, 22). In Scholastic terms, this appeal to the moral sense of the people is known as the "authorization" principle. While Leo made use of the principle that all moral law derives ultimately from God, he never appealed to the mediation of the moral aspects of civil law by civil society. In fact, Leo never appreciably appealed to a society-state distinction, with the state limited by society (1952b, 551). Or did he?

Murray's next two articles turned somewhat abruptly to a consideration of the role of the state toward various orders of culture, or "civil society" in his earlier terminology. He contrasted the Leonine treatment of the state role toward the economic order (a nonpolitical order) as found in *Rerum Novarum*[15] with Leo's treatment of the state's role toward education and religion.

Only in *Rerum Novarum* did Leo consistently maintain a distinction between the state and the socioeconomic order, and incidentally, a clear political definition of the state.[16] He attempted to steer between the *laissez-faire* denial of the right of state intervention in the economic order (on grounds of moral danger), and the socialist, totalitarian attempt to subject the economy thoroughly to state control through constant intervention by political officials. In situations of grave economic injustice, the state can and must intervene in the economic social processes, but only in grave situations and as a last resort (1953e, 552). As for the normal relations of state and the economy, the state has an obligation to recognize the relative autonomy of the economy and to encourage the development and maturation of those intermediate institutions which contribute to economic growth. The principle which limits the state is

> ... the rightful and necessary freedom of society in all its associational forms to direct and govern itself .... The freedom of society is an essential element of the common good, ... for in society, not in government, reside the vital energies which make for public prosperity (1953e, 554).

Neither absolute autonomy nor absolute right of intervention may be claimed by the economy or by the state. The state fulfills its political function when it intervenes within the limits of coercive law, for the control of gross injustice. If the economic order is to function most effectively and in fact most morally, it must be given freedom from total submission to state control; like any other order of culture it operates best by free acceptance of the common good goals by those who participate in the economy.

Now, if Leo called for severe state intervention in the cultural orders of education and religion, what is the basis for that call? In light of *Rerum Novarum*, that call cannot be based on the essential moral responsibilities of the state with its limited instrument, civil law. All orders of culture, including the economy, have a general right to autonomy, and function most properly within the possibility of free acceptance and development of the goods offered by those orders (1954c, 29).[17] The most important forces for moral and religious good in civic life arise from free, vitalistic functioning (1953e, 556), not from state control and direction. It cannot be that Leo directed the call for intervention to one kind of state and the demand for restraint to another, for both calls were directed to both democratically and monarchically defined manners of governance. The only possible source for the demand for intervention can be Leo's perception of the factual nature of the people, of civil society. Leo perhaps correctly judged the citizens of Catholic nations to be an "illiterate mass," a people of childlike simplicity and ignorance (1954c, 16, 19). For the protection of such immature societies, Leo appealed to a paternal role for government (1954c, 23). He considered the citizen only in the aspect of a passive political subject, not as an active participant in political processes. In such a context, docility became the only moral norm for political membership. Further, even though the *studium*, as the proper instrument for societal maturation, should exist independently of state intervention, in fact the *studium* had been absorbed into state control (1954c, 31). Leo concluded that the state should guide the education of the masses. And, since education takes a considerable time, and since the danger presented by the Sects was immediate, the state should suppress public Sectarian propaganda; it should curtail freedoms of speech, press, and assembly.

Finally, Murray argued that, although Leo based his primary claim for freedom of the church on divine right conferred by Christ, he also based such freedom on the political limitations of government—religion operates for the temporal common good of society when it is granted the fullest freedom, as with any other cultural order (1953e, 562). This protection of the church's right to free activity is the only essential role of the state vis-à-vis the church. All other claims by Leo were again based on a judgment of the religious and moral immaturity of so-called Catholic peoples. While Leo pushed for better clerical and lay education, the present danger to uniform, if weak, Catholic social faith led him to call for a paternal protection of the masses by state means.

By 1954 this long, complicated argument had finally reached a conclusion which was acceptable to Murray, if not to his opponents. The church's endorsement of establishment and intolerance was based not simply on theological principles, but more directly on the changing reality and understanding of the state, as well as on the changing reality and understanding of civil society. In the last, suppressed Leonine article, Murray took on three Leonine propositions (which again incidentally had been used by others in support of establishment and intolerance as ideals of Catholic political theory), but the very casting of those propositions signaled on Murray's part a finally firm distinction between society and state.[18] Against the theological and ethical claims of continental democratic monism, Leo countered that:

> ... (1) *society*, no less than the individual, is subject to the sovereignty of God: hence his development of the theme of public religion ... (2) that the state—the order of human law, and government as its effective author— is part of the moral universe, subject to the law of God, hence his theme of divine law as "the principle of the whole juridical order." ... (3) that *society* is part of the present Christian economy, subject to the law of Christ; hence his central theme, the traditional thesis that there are two societies, two laws, and two authorities, with all the implications of this thesis (1955a, gal. 5, Q-95) (numeration and highlighting are my own).

Regarding public religion (1), Murray distinguished the spontaneous, free expression of collective public faith (on a clear analogue with the individual faith expression in the cooperation articles) from juridical establishment, the latter of which is not an act of faith, but a matter of temporal law (1955a, gal. 5, Q-33).[19] Similarly, a societal recognition of the law of Christ (3) as another distinct order of meaning will entail a spontaneous permeation of all orders of culture by the values expressed in that law.[20] But such permeation will be consistent with the means and the goals of religious faith, the spiritual influence over the temporal, and free acts of faith and worship. The principle that the state stands under divine law (2) is understood by Murray as an expression of Christian constitutionalism, that the state is at once limited by an order of law outside itself and is an instrument of that law, at least within the narrow perimeters of its own competence (1955a, gal. 9, R-40). Christian constitutionalism yields both an ethical and a juridical norm. (Leo presented only the ethical norm, because of the type of debate in which he was involved.)

The situating of the term "society" within the first and third propositions is, in Murray's phrase, a "nicety" which Leo did not always observe in his theological and ethical arguments. Ultimately, he missed the significance of the society-state distinction because he viewed Catholic nations to be truly and thoroughly composed of Catholic peoples, and he judged these people to be defenseless against those external forces which worked viciously to turn them against the divine and revealed laws of God (1955a, gal. 16, R-81). Since they constituted a Catholic society, a true expression of their own faith would be a Catholic state. And since they were defenseless, establishment and intolerance were proper means of preserving that spontaneous faith.

Murray concluded, then, that Leo's argument was conditioned by the political and social forms which he confronted in his own times and was further limited by an incomplete theory of law. The remainder of the fifth Leonine article, another article entitled "On the Structure of the Church-State Problem," and a talk given at Catholic University pushed the analysis of church-state history into the twentieth century, before Murray was effectively, if temporarily, removed from the debate. The immediate occasion for these last advances into historical analysis was an article by Alfredo Cardinal Ottaviani (Ottaviani 1953) in which the "ideal" (thesis-hypothesis) theory was presented with considerable force. Claiming that he was not presenting the argument of any particular theologian, the latter portion of the fifth Leo article began with an outline of what Murray called a "disjunctive" theory.[21] The major features of his argument should be at this point familiar: two different criteria governing the juridical forms, with the "ideal" solution being establishment (and intolerance), guided by the principle, in Murray's terms, "as much intolerance as possible, as much freedom as necessary." Establishment was viewed as a doctrine, an aspect of the eternal teachings of the church which should, if the social situation allowed, be enforced with the full strength of the law (1955a, gal. 24, S-35).[22] Key to the position was the judgment that tolerance itself is an evil, a lesser evil which must be accepted in sharply, religiously divided communities.

Against this position Murray claimed the authority of Pope Pius XII, as presented in the latter's 1953 talk to Italian jurists (1955a, gal. 25, S-2).[23] Pius' claim that he himself had ultimate say in matters of church and state was interpreted by Murray as a rebuke of Ottaviani's article.[24] Murray further suggested that Pius, unlike Leo, demonstrated a clear notion of the limits of law, both in what can be accomplished by use of force and in the limited good which is law's proper object, namely, civil peace (1955a, gal. 28, S-11).[25] Both of these limits are a reclamation of the Scholastic, Thomistic tradition of civil law. Further, tolerance is not a lesser evil, but rather a practice of civic virtue within the limits of civil power. In some situations or *quaestiones facti,* "human authority has neither mandate nor duty nor *right* to use its coercive power against error and evil" (1955a, gal. 27, S-33). While the governing norms of the church are solely those of moral and religious truth, law has the added norm (and primary norm)[26] of public welfare and, more limitedly, public peace. Pius insisted that Catholic jurists form laws out of the principles of Catholic social theory, but granted to the jurists the autonomous obligation to judge the effective application of those principles within their own political and social situations.[27] All legal forms (including establishment and separation, are hypotheses; the only "ideal" or "thesis" content of Catholic thought is the governing principles (1955a, gal. 30, S-60; 1954d, 7). Any argument that proceeds to establishment or separation for a particular national community must advance from the same set of starting principles; such is a "unitive" theory of church ethical determination.

Murray's use of the jurist talk was no doubt sufficiently upsetting to some. But, he heightened and deepened his understanding of the tradition as a struggle against political and social monism. In all its confrontations with political power, the church has consistently posited "its traditional doctrine of a juridical and social dualism characterized by the primacy of the spiritual over the political" (1954b, 11). This doctrine of dualism became an effective force under Gelasius, in his opposition to the classical monistic theory of the state as the single perfect society, as advanced by Anastasius (1954b, 12).[28] John of Paris and Bellarmine opposed monisms advanced both by regalists and by caesaropapists—monistic claims arising from either the state or the church.[29] Leo XIII's argument was against democratic, totalitarian monism (1954b, 19–20). By the time of Pius XII, however, the cause of social monism has been taken up by a new political force and the social community under attack has shifted. Whereas Leo faced monistic claims limited to individual nation-states, Pius confronts the international monistic claims of communism (1954b, 25). The common good under challenge is not simply that of individual states, but the larger common good of the international society.

Murray had earlier argued that advances in communication and travel had established a natural international community, which, as an "intention of nature," demanded institutionalization in a common order of law (1944d). Pius' particular contributions to the tradition were twofold: the recognition that this new, international social community is the most pressing concern of the universal church, and his insight that the proper object or goal of the demanded juridical order, as with all juridical orders, is public peace (1955a, gal. 25, S-2). Now, if the most important common good involved in any juridical argument must be the international, then arguments concerning establishment or separation must take account of the international effects of even particular national, juridical institutions (1955a, gal. 30, S-60).[30] That is, even the local churches within a country such as Spain must also consider the situation of the church in its universality and the effect that such establishment has on the position of the church within the international community. It might well be that a particular national community could conclude to establishment within their own territorial boundaries, but Pius has frankly admitted that the most important, relevant community or society of moral determination is religiously pluralistic (1955a, gal. 25, S-2; 1954d, 8). Endorsement of juridical forms by geographically limited churches must not jeopardize the universal position of the church, nor claim to be more Catholic than the pope.

Murray also explicitly suggested, for the first time, a certain autonomy for a political society in the ethical evaluation and determination of its own temporal good. Any form of institutionalized church-state relations must be advantageous to both the state and the church (1955a, gal. 23, S-5). The form of institutionalization will be mutually arrived at, the state guided by its primary principle of peace and the church guided by its principle of freedom. Harmony or *concordia* between these two goods is a product of prudential judgment and mutual adjustment between two sets of independently based goods (1955a, gal. 9, S-31). All the church requires of the state is to recognize the principle of social dualism, or, more specifically, to affirm that the social good is not the absolute preserve of the state.[31]

Murray further situated those who would claim establishment and intolerance as Catholic "ideals" in the same camp with social or political monists. Pushed to its extreme, and to its perhaps logical conclusion, the "ideal" theorists are "Catholic Jacobins,"[32] attempting no less than the French Jacobins to pound in a social monism by coercive means. Murray's own theory of collective faith rejected the use of temporal means for such spiritual ends. Even a Catholic form of majoritarianism (legally forcing the will of a majority on a minority), he suggested, is a form of totalitarianism, for which the church could pay dearly.

Finally, who or what in the temporal arena can effectively challenge the monistic tendencies of the state and of even some members of the church? Here we approach the somewhat fragile and unexamined heart of Murray's social theory, the assertion of the importance of the people's moral will. According to Murray, the only power which can effectively confront modern monism is "the spiritual and moral power inherent in the organized conscience of society, the people, whereby the purposes and actions of government are to be judged, directed, and corrected." Social dualism must now be maintained by the "method of freedom, ... the ordered set of free institutions now known as democratic," under the slogan "A free Church amid a free *people"* (1954b, 28). Murray further suggested that this contemporary moral sense of the people places an obligation on the church. Adopting Sturzo's claim that civil democratic freedoms have been unbreakably linked in modern social consciousness to the church's own freedom, Murray called for a recognition that the church's own agenda of preserving its freedom can only rise or fall with the preservation of those democratic rights, including civil religious freedom (1954b, 26). But the subject of consensus as a moral will is to be taken up in the next chapter. Suffice it here to note that Murray has claimed some type of priority for that civilly developed moral sense, over and against the dominant ethical sense of the church.

Thus Murray ended, if somewhat incompletely, his early 1950s' theological argument for the separation of church and state. My own presentation of his American constitutional and consensus analysis has been delayed for a detailed examination in chapter 3, even though it is an important factor in his understanding of the twentieth century problem. It is clear even within the Leonine articles, however, that another socially held, and constitutionally supported, theory of the state might possibly ground democratic freedoms in such a manner that the church could at least live with those freedoms. In the third Leonine article, Murray claimed that the American First Amendment was not based on an ecclesiology, neither on a restriction of the church to the private arena nor on a judgment that all denominations stand equally before God (1953c, 152–53). If that is so, then the main force of Leo's argument would not be applicable to American democratic forms of separation; no battle over theological principles need be, nor can be, engaged. All of this will be considered in the next two chapters.

Likewise, only brief consideration has been given to Murray's and Sturzo's claim that civil, democratic freedoms have been linked to the church's freedom. This also will be treated later in my consideration of Murray's conciliar writings. And, finally, I will later take up the question of the maturity of civil society, the ultimate keystone of Murray's defense of modern separation theory. Here "societal maturity" has been defined primarily in the relation of a people to political forms, not to the moral law itself.

IV. CONCLUSION: FORMULATING SOCIAL CONCEPTS.   In his attempt to form a compelling argument for religious liberty, Murray has moved from an appeal to prudential or "political" judgment to a reexamination, redefinition and discovery of various political, ethical and social concepts. In his first, "essentialistic" argument, he adapted the notion of historical, prudential judgment from the cooperation debate to the more complex realm of factors involved in church-state relations. He found, however, that his sharp distinction between theoretical and practical argumentation did not yield such a compelling judgment. In his turn to historical studies, he found that the understanding and judgments of political forms likewise were involved in the historical change, development, and decline, first concerning the state, then concerning the society that "authorizes" the actions and the shape of the state. By bringing the "theoretical" factors of his abstract arguments into the historical stream, he began to break away from an overly institutionalized notion of the important forces of social development, turning more to the meanings that constitute social realities. The notion of social consensus—which in the cooperation discussion had simply entailed conceptions of just ordering, and in the first "essential" argument had been the degree of common religious commitment (and in both had been subsequent to theoretical arguments)—has in this later argument begun to take on a life of its own: the basis out of which institutional realities are defined and controlled. At the end of this later argument, Murray was moving toward a notion of social consensus as controlling "theoretical" arguments, and as therefore controlling the church's own judgments, even though that consensus might arise outside the church's own boundaries; he was developing a distinctly social conception of human cognition. Murray will again take up and more clearly develop these ideas during the Second Vatican Council. I hope the preceding has made clear that Murray was forced to reformulate both his political and his social categories, if he was to deal adequately with the social problems which he faced. His own immersion in the tradition's arguments, and the social arena in which he himself was arguing, called for the emergence of such concepts.

Now, one of the ongoing objections to Murray's political theory is that he located *the* contact point between church and state in the individual person, thereby leaving his theory essentially individualistic. Throughout these seven years of articles, he does repeatedly make such an appeal. The church directs its message to the conscience of the individual; the state must allow for harmony within the individual, with the latter's orientation to two different ends. However, in response to that objection, and in an attempt to highlight the growing role of social categories in his own argument, I will conclude this chapter with a discussion of Murray's developing conceptualization of "society," to be followed by a brief comment on his as yet rather hidden basis for moral autonomy.

Murray has attempted to distinguished civil and ecclesiastical societies according to four different categorizations. The first, "essentialistic" argument developed within what Murray called (1) "moral" definitions of those societies. The remaining three definitions arose in the historical argument. They were distinctions (2) according to the origins of each society (one in creation; the other in redemption), (3) according to ends (common good and eternal beatitude), and (4) according to means or instrumentality (coercive versus spiritual).

The first argument focused on the moral: the individual lives within a universe made up of two primary moral authorities, the individual conscience (or the church) and the state. However, this moral dualism began to dissolve when the question was shifted to moral authority within a revealed universe, under the principle of the primacy of the spiritual. When Murray shifted from an individual-social division of the natural law universe to an attempted distinction between two concrete social institutions, either the church stood in danger of restriction to the individual sphere, or the state lost all indices of autonomy from the church. As Murray later accused Leo, this first argument was restricted to the terms defined by a specific historical problem: the totalitarian claims of nineteenth century European democracy. Much of the nature of law, of the state, and of society were ignored because of the restricted type of debate in which he (and Leo) were engaged. The first argument "failed" because of the limited historical problematic in which it was framed (and also because of the individualism implicit in grounding a social right on a narrow, faculty psychology definition of conscience, itself a reflection of that problematic).

In his second argument, however, Murray did not lose what he considered fundamental to the first—the claim that the temporal order stands under the moral authority of the spiritual, God and the church. That which can and must obey and worship God is not, however, the state, but rather a social reality which grounds the state. The state remains indirectly under critique of the church, but only through the church's direct access to that other reality. And what is that reality? It is civil society, not the individual. Murray redirected the church's claims of moral primacy and of moral import beyond the state to that society by denying to the state an even analogous personality.

Throughout Murray's arguments, the distinction according to origins assumed a greater and greater importance. The distinction, a corrective principle for his and others' arguments, facilitated a shift in his argument from a "solipsistic ontology" (with focus on the hermetically conceived cognition of the individual subject), to a "universe" which he himself would later call a "social ontology."[33] In the arguments of his Catholic opponents, the primary and lexically ordered project of the church was defense of the proposition that

Catholicism is the one true church, the source of redemption within the new, revealed order. Concentrated on the confession of this truth claim, they left unexamined their own political theory, retaining a highly personified notion of the state. Murray himself initially shared this supporting epistemological and political theory. But, even in his essentialistic argument, he insisted on the dual aspects of the ethical universe (in line with the distinction according to origins), allowing him to justify the twin nonlexically defined missions of the church (integrity and common good). In his historical argument, the church's primary public project became the promotion and defense of this dualistic structuring of the social environment, as the latter has been changed by God's historic intervention. Social dualism (even derived as it is from the fact of revelation), with its structural implications, required the development of languages that are social, that are proportionate to the actual problematic of church-state relations (concrete institutional interactions, defined in terms of mutual freedom and influence, political force and civil law). Once Murray had developed those social and political categories, he was then able to turn the spiritual primacy principle against Connell. The distinction according to origins directed Murray to various aspects of social reality, then to the languages appropriate to that reality. It facilitated his development of a social ethics. And by clarifying his political and social conceptions, Murray was drawn toward another arena in which questions of individual and social truth claims could be more properly addressed—that is, toward civil society.

Murray's use of the ends, finalities, or teleological distinction underwent much more transformation. By definition, the institutions of the temporal order will pass away; likewise, the church as a specific institution will end with the end of time. Therefore, the distinction according to ends does not concern the terminus of either institution, considered as an institution in itself. Neither the state nor the church has its ultimate ends in the supernatural order. Murray has used the ends distinction in both arguments, rather, to define and limit the missions of both church and state. In the essentialistic argument, the mission of the state is the protection and promotion of the common good, a reality that is (as yet unclearly) distinct from the state. In the historical argument, the mission of the state is restricted to the maintenance of public peace. The promotion of the common good has been handed to other forces. Again, in the essentialistic argument, Murray did, following Leo, describe the mission of the church as directed to the enlightenment of conscience, conceived in an individualistic manner. But, it is a mild irony of Murray's historical argument that an attitudinal orientation of Leo himself spurred Murray to an abandonment of that individual point of contact. Leo's compassion for the Catholic peoples allowed Murray to reformulate the principal recipient of the church's mission to be, rather, the people, the society behind the state. Thus in the last Leo article, the mission of the church, along with the conception of public faith, concentrates on civil society, not the individual. Again, Murray needed this social conception to ground his argument for civil religious freedom.

Finally, even though Murray's initial conception of the means distinction was formulated with individual human consciousness in mind, the recipient of those means proper to the church was quickly socialized. By establishing the use of coercive, civil law as only a contingent right of the church, dependent on the real-world lack of institutions to counter violence, Murray could then claim spiritual power to be, in essence, free of such coercive means (owing both to the nature of faith and to the temporal autonomy of the state as a perfect society). The problem, of course, is the determination of political maturity. In his first three articles, political maturity seemed to be constituted by a system of checks and balances on police power, means by which an unjust officeholder could be removed from office. This resolution of the maturity problem centered on technical and institutional issues. By the mid-1950s, the maturity of political society, the "people" as a spiritual unity capable of constitutionally and juridically limiting the use of police power, has become an added index of temporal autonomy, built around notions of consensus rather than technique. Adequate technical means and consensus,[34] therefore, remove the church from the occasionally rightful assumption of means which are not proper to her own power, allowing her unambiguously to effect free conversion of individual and collective human conscience. The means proper to both individual and social intelligence are those of discussion and persuasion, not those of force.

So Murray did begin his discussion of religious liberty with an individualistic contact point, as he began with an individualistic notion of human cognition. But, in his encounter with the tradition, and with the Catholic "majority" argument for intolerance, he recognized that the "disjunctivists" had misunderstood the dynamisms and forces which constitute a "Catholic society." A people are Catholic insofar as their faith is freely and spontaneously manifest within all social institutions and actions. The church, then, addresses a people, seeking a collective, free response. Unfortunately, Murray did not yet have a clear set of categories by which to deal with a Christian people. He had used the term "temporal people" as a synonym for political society, not for civil society; and in fact, he tended to confuse the latter two terms. But surely "Christian people," as he used the term, is more closely parallel to civil society than to a political society or people (as also the recipients of the church's mission are more closely akin to civil rather than political society). Be that as it may, the socializing of Murray's political and cognitional theory seems obvious.

One last item remains. It should be noted that there is a bit of a "sleeper" in Murray's argument that will awaken during the council. He never did make much use of the notion of subsidiary institutions. There is, however, a move toward what might be called a "moral subsidiarity" within this argument. First, it is wrapped up in his gradual redefinition of the state. Murray initially argued that, by its limitation to the temporal common good, the state has no right of intervention in private matters. Later, the state was viewed as limited by its proper instrument, coercive law, to the external (nonspiritual) aspects of human reality, and eventually to the even more limited concept of public peace. Then the state was constitutionally limited by the abiding moral sense of the people, as an expression of the authorization principle. And finally, the Leonine socioeconomic consideration suggested that within society itself there are autonomous or semiautonomous sources of moral as well as of technical direction, which are best left with as much freedom as possible, not only vis-à-vis the state, but also vis-à-vis society at large. Some of these are fairly individualistic, such as the family, but some are complexes of institutions which extend through the full spatial and cultural range of a particular society, such as the economy. Murray did not distinguish between the two types of subsidiary centers of moral insight, but he increasingly called for their relative autonomy and freedom, much as he did for the family in the first, essential argument. The state, then, is limited by society and society itself is limited by the moral and technical efficiencies of its own parts. "As much freedom as possible."

Second, the groundwork has been laid for the application of a "moral subsidiarity" principle to the church itself,[35] at least in the church's external dealings. Murray had, in the essentialistic argument, claimed that the theological argument would never contradict the ethical argument, that the latter offered some limitation over the former. With the ethical argument now placed within social history, the conceptual possibility emerges that new value configurations arising within new social and political forms can place moral demands on the church for recognition and encouragement, as an aspect of the church's care for the common temporal good. When Murray next surfaces from his period of quiet, Sturzo's claim of the consensual conjoining of ecclesiological freedom with democratic freedoms will offer just such a point of departure. But this is another subject, for another chapter.

Murray has now conceptually identified society and its relation to the political. He has suggested that society is the moral center of the temporal order, through which that order comes to self-definition, and by which it adjusts to social, economic, and political changes. Yet Murray has much to learn concerning the developmental dynamics of social meaning. In the next chapter I will examine the ebb and flow of social self-definition as Murray discovered and defined the process within the quite temporal, impermanent reality of American society.

Chapter Three

THE AUTHORIZATION PRINCIPLE:

Expeditions within an Historical Society

While Murray was debating the religious liberty issue within the Roman Catholic Church, he also became involved in many different American social discussions, ranging through the topical concerns of the time: parochial school aid, constitutional law, censorship, nuclear war, and a host of others. These discussions began in the mid-1940s along with the religious liberty debate, but continued through the period of his silencing (1954) to the election of John F. Kennedy to the United States presidency. Most of those issues were eventually incorporated in some form into his 1960 *We Hold These Truths* (1960a), after having first found publication in moderately popular journals such as *America* and *Thought*. This popular forum rightly suggests that Murray's arguments were consciously advanced with the public in mind, in the hope that they would be socially effective.

Now, it makes fascinating reading to trace all these articles and correspondence sequentially, through the many issues and against the background of Murray's developing political, social, and ethical theories. Almost every article contains a new insight, a preliminary breakthrough into, or application of, his particular theories. However, in this chapter, I simply want to point out the growing centrality within Murray's various arguments of the Thomistic social authorization principle (the claim that the people are the ultimate judges of the king's justice), and the rather practical problems he found with it. For the sake of brevity, I must presume much of the content of those many issues, although each argument does deserve closer attention in its own right.

My topic, then, is the growing theoretical and practical role of the authorization principle in Murray's practice of public debate. The importance of that principle for his religious liberty argument has already been noted. Authorization dialectically unlocked the state/society distinction and emerged in a more complete form from that distinction. Within his ecclesiological circles, therefore, Murray had much invested in it. Here he will try practicing this authorization principle, gaining a concrete appreciation of its role in the public, civil forum, and attempting to act in that forum in ways contributing to the forum's intellectual and moral growth.

The following presentation is divided into three parts: (1) Murray's growing use of authorization within his civil arguments; (2) his "socializing" of the natural law theory by conjoining it with a consensus theory, and (3) the practical changes which the principle brought into his own manner of public arguing, including changes in the priorities that he set for those arguments.

It should be noted at the beginning that Murray was operating within a principle that he considered essential to democratic living, a distinctly American principle which grounds America's self-under-standing (much as he tried to situate the dualism principle within the church). In this context he did not question that principle; rather, he opposed philosophies, theologies, and social practices that wittingly or unwittingly appeared to endanger the public recognition and practice of authorization. Murray attempted here to define, defend, and advance the recognition of moral authorization and its concomitant social reality, "consensus." He would not be forced to defend the soundness of the principle itself until the Second Vatican Council. These internal American discussions, however, prepared the way for his conciliar arguments.

I. GROWING USE OF THE AUTHORIZATION PRINCIPLE.   I will here briefly survey Murray's appeal to the authorization principle within three specific arguments: (a) an American education debate; (b) a censorship debate; and (c) the mid-1950s confrontation with international communism. In the first two, he tended to presume the existence of an American moral consensus; in the last, he called in anguish for the development of such a consensus.

A. The American Educational Debate.   About the same time Murray was developing his first religious liberty argument in polemical exercises with Fenton and Shea, he was also involved in a disagreement over the meaning of the American Declaration of Independence, the Constitution, and the First and Fourteenth Amendments. The immediate occasions for the argument were the Supreme Court decisions in the 1947 Everson and 1948 McCollum cases,[1] the former allowing busing of parochial students to private schools, the latter denying the use of public school property for off-hours, voluntary religious instruction.

Murray entered the debate in December 1946, with a critique of Dr. M. Searle Bates' theoretical argument for the separation of church and state, as the theory was presented in *Religious Liberty: An Inquiry* (Bates 1945).[2] In Bates' argument, Murray contended, "It appears that the First Amendment canonizes Liberal Protestant ecclesiology in an extreme form, and anathematizes as un-American all dissenters" (1946e, 261). One must hold, if one subscribes to the American Constitution, that "all churches are simply voluntary societies, of equally human origin and of equal value in the sight of God." This for Murray is a theological presupposition and quite foreign to the original intent of the Constitution and First Amendment. Murray, then, rejected Bates' argument for its alleged ecclesiological premise, and he further appealed to the intention of the Founding Fathers.

Murray considered the First Amendment to be simply good ethics and politics (based on reason) (1946e, 263). In the present debate, however, he was not ultimately concerned with Protestant theological interpretations, but rather with secularistic "theologies" of democracy. Even in response to the "positive" Everson decision, Murray's major target was Mr. Justice Rutledge's minority opinion, which Murray considered "a more than faintly doctrinaire piece of historicism" (1947c, 628). The opinion was a "piece of historicism" because it reflected certain nineteenth century notions of religious liberty which were not in line with the intention of the framers of the American Constitution. And Murray's qualified endorsement of the Supreme Court was not long lasting. In a closely argued and very impassioned response to the McCollum decision (1949i), he revisited the majority opinion in the Everson case, and found behind all present Supreme Court arguments an historical fallacy, an absolute sectarianism, and a non-American statism. Again, the historical fallacy lay in the attribution of Madison's and Virginia's doctrinaire definition of religion (as purely a matter of internal conviction) to the overall intent of the constitutional framers (1949i, 29, 41–43). Murray maintained that, regardless of Madison's own personal religious beliefs, that which won national affirmation was a political and pragmatic attempt at securing the temporal, public good; the First Amendment was a statement with political, not religious, reference. The Supreme Court's argument, then, was historically inaccurate.

Second, Murray criticized the McCollum decision for in large part abandoning the historical argument. In the opinion of Justice Frankfurter, the current problem was to reinterpret the amendment in light of modern social consciousness (1949i, 25–26). And the consciousness that dictates juridical and public educational policy is secularistic. Its social carriers are selected sectors of the American educational establishment, like the American Federation of Teachers, for whom diversity in the religious sphere is destructive of democratic unity. In the philosophy adopted and developed by Frankfurter, the public school system is the "sacrament" of a "religion of democracy." All those who do not participate in the public school system are in a sense heretical, having chosen to live beyond the pale of the religiously exclusive creed of secularism. The central absolute of that creed is nonestablishment, with no aid in any form its corollary; free exercise, in the face of nonestablishment absolutism, is reduced to irrelevance. According to Murray, then, an absolutism of the nonestablishment clause indicated an absolute quasi-religious philosophy whereby "the First Amendment has been stood on its head. And in that position it cannot but gurgle juridical nonsense" (1949i, 33).

Finally, this "juridical nonsense" was evident primarily in the Court's insensitivity to the truly pluralistic nature of American society, as well as to the just claims of parental rights. On the one hand, an absolutist religious philosophy was being imposed on society under penalty of at least economic disabilities, all in the name of a neutrality toward religion which was actually a "neutrality against religion." On the other, the Court's rulings were a violation, in the name of democracy, of the rights of parents in the education of their children (1949i, 36). Although the Court heard arguments based on the rights of parents, it in no way addressed the problem of such rights in any of its opinions. The question of rights was swallowed up in the absolutism of the Court's statist definition of nonestablishment.

Murray attempted, then, to base this early argument on what he considered the past consensus of the founding fathers, with the presupposition that the present laws should reflect that past consensus. But, he also appealed to the religiously pluralistic composition of American society as related to the justice question. His rejection of secularism here is in line with those similar rejections in the essentialistic religious liberty argument.

Murray's reliance on an appeal to the founding national consensus was also not long-lasting. In 1956 Murray published "The School Problem in the Mid-Twentieth Century"—which, with revisions, became a chapter in *We Hold These Truths*: "Is It Justice?." He asserted again that one cannot read a governmental hostility to religion into the intent of the founding fathers (1956b; 1960a, 151).[3] Further, the present constitutional problems in the arena of education are of relatively recent development. The prior norm for American education was indeed religiously based schools. But now that government has entered the educational arena, the state must be in some sense cognizant of the spiritual needs of its people, since those needs remain real and the state has assumed the primary facilitative role for education. If the state appropriates funds for public education in the name of public welfare, then aid to the development of religious consciousness as a means to free exercise must be granted to parochial education as well as to public education (1960a, 153). Murray had two bases for this judgment.

The first is a matter of justice. Despite the title of the 1960 chapter ("Is It Justice?"), Murray quickly disposed of the question. The denial of public funds for parochial schools has always been and will always be against the dictates of distributive justice (1960a, 145–46). Similar to the racial discrimination problem, unequal distribution of publicly obtained funds is objectively and permanently unjust.

A "sociological" case (1960a, 147),[4] however, can be made for previous funding restrictions. In an earlier age, America understood itself to be a Protestant nation. As a reflection of a Protestant self-understanding or consensus, public funds were given to a predominantly Protestant oriented public school system. But the foundational religious consensus of this nation has changed. Relying on the thesis of Will Herberg (1960a, 144), Murray contended that America now understands itself as genuinely pluralistic, with Catholics, Protestants, and Jews having equal political and social rights, and as equally sharing in the formation of the spiritual basis of our society.

Throughout the rest of his life, Murray's dealing with school aid and religion in the public schools and universities would be based on this appeal to the "present consensus." In 1952, Murray entered into correspondence with Robert MacIver. The occasion was a Columbia University sponsored American Academic Freedom Project,[5] the point of which appears to have been the shaping of a case for academic freedom (in a fairly absolute sense), while at the same time finding grounds on which to exclude Communist "propaganda" from within the university walls. The problem, then, concerned the restriction of free speech within the democratically organized university, that is, a limited type of censorship within the educational community.

Murray attempted to defend both the notion that a Catholic university could be an arena for free and intellectually honest academic inquiry, and the notion that religion could be, and must be, studied in state schools, even claiming that in those state schools the teaching of religion must be by those who themselves believe. In a discussion that I will more closely examine further on, Murray judged that the academic establishment had sabotaged its possible positive social role by adopting scientistic premises (thereby alienating itself from the people) or by its own fundamental internal divisions (resulting in an inability to communicate among itself, much less with civil society) (1954a, #8). In either case, it has relinquished its role of moral leadership within democratic society. Therefore, the best that a university can be expected to do is be a neutral forum in which the religious diversity of civil society comes to expression, and in which the different logics of faith can be examined and compared, with all points of view "fairly" and "fully" presented (1954a, #7). The people will only accept from the university a commitment to "cultivate 'sincerity' of mind, habits of disciplined thought and civilized mannerly discussion . . . ," teaching the student how to think, not what to think (1954a, #7). Just as the state should be restricted to the facilitation of public religious discussion (not determining its content), so ought the academic community, but for somewhat different reasons.

From 1949 to 1956, the basis of Murray's calls for educational reform has shifted from an appeal to tradition (the intent of the founding fathers) to an appeal to the present social consensus, after earlier rejecting a similar appeal by Frankfurter.

B. Censorship: The Use of Law for Ethical Objectives Other than Public Order.
In both his religious liberty and American education debates, the notion of social consensus and the alleged content of the American consensus were brought to bear as collective value commitments which place limits first on the state, then on the educational establishment. Murray increasingly restricted the state to the role of simple maintenance of public peace, within which social ethical debates could take place. And the university was itself to be simply a forum where all to which the human mind was open could be addressed, again analogously establishing a field of public peace. However, he was soon thrust into another debate, wherein he had to address the question of nonpublic order goods entering the political forum, i.e., the enforcement of moral requirements not immediately related to public peace. The issue was literary censorship.

Murray's 1956 article, "Literature and Censorship," was his second most widely published pre-Vatican II study, and found its way into *We Hold These Truths* under the title "Should There Be a Law?" (1956e). Here he attempted to make the case that the natural law theory or the "tradition of reason"[6] is the only theory which can supply a basis for public discussions and enforcement of moral values. The theory's capacity to supply such a basis rests in its notion of prudential determination and in its distinction between the moral and the legal orders.

After somewhat lavish praise for the American recognition that the order of law (government) is constrained by a distinct moral order, and for the mechanism by which that moral order directs the law (the people's participation in law-making), Murray criticized the "Protestant notion that whatever is moral should be law and whatever is law is moral" (1960a, 156–58). This confusion of law and morality, and the further derivative confusion of public and private morality, "ensues in a knavish denial that there is any such thing as a public morality" which operates within its own limited field and by its own particular rules and dynamisms. To properly discuss the issue of censorship, one must have a right theory of reasoning which can distinguish between private and public moral behavior. If the realms remain confused in public thinking, we will repeat those disastrous Protestant experiments in the moral direction of American society, such as Prohibition and the New England birth control statutes.

Any discussion of censorship is primarily a consideration of the application of police power, and as such is a consideration of what can actually be achieved through the means of civil law (1960a, 159). When we "have made our case that some literary influences are socially corruptive, we have only reached the threshold of the problem of social freedom" and social morality (1960a, 161). It has been the genius of the American polity that law as constraint may be imposed only for the sake of freedom, that this tool which is proper to government is directed to the fullest possible fulfillment of free exercise within society. In a discussion of constraint, one is involved in the weighing and balancing of conflicting claims to free exercise. The imposition of constraints follows from a complex moral judgment which is called "prudence" (1960a, 171).[7] Even the laws which regulate freedoms, then, are acts of reason: reason governs that distinct social reality.

But not all uses of law are solely for the purpose of regulating conflicting claims for free expression or exercise. Social reason functions in the further weighing or balancing of those freedoms with the dictates of the public moral consensus. In the "tradition of reason," public coercive restraint is limited by the limited field of juridical application (to acts in the public forum) and by the constraint of the societal moral consensus. Law can never be effective in public education or in public control when there is lacking a public consensus on the moral issue under discussion. The application of the law to an issue such as prohibition of alcohol not only did not limit public immorality due to alcohol abuse, it led to a breakdown in respect for law and for the moral uses of law. The prudential judgment which forms public law encompasses, then, the values in conflict *and* the consensus which determines a law's effectiveness. And this judgment is still reasonable; it is based on publicly discussable criteria.

According to Murray, only the underlying epistemological theory of the tradition of reason can maintain the recognition that issues of public morality are solved by reason, not by force. He criticized some Catholic groups that "look more like power groups, an image of force groups, not of reasonable people" (1960a, 171).[8] The effectiveness of morally directed laws depends on two distinct criteria which are ignored in power approaches to social reformation. The most immediate criterion is the public recognition that a proposed law is a reasonable, prudential judgment. That reasonableness must be perceived socially, which means public discussion of the reasons for such judgments. Remotely, this effectiveness rests further on the recognition that a case is presented within an affirmation of the centrality of freedom in the social sphere—one of the most general truths which constitute us as a people and which remain preliminary to the adoption of any particular social policy. America has opted for free, reasonable exchange as the governing mode of public, ethical determination. The people's underlying presumption in favor of reason exercised in freedom will override any attempt at nonconsensual enforcement.[9] The proper means of establishing effective public policy are not immediately those of law, but rather those of argument and persuasion (1960a, 168). Agreement must be reached or reasonably attempted, or the primary norm of the juridical, the preservation of public peace, will be violated. If collective agreement over a specific issue has not been achieved, then the natural law reasonableness of the people will rebel against the apparent arbitrariness of the law. If the surrounding discussion has not been free/reasonable, then the method of juridical formulation will be alienated from the valid American commitment to freedom/reason, and again lead to a rightful disturbance of the public peace. In either case, the result will be significant public spurning of that law.

The censorship debate led Murray beyond the simple juridical norm of the "goods of order," as these were developed in the religious liberty discussion. Moral values which are not immediately goods of order can reach the public legal forum, if there is sufficient agreement in the body politic on the correctness of specific moral judgments and if the formation of those collective judgments has been publicly reasonable. But the ultimate index for juridical imposition remains proper to the juridical order, namely, the public peace. In Murray's three moral norms for the direction of law (peace, common morality, and justice), the second has, within limits of law, been subjected to the first.

As Murray argued to the constraint of "common morality" by "public order," he likewise uncovered a hierarchically ordered notion of consensual commitment, each order of which might in its own right shape the juridical order. The first is the general commitment of Americans to the methods of freedom. Murray was here moving toward a notion of a general, social ethical commitment that sets up foundational premises for any argument of specific ethical issues. Since he held that this preference for the "methods of freedom" is an historically developed, ethically justified perspective, some manners of arguing or publicly enforcing specific ethical judgments might be immoral in their manner of presentation, even though morally correct concerning the specific issue. They would be violations of the morally affirmed "methods of freedom." His argument concerns not only the pragmatic effectiveness of a public presentation, but further, the moral content of that presentation against the general moral awareness of that historical society. He does not try to justify this general commitment, only to demonstrate that its violation can doom even the best arguments over specific issues.

A second level of general value commitments pertain to the more specific realm of nonpublic values, which he held can and must be argued in the public forum, and the enforcement of which is dependent on the social acceptance of those arguments and evaluations. He allows some censorship, while retaining tight rein over government. Such an argument required a notion of governing consensus concerning both the methods by which public arguments are advanced and the values involved in specific issues. Murray recognizes, then, at least two levels of ethically justifiable premises which must enter into public determinations, and as such complicate those determinations.

This 1956 argument was rather abstract, but Murray was willing to act on it. In the early 1960s, a Massachusetts attempt to liberalize birth control laws gave Murray an opportunity to place ecclesiological recommendations concerning that law within his theory of juridical limits and positive social consensus. Richard Cardinal Cushing asked for Murray's recommendations concerning an amendment which would have eliminated penalties of up to two and one-half years imprisonment and/or up to one thousand dollar fines for sale and supplying of artificial contraceptive devices (Massachusetts General Law, 272, par. 20, 21, 21a).

Although at this time Murray seems to have maintained that artificial birth control is immoral, he argued that "the case for affirming contraception to be a matter of private morality is sufficiently conclusive in our present circumstances" (1965f, 2) so that the case does not fall immediately within the field of public morality with the latter's indices of public peace and justice. Again, the original birth control statutes were attempts to regulate private forms of behavior in an arena (the bedroom) in which laws are "unenforceable and ineffective." Generally, Murray judged, in the field of sex morality, the "public educative value of law seems to be almost nil." But most importantly:

> . . . the practice, undertaken in the interests of "responsible parenthood," has received official sanction by many religious groups within the community. It is difficult to see how the state can forbid, as contrary to public morality, a practice that numerous religious leaders approve as

morally right. The stand taken by these religious groups may be lamentable from the Catholic moral point of view. But it is decisive from the point of view of law and jurisprudence, for which the norm of "generally accepted standards" is controlling (1965f, 2).

He then recommended Catholic support for the amendment, but further suggested that Catholics make the basis for their support clear, that they in no way condoned artificial birth control as a moral good, but rather that their support of the bill is based on principles of law, jurisprudence, and religious freedom (1965f, 3).[10] Finally, it is up to Catholics "to lift the standards of public morality in all its dimensions, not by appealing to law and police action, but by the integrity of their Christian lives. This in order to set the birth control issue in its proper perspective" (1965f, 4), or, one might say, to remove the debate from the arena of force to that of argument.

C. Communism and the Present Danger.   In the American education argument, Murray argued from the present American social consensus to the presentation of religious issues even within secular schools. Then, in the censorship debate, he tried to adjust his political theory to the public juridical expression of some moral judgments, although always within the confines of public peace. Finally, like most Americans in the late 1950s, Murray was immersed in Cold War rhetoric and the problems which arose out of the East/West confrontation. In 1957 Murray received an appointment to the Committee of Consultants on Basic Issues of the Fund for the Republic, the parent group for Robert Hutchins' Center for the Study of Democratic Institutions. The appointment and subsequent discussion led Murray to question long-term democratic social and political viability in the face of militant international communism. He again turned to the question of the American consensus.

Out of Murray's committee studies, he isolated four elements which guide Soviet foreign policy. The first is the Soviet conviction that power is to be unrestrained by any Western notion of law (1958c; 1960a, 222f). The state is to take any available means toward securing its objectives, independently of any notions of justice and human rights. Second, Russia is unique as an *imperium* in that all its moves in the political forum are to be conducted in accordance with Leninist theory. Even now, "there is no convincing evidence that Mr. Khrushchev represents apostasy or even heresy." Third, there is the Russian imperialistic doctrine, the doctrine of world revolution, which orients the Soviet Union to world domination through whatever means are available. And, fourth, Russia views itself as "inheritors both of Tsarist imperialism and of mystical Panslavist Messianism." It sees its purpose in the scheme of things to be the elimination of that culture which is generally called the "West." A third epoch will abolish and supplant what are called the two Western epochs: feudalism and capitalism. Murray then gave several examples of Soviet policy decisions that remain unintelligible to Western politicians (1960a, 227).

The reason for the Western misunderstanding of Russian activities rests in the Western inability to visualize doctrine controlling policy. While Americans sit down at a negotiating table hoping to strike a pragmatic compromise ("We still talk too much"), a Communist will push, stonewall, or leave the table, all determined by his dogmatic vision (1960a, 234–35). Further, the Westerner's lack of doctrine, or his exclusive faith in democratic procedures, leaves him with no clear principles on which to form his own policy decisions. So, in the face of a consistent dogma, the Westerner crumbles. The initiative constantly remains with the East. At best we have faith in our technology, but technology with no clear directing principles leads only to overarming and increasing the danger of war, and so is "irredeemably immoral."

Much more will be said further on concerning Murray's growing despair over the American experiment. Important to us here, however, is the urgency in which he casts his argument. The Soviet Union has demonstrated that even "a damnable philosophy is more effective than no philosophy" (1958b, 1960a, 91). For the advancement of "reason" in the public debate, he introduced the natural law notions of proportionality, from within the just war theory. The argument itself need not detain us here, but it should be highlighted that Murray's principle target was, again, the American ethos guaranteeing that any use of nuclear weapons, or even any attempts at nuclear disarmament, would be immoral, i.e., irrational. Americans, he claimed, can think only in terms of unconditionality: one either annihilates one's enemy or totally, absolutely surrenders to him. Even among Catholics, there "was no substantial effort made to clarify by moral judgment the thickening mood of savage violence that made possible the atrocities of Hiroshima and Nagasaki" (1958d; 1960a, 265). And the entire policy of unconditional surrender was a violation of those moral limitations which natural law, just war theory has clarified (1960a, 266–67). This absolutist mentality is borne of a lack of doctrine. But, more importantly, it indicates "an abdication of moral reason which could direct the use of power." We have no sense of the restrained use of force or the criteria by which force could be used morally because we do not discuss public values in public. Only a public discussion of those commitments which make us a moral people can lead the way out of the Cold War.[11]

So, by 1960 Murray had many more of his arguments, beyond that of religious liberty, grounded in a growing consensus theory. He attempted to argue that America was founded in a consensus and could only survive by means of a redeveloped consensus. In the third section of this chapter, I will again take up the problems which he found with that consensus. But first, Murray's reinterpretation of the natural law in light of that consensus theory deserves some attention.

II. THE IMPACT OF CONSENSUS THEORY ON NATURAL LAW THEORY.

Although it may be true that the best theories are not defined *solely* by their opponents, it is nonetheless also true that theories do develop within historical environments, and as such generally take account, if they are to be socially effective, of the author's opponents. Murray's theoretical considerations are no exception. Much of *We Hold These Truths* is a collection of essays dealing with the issues that were just examined, but the heart of his argument is developed in three essays of a theoretical bent. The last essay of the book, "The Doctrine Lives: The Eternal Return of Natural Law," was actually the first written (1950a), and as such set the direction for the entire book, and for the entire decade. To grasp the changes in Murray's own theory of natural law, I will compare the 1950 argument with another advanced in 1954, then with another article that was not published previously to *We Hold These Truths*.

The agenda of "The Doctrine Lives" was set in the third of three articles in the *Yale Scientific Magazine*, under the general title of "On the Necessity of Not Believing." The three articles dealt with the proposition that, given our modern understanding of human rationality, belief in any nonempirically verifiable truth-claims is impossible. Murray characterized the first article by Homer W. Smith (Smith 1949) as a nontriumphalistic "scientific Monism," based on the proposition that "the methods and findings of the biological and physical sciences . . . are the only valid methods of intellectual inquiry, leading to the only valid findings" (1949a, 12). Thus, intellectual integrity demands a rejection of religiously based belief.[12] In the second article (Greene 1949), Theodore M. Greene agreed that our modern understanding of human intelligence has destroyed truth claims which arise from any modes of knowing other than scientific inquiry (1949a, 12). On the other hand, Greene also claimed that the human person must risk a commitment to some unsubstantiated truths for the sake of human and humane living. Murray understood Greene's last claim to be a Kantian manner of founding religious and moral truths, and a totally unacceptable, or at least unnecessary, epistemological position.

Murray had several grounds for rejecting the previous two arguments, not the least of which were the totalitarian truth claims, the "monism," he found in Smith, claims paralleling those of French political totalitarianism (1949a, 30). But already Murray's concern is clearly with the public forum. By denying reason's penetration of religious and moral realities, both Greene and Smith put the human person in the impossible position of confronting atheistic humanism without any intellectual resources, and, in the present age, we now confront an atheism which is out to trample Western civilization. His concern was with the social effects of those epistemological presuppositions, the ultimate moral relativism and social confusion which result from scientism or fideistic positivism.

In "The Doctrine Lives" Murray outlined four possible epistemological positions: (1) the "old rationalism" (socially unaware Lockeanism), (2) Marxism, (3) the "new rationalism" (scientism), and (4) natural law, and then attempted to establish a dialectics of choice between them. Murray's presentation of the natural law theory is based on a rather individualistic epistemological theory, typical of that used in his "essentialistic" religious liberty debate. But already there is an underlying social concern. What recommends the theory is that, like the Declaration of Independence and the Constitution, it is based on a realistic epistemology.

> Natural law supposes a realistic epistemology, that asserts the real to be the measure of knowledge, and also asserts the possibility of intelligence reaching the real, i.e, the nature of things—in the case, the nature of man as a unitary and constant concept beneath all individual differences (1960a, 327).[13]

The theory presumes that the mind is not simply the creator of social reality: rather, social reality imposes certain demands or exigencies on human understanding. Yet the reality which is the basis for natural law is immanent to humanity, not imposed in a positivistic fashion. That reality is the human person as a knowing and feeling subject (not simply as a survivor) and as a social being. Just as Murray had earlier argued that international forms of sociality necessitated and preexisted the establishment of an international legal structure (1944d, 813–14), so here in the social drives of the human person lay natural, pre-given demands on human moral intelligence. For the person, then, both as an individual and in society, there exist pre-given orders of good and right, before intelligence recognizes them and practical reason formulates an order of civil law in support of them. Any human being who makes a moral claim against common moral opinion or against legal systems must and does appeal to a pre-given and finally absolute order of justice which is normative for human self-under-standing. The first dictates of the social order are, then, more specifically *suum cuique,* and more generally, "justice is to be done and injustice is to be avoided" (1960a, 332). From this general starting point in the social, moral arena follow the principles of (1) the supremacy of law as a product of reason, not simply of will, (2) the political authority of the community, (3) the limited political role of the ruler, and (4) the principle of constitutionality with its agreement or contractual overtones (1960a, 333). While these principles must be discovered and developed, they escape the relativism of the rational-istic theories in that an appeal is made beyond social will to an order of justice which exists before social will and which ought to be formative of that will.

If the realistic epistemology of natural law theory offers a nonrelativistic basis for those rights and legal structures which we hold to be true, the theory likewise grounds the transcendental reference which we have also declared to be one of our fundamental truths. Unlike the thin rationalisms of both the old and, particularly, the new varieties, natural law theory is "immanent in the nature of man, but transcendental in its reference" (1960a, 329). Man is open in his rationality to an order of being which escapes the narrow definitions of reason of Lockean, Marxian, or scientific empiricism. We as a people have found the ultimate grounding of our rights to be in an order of being which is not simply idealistic, nor simply temporal, but in the creative will of God. Anything short of such a final reference, Murray implies, will lead to a relativism and finally to enslavement by despotism or majoritarianism.

It is obvious in the present article that Murray's main concern was with socially foundational epistemological theories which exclude reason's role in a distinctly social object (human interactions which are not reducible to individual drives) and in its perception/formulation of a transtemporal order of reality (an order of justice which would derive from the eternal reality of God). The people must be able to know social reality and to affirm its certainty, both actions for the sake of social well-being. In 1950, it was the "realism" of the natural law theory, as a counter to relativism and confusion, that recommended the theory. By 1958 (and for reasons yet to be examined), Murray recognized that the truths which are the ground of the American consensus can no longer be affirmed with the same "naive realism" with which they were formerly affirmed (1958a; 1960a, 5). But at that point he proposed a "critical realism," again to counter the relativisms of scientism and "neo-Kantianism."[14]

As noted earlier, in the mid-1950s, Murray was attempting to recommend the American forms of separation to his own church. In a

1954 article, he attempted to support this recommendation by examining the compatibility between Catholic social and political beliefs and the foundational beliefs of the Republic. Perhaps prudently, he began with the claim that his own perspective was not the question of the acceptability of Catholicism to America. Such would be a gross impertinence and an invalid question. Rather,

> ... the question is whether American democracy—in our case as involving a theory of pluralism—is compatible with Catholicism. No other manner of putting the question would be acceptable to anyone who places the imperatives of consciences, which mediate the law of God, above the imperatives whose origins are in human law and sentiment (1954e, 14).

His manner of demonstrating the compatibility of American Constitutionalism with Catholicism was to trace back the governing philosophy of both to a common root in Catholic medieval thought, thereby claiming that "your founding tradition is really ours." Relying heavily on Clinton Rossiter's *Seedtime of the Republic* (1953), Murray mapped out four beliefs which were foundational to (and presently held by) the Republic (1954e; 1960a, 28–37), echoing in part the 1950 listing of four essential principles (1960a, 333), but now with stronger emphasis on the moral agency of the people. These beliefs were: (1) The nation in all of its activities looks to the sovereignty of God as the "first structural principle of its organization." This principle has been reiterated even in our day by American presidents, constituting America as distinct from Jacobin Europe. (2) The purposes of government are political, in the sense that the right to command is dependent on adherence to the law, that the king or government officials are subject to the order of law, not purely creators of it. (3) The validation of the moral content of law is carried out by the people. Even in the medieval period, this principle of moral consent and affirmation was at least in theory (St. Thomas) operative. (4) Only a virtuous people can be free, that is, "only when the people as a whole are inwardly governed by the recognition of the universal moral law," can government fully operate in its pursuit of its (limited) common good.

American Constitutionalism added further specifications to these four foundational medieval principles. To the principle of constraint by law was added the fact of a written constitution explicitly ratified by the people. "By the Constitution the people define the areas where authority is legitimate and the areas where liberty is lawful" (1960a, 32). The state has been separated from society and limited in its offices toward society by an order of law. And to the principle of consent was added the further specification of consent to legislation through representative government. This involved a "great act of faith in the moral sense of the people," in their ability to "judge, direct, and correct" the processes of government (1960a, 34).[15] Further, the means by which the people's participation in government is to be defended are such democratic institutions as free speech and free press. But the grounding of those freedoms was not "eighteenth-century individualistic rationalism." These freedoms were thought to be "social necessities" (1960a, 34), "exigencies of civil conversation" (1960a, 45), requirements for the efficient and moral operation of society. The American emphasis on procedural rights was an attempt to guarantee that all citizens would be equally subject to the common order of law, and active in its explicitation.

Because the four foundational principles are part of the medieval natural law theory, and because the further specifications are reasonable, a Catholic can, on the basis of the substance of the consensus itself, positively accept American constitutional theory and the truths there embodied. The theory has been the "product of Christian history," not a child of rationalism. "Historically, this tradition has found and still finds its intellectual home within the Catholic Church" (1960a, 41).[16] "The ideas expressed are native to [the Catholic's] own universe of discourse. Even the accent, being American, suits his tongue."

From 1950 to 1954, Murray has shifted his focus from a set of truths which will save American society, to an understanding of that society as an outgrowth of that natural law theory, a growth which has taken place within a specific social and political history. By 1960, Murray had himself developed strong doubts about the nature, content, and existence of an American moral consensus. But in the newest article for *We Hold These Truths*, he attempted to argue that there exists in America a moral consensus directing at least domestic economic practice. He claimed with the support of Adolf Berle (1959) that the spontaneous controls by which American industries curtail and direct their activities, particularly in areas which have not been juridically defined, can only be understood within a concept of social, moral consensus. According to Berle, this consensus is not in every instance nor even often a democratically expressed majority opinion. It is rather a determination of the "Lords Spiritual," a reasonable determination adopted by businessmen who are at once businessmen and human, rational beings (1960a, 100–07).

Murray's concern, however, was not with the existence or even with the content of this American consensus, but rather with the structure, dynamics, and location of that consensus. The consensus

itself is experienced, by businessmen and others, as an authority, as
making behavioral demands which are not necessarily supported by
civil penalties. This consensus, however, is not simply a matter of
experience. It includes an "understanding" of humanity in its individual and social aspects. But most properly, a national consensus is a
series of value "judgments" based on the "experience" of human living
and the understanding of that experience.[17] The judgments (or the
principles expressing the judgments) grow out of various experiential
complexes. The first and second levels of judgments/principles concern the behavior which is most immediate to the individual: the basic
choice of ethical orientation and the implications of that orientation
for interpersonal experience (1960a, 109–10).[18] Within the realm of
interpersonal, common experience, understandings, and judgments of
moral worth are accessible to every rational individual, *"ut in pluribus,* in
the case of most men."

In situations which are uncommon, or removed from the realm of
immediate, interpersonal interaction, ordinary men and women lack
the analytic ability or the leisure to clarify the multiple conflicting
values and the implications of possible modes of action (1960a,
110–11). These third and fourth levels of value judgments are at once
more specific and more remote. They are more specific in that they are
tied to particular institutional and cultural complexes not easily, nor
appropriately, generalized. They are remote in that only the "wise"
men and women of exceptional understanding and judgment can fully
and rationally explore their complexity. The role of the wise within
any society is one of analysis, judgment, and also of education. "The
wise must teach [the remote natural law principles] to those of lesser
reflectiveness" (1960a, 115). The mediator of these principles or
judgments to the social order are an elite of that order. This dynamic
relationship between the wise and the people is true of any social body.

Now, a central judgment/principle of the Western liberal tradition
of ethical reflection has been the affirmation that the people, not
directly the wise, are the immediate source of moral validation of
specific institutional forms (1960a, 119). Again, the American specification of that principle has been the validation of legislation as well as
of constitutions by the people. Murray did not here question the
validity of this principle or specification. Needed for its functioning,
however, is the further judgment of the reasonableness of the people.
Here Murray equated the Thomistic natural law principle of "the
rational soul" as the "proper form of man" and Berle's understanding
of American social justification. According to Thomas, it is man's
reasonableness, his argument to judgment on the basis of publicly
verifiable evidence, that constitutes the human person as human. And

it is "this quality of being in accord with reason [that] is the *non-contingent element* in the body of thought that constitutes the consensus" (1960a, 119).[19] The people (e.g., businessmen) "can grasp the reasonableness of the conclusions reached by the wise, even if they are incapable of the 'careful inquiry' that led the wise to those conclusions" (1960a, 120). They will "naturally" seek to establish the legitimacy of their power and also to have their use of power publicly recognized as legitimate (1960a, 121), avoiding any public image of unreasonableness. All people are at bottom natural law practitioners, attempting to have their own activities appear in the social arena as reasonable, even if they secretly view their own activities as evil. Reason is the final court of appeal in a democratically organized society.

Murray unfortunately did not discuss the type of criteria or methods by which the people recognize the reasonableness of an argument or judgments. Does such recognition and affirmation rest on the perceived moral goodness of the wise (the wise as good), or on an unthematized awareness of the adequacy of a judgment to a situation (the proposed act as good)? He does appear to claim that the people will inchoately and unthematically be able themselves to judge the degree to which proposed conclusions are supported by evidence and argument, perhaps in line with Lonergan's notion of "common sense" and "common sense judgments."[20]

Murray still could not answer the question: "Who are these wise men today?" In the medieval period, the wise were the people of the *Studium*. It was "not the function of the Church as such to elaborate the public consensus, which is a body of rational knowledge, a structure of rational imperatives ... " (1960a, 121).[21] To the *Studium* fell the task of "defining what justice is, and what the freedom of the people requires in changing circumstances" (1960a, 122). But in our present age, "all one can say is that they are men who have a 'care,' but who are not 'interested parties' (in the usual sense of the latter term)" (1960a, 123). As will be discussed later, neither the American academic community, nor Protestants, nor Catholics had demonstrated to Murray the practice of reasonable argument, the tradition of civility or reason.

However, by 1960 Murray had bound the authorization principle with the natural law theory of moral knowledge. He did so with respect to (1) the former's legitimization by the latter, (2) their common historical roots, and (3) the major preoccupation of both with the engagement of moral discrimination. Now, not only were Murray's specific ethical arguments based on authorization; his theory of social knowledge and social morality were likewise linked with it. I will now examine challenges to the authorization principle, the pivot for many of his practical and theoretical arguments.

III. DANGERS AND CHALLENGES TO THE AUTHORIZATION PRINCIPLE. What hinders the moral direction of civil society by the people? What forces interfere with the exercise of the authorization principle? The forces Murray gradually found himself confronting, for the sake of a more socially/morally active American people, can be divided into two categories: (a) the styles of public discourse practiced by antagonists and (b) group attitudes which determine both the style and the possibility of such discourse. Murray had firsthand experience with both sets of problems, since he himself practiced styles of argument and shared in attitudes which hindered discourse.

A. The Social-Ethical Immorality of Polemics.   I have already reviewed Murray's first critique of the American Protestant understanding of the First Amendment. Murray interpreted Bates as claiming that the original ecclesiological intent of the amendment was to affirm that all churches are of equal religious value, a theological principle clearly unacceptable to Catholics. The First Amendment is rather a tool for the temporal order, a law, to protect the order of religion from political monism and to foster a limited temporal end, namely, public peace.

But, Murray never seriously addressed Protestant justifications of religious liberty or of the First Amendment. Several factors hindered such a confrontation: the polemical nature of the school aid debate, Murray's own apparent enjoyment of the polemics, his preoccupation with secularism, and his conviction that no theological, i.e., ecclesiological, conversation between Protestants and Catholics was possible. (The first three of these will concern us here; the last will be faced in chapter 5.)

In response to a 1946 *Christian Century* editorial which concluded that a Wisconsin bill (allowing public funds for parochial school busing) "is the thin edge of the wedge which, when driven all the way in, will split American democracy wide open" ("The Wisconsin Bus Bill" 1946, 1302), Murray did attempt to argue that the significant "wall" in aid questions was not that between religion and the state, but rather that between the parents' rights and the state's rights in the matter of education. And any law which would de facto severely limit the parents' choice between public and accredited private schools would be a constitutional violation of the parental rights and a handing of a child's education to the absolute control of the state—thus a form of Continental statism. But Murray found, at the core of the Protestant arguments, images such as the "camel's nose" and "wedge" which evoke not an argument over rights, but rather only fear (1947b, 541). The "origins [of the Protestant argument] are in fear—that deep, irrational at times and in certain individuals almost pathological fear that Newman long ago pointed out to be part of the 'anti-romanism' that seems to be inseparable from Protestantism" (1947b, 542).

A year later, in response to "a Manifesto by a new organization called 'Protestants and Other Americans United for Separation of Church and State' (hereafter referred to as PU)" (1948a, 513),[22] any attempt at serious argument dissolved, at least temporarily. In response to admittedly provocative charges, Murray attempted to situate the content and tone of the "Manifesto" within 150 years of American Protestant nativism. Consistent with nineteenth century nativist movements, the sole basis of argument is the "ancient scare technique, very effective against government (the shout through the palace windows: 'If thou release this man, thou art not Caesar's friend!')," an attempt at the formulation of "policy-through nightmare" (1948a, 513–14). The main effect of such Protestant tactics has been "the progressive secularization of American society, particularly of education." Yet the real enemy is not Catholicism, but rather that "secularism that bears within itself the seeds of future tyrannies" (1948a, 515). The one important claim that Murray made was that a "policy through nightmare approach is not part of the rational, responsible democratic process," admitting for the first time some significance to a concern over such processes.[23]

And again in response to W. Russell Bowie's "The Catholic Position" (Bowie 1949), Murray found the basis of Bowie's argument to be "that hostility to the Catholic Church [which] is profoundly lodged in the Protestant collective unconscious, in consequence perhaps of some natal trauma" (1949f, 276). Murray "concurs" with Paul Tillich's statement that "Protestantism is merely on the defensive," but finds that defensiveness to be simply a reflection of Protestantism's inability to define itself in any positive manner. It can only understand itself in opposition to Catholicism. Protestantism, Murray claimed, has never known what it was for. Bowie's real bone of contention is not the church-state position of the Roman Church nor the fear that a Catholic America would reduce Protestants to the rank of second-class citizens. What he really fears is the Catholic claim to be the one, true church, the Catholic view of Protestantism as a "second-class religion" (1949f, 282).[24]

Murray's exercise of religious macho evoked a predictable reaction. In response to 52 letters (all of which appear to have been negative), a somewhat chastened Murray apologized for appearing flippant in a debate which "is much too serious to be taken too seriously" (1949f, 637). Adversarial arguments, he added, if conducted solely in polemical metaphors, do not help raise the discussion to a reasonable and reasoning level. Nor was Murray able to hide his own

major theological preoccupations. In his response, as well as throughout these articles, he questioned again and again the alliance between
modern democratic secularism and liberal Protestantism. And the one
name that stands out among others in this alliance was that of Paul
Blanshard.

To Murray, Blanshard represented a "new Nativism," the "in-
spiration of which is not Protestant bigotry, but the secularistic
positivism that deplores bigotry, at the same time that it achieves a
closure of mind and an edge of antagonism that would be the envy of a
Bible-belt circuit rider" (1949e, 233). Whereas the old nativism held
that "Catholicism was anti-American fundamentally because America
was Protestant, and Catholicism was anti-Protestant," the new
nativism holds that Catholicism is anti-American because the church
claims there to be a source of truth beyond democratic majoritarianism and scientific naturalism (1951b, 216). Blanshard's central notion
of freedom admits of no moral authority outside of political will; that
is, his understanding of morality reduces to power. He can understand
the church, therefore, only in terms of power, and the church as a
power organization must be subjected to the autonomous will of the
democratic state. The public control of society must be given over to
scientific and democratic methods, with the church limited to the
sacristy or to the purely interior forum of the human person (1951b,
218-19).[25] But even more than this subjection and limitation, the
church must be internally transformed into a democratic institution,
allowing no religious authority outside of majority vote. In a word,
Blanshard is a social monist who challenges the perennial Christian
doctrine of social dualism. The ultimate index by which he condemns
the internal structure or the moral directives of the church is that the
church is un-American, not that it is false or wrong.

Both Bowie and Blanshard are united in what they are against: the
Catholic Church. But whereas Bowie does not know what he is for,
Blanshard wants to replace revealed religion by a religion of democracy. And Blanshard is an "undiluted secularist who has just been
coopted into the ranks of the Fathers of the Protestant Church. (His
book, *American Freedom and Catholic Power*, seems to have been published
with the silent imprimatur of a multitude of Protestant clergymen;
and Dr. Bowie reverently quotes it.)" (1949f, 277).

This first Catholic-Protestant exchange was buried under Protestant suspicions of absolute authoritarianism combined with political
power and of Catholic fears of the divinization of contentless political
process. For a time any calls for "due process" or "procedural
requirements" sounded to Murray to be modern apostasies from both
natural and revealed truths. It is little wonder that he himself moved

so slowly to a concern for, and an examination of, such processes in social formation. He simply fought back with his considerable polemical skills.

However, Murray's early 1950s exchanges with MacIver (previously mentioned in another context) seem to have initiated a break with the polemical habit, through a serious mutual attempt to find a common ground for academic liberty. Their exchanges swirled around the possibility and advisability of grounding academic freedom on the premise that all could agree that scientific methods yield true results, even if the American academic community could not similarly affirm the validity of other forms of knowledge. To Murray this all sounded too much like scientism (the claim that only empirical methods yield true knowledge), and he objected to the purely *laissez faire* notion of freedom that appears to derive from scientism. However, Murray's own appreciation of America's intellectual disunity was deepened by their conversation. Twice he suggested that it might be time to end the exchange, for "I seem to be failing to make myself clear ..." (1954a, #3), "our minds are not meeting—in the sense, I mean, that they are not even clashing" (1954a, #10). It is little wonder, then, that he began to emphasize the incompatibility of the different perspectives within the academic community itself. It was time to admit that "today in America there is really no such thing as an intellectual community (the fact that lies at the bottom of all our difficulties in communication; within a community one can always communicate)" (1954a, #7).

There was some concurrence over policy recommendations between Murray's pragmatic argument for the university as a forum in which all opinions are "fully" and "fairly" presented (1954a, #7), and MacIver's insistence that, in its mode of operation, the university should not preclude any significant questioning. Even with this policy agreement, however, MacIver's and Murray's last exchanges reflected the frustration of both with the argument. MacIver's discussion was still cast in terms of the (possible) imposition of restrictions by external authorities (whether religious, political, or social) (MacIver 1954a, #9), while Murray was still preoccupied with the (actual) restrictions placed on academic investigation by the dominant epistemological commitment of the American academic community (1954a, #10). Murray himself admitted the concurrence on policy, and suggested that their major point of difference centered on "how the mind itself should be governed in its search for the totality of truth on all the various levels of truth" (1954a, #12).

> I would hold that the freedom of intelligence stands in polarity to certain laws of intelligence . . . and these laws are discoverable in objective reality: they are themselves part of the truth that intelligence must seek, without prejudice.

But this quest for the very dynamics of human rationality is an issue which must await future development; only a pragmatic argument for intellectual freedom is presently possible within contemporary American society.

The Murray-MacIver exchanges were important for three reasons. First, the discussions between Catholic Murray and Protestant MacIver were not overburdened with what appears to have been the dominant polemical tones of the day. Second, the very civility of the exchanges compelled Murray to push his notion of pluralism beyond disparate religious creeds to an acknowledgment that mutual agreement was lacking even over foundational ethical issues. And third, he was forced toward policy statements that sounded much like those procedural requirements which he had at first rejected as dictates of a democratic "religion."

Murray's uneasy acceptance of procedural requirements grew, and the practice of polemics further abated, in the context of a later discussion concerning literary censorship. In that debate, Murray was caught between "practical secularists" and Catholics who were not living up to "their own" social theory. John Fischer, in a *Harper's* magazine editorial (Fisher 1956), criticized "a little band of Catholics" who were "conducting shocking attacks on the rights of their fellow citizens." The group under discussion was the National Organization for Decent Literature, which published recommendations and condemnations concerning adolescent reading. Much to Murray's own embarrassment, Fischer had appealed to four procedural rules in his condemnation of NODL's "lynching" of books, four procedural principles that Murray had presented in his major censorship article.[26]

In "The Bad Arguments Intelligent Men Make," Murray expressed disdain for Fischer's "tactic of unreason," his "argument by cuss word" (1956j, 120). But he also criticized the use of NODL's book recommendations by certain rustic sheriffs and fanatics in their attempts to shut down or boycott "adult" book stores, both of which tactics Murray considered means of coercion. Murray lamented that for Fischer and the fanatics, "there is really no argument at all—at least not yet. The two sides are not talking about the same thing" (1956j, 121). Fischer argued the primacy of procedure over substance, the Catholics the primacy of substance over procedure. Fischer did not want to admit the depth of the problem, while the Catholics did not want to advance public consensus by the means proper to the development of public argument.

Thus the argument fulfils the customary American pattern. The next step is for the contestants to retire from the field, either in sorrow or in anger or in both. Thereafter their partisans move in. Epithets are bandied; labels are exchanged; non-sequitur's proliferate. Until finally, both sides mutter disgustedly, "So's your old man." And there is, for a time, a sullen silence (1956j, 121).

In terms of important issues, each side was hitting on valid aspects of the social, ethical problem—but both missed the problem in its entirety. But in terms of social method, "Mr. Fischer is the more right." In the selection of means, Catholics are bound by the virtue of prudence to a "concrete rightness of method" in the pursuit of moral aims. Instead of coercion, Catholics should "inject the Catholic tradition of rationality into a mass democracy that is rapidly slipping its moorings in reason" (1956j, 123). Beyond the issue of sexual morality or rights, Murray perceived deeper dangers for American society.

I believe that nothing is more damaging to democracy than lack of rationality in public argument. The foundations of our society are indeed laid in an identifiable consensus. But they are more importantly laid in a reasonable *disposition* to argue our many disagreements in intelligent and temperate fashion.... I believe that whatever corrupts rational public argument corrupts democracy (1956j, 120).

The rebuttals Murray received in his *Christian Century* exchanges, the experience with MacIver, and his confrontation with "irrational" Catholics, all combined with his own use of the authorization principle to shape in him a deepening concern with the state of American public conversation, while also helping him to transform his own understanding of democratic rights from "vacuous proceduralism" to ethical procedural requirements. From 1960 on, he would be directed by an almost compulsive drive to rise above the polemical tones of church and civil society debates.

But Murray's concern was not simply with polemical styles that reduce the public forum to a state of war. He had yet to confront the more directly social sources of moral disintegration that he found rampant in his own American environment.

B. Attitudes Which Endanger Democratic Moral Direction.   Murray rejected any attempts to found the American social consensus on the basis of Protestant ecclesiological principles. This he considered to be a theological base, and unacceptable to American Catholics. He also rejected what he considered the secularistic foundations offered by the educational establishment and by the Supreme Court, since these foundations were contrary to the natural law. Both rejections were based on religious grounds (though differently founded in revelation and reason, respectively). Through the 1950s, Murray found further grounds for his criticism of the various groups that vied for America's public consciousness. There was, of course, the practice of polemics that obscured the real issues at stake in a social problem. But behind such practices lie attitudes that legitimate a refusal to think publicly, together.

After having mingled with Reinhold Niebuhr in the context of the Fund for the Republic nuclear war discussion, Murray once again went after a version of American Protestantism (Neo-Orthodoxy), but for reasons that deserve some attention. As already noted, Murray condemned the lack of ability on the part of the American people to think their way into and through the problem of military force. This could be attributed simply to a disdain for serious thought. However, by 1960 Murray located another culprit. He began by admitting that the ethical theory governing the nineteenth century had in fact grown out of fundamentalist Protestantism.[27] Such an ethic was voluntaristic (an act was good or evil because God commanded it, with reason never able to penetrate to the actual moral quality of the act), subjectivist (the intention was what counted, not the act's moral qualities), and governed by the sole criterion of "altruism" (1960a, 276–77). In effect, such a theory was at core individualistic, based on the rather naive presupposition that personal values could be directly transferred to the social order. At best, that ethic, based as it was solely on biblical imperatives, could generate only an "interpersonal" ethics, blind to the institutions and forces of modern society. This ethic has for the most part been recognized as a "simplism."

That fundamentalist ethic has now been replaced by an ethic whose highest category is the term "ambiguous." It is based, as was the old fundamentalism, on three premises: (1) a false dichotomizing of the private and public arenas of morality; (2) a faulty concept of "self-interest"; and (3) an abhorrence for, and demonization of, power (1960a, 279–81). It is particularly this last issue (that of power) which, according to Murray, vitiates the social effectiveness of the "ambiguists." To venture out into the international field entails the acceptance of national self-interest as an integral feature of a nation's policy, and also the use of law and coercive restraint as means for advancing that interest. But, with the ambiguist's views of the public sector, self-interest, and power, the only possible response to a difficult international incident is that it

> . . . appears as a "predicament," full of "ironies," sown with "dilemmas," to be stated only in "paradox," and to be dealt with "only at one's hazard,"

because in the situations "creative and destructive possibilities" are inextricably mixed, and therefore policy and action of whatever kind can only be "morally ambiguous" (1960a, 283).

If one refuses to use power, then one is " 'irresponsible,' and therefore [becomes] more guilty yet" (1960a, 282).

One might concur with Murray when he admitted that he had some difficulty entering into the argument,[28] but he offered three such entries (1960a, 285–86). The first concerns the individual/political dichotomy. One is not less Christian for going beyond those personal and familial ethical norms presented in the bible. The political arena is something less than the Kingdom of God; it is a temporal reality with its limited means and limited goals. But these means and these goals, as well as their limited possibilities, derive from the reality of political society itself, as man has been created for and has a natural drive toward such society.

Second, self-interest as a motive for national action is not in itself wrong or evil. In fact, the norm of self-interest is a good canon for moral as well as political discernment (1960a, 286–87). It becomes evil when self-interest becomes the classical *raison d'etat*, when it becomes the sole criterion of national action. The tradition of reason situates self-interest within the larger realm of social reason, in the international common good. The meshing of national and international interest is a complicated task ("The casuistry is endlessly difficult"), but the drive toward a national policy which is in line with the international good sustains the moral orientation of national policy, and sets a very real and, although difficult, realizable goal for national action.[29]

And, finally, power is an instrument, morally neutral in itself (1960a, 288–89). One can develop criteria which will distinguish between "force" and "violence." Again, the working out of these norms, much less their adoption within the international community, are immensely difficult tasks. But without an attempt at forming mutually intelligible canons for judgment, the entire political field becomes nothing more than barbaric. The norms, as institutionalized by laws, establish a thin wall or margin between chaos and public welfare, "but the margin makes the difference" (1960a, 189).

Obviously, that which had bothered Murray most about Niebuhr's social and moral theory was the effect that it might have on the public forum. Reason for Murray was the sole source of ethically directed will in politics. It is that which leads the individual or nation beyond enclosed self-interest (in his "classic" sense). And the forces of destruction can be held back only by publicly recognizable criteria of restraint. It is not surprising, then, that Murray's last criticism of the "ambiguists" is that they erode the "moral footing from beneath the political principle of consent" (1960a, 293). Neo-Orthodox ethics is not really an ethics, but rather a vision of society in which ethical choice is impossible. "All norms vanish amid the multiplying paradoxes; and all discrimination is swallowed up in the cavernous interior of the constantly recurrent verdict: 'This action is morally ambiguous'" (1960a, 292). It contributes to the disintegration of the collective faith in the people as moral agents, in a society which was structurally designed for the workings of such agency. Such an ethics leads to the disappearance of criteria which might guide social, ethical thought; intelligence is replaced by an "all-pervasive fog."

Murray's criticism of American Neo-Orthodoxy, be it noted, was not theological. (He was not yet ready to enter or advance such a discussion.) His concern was with the social-epistemological implications of its theory of value determination and value discussion. He was defending the authorization principle—that the people can come to rationally defensible particular moral judgments and general value commitments.

Where, then, could Murray turn for practitioners of the tradition of reason? Early in the 1950s he had claimed that if America ever lost its tradition of reason, the Roman Catholic community was standing by to maintain and preserve it (1960a, 43). As he faced the frustrations of his conversations with MacIver and others, he began to elicit support for the tradition of reason from sectors within his religious community. Catholic laymen, an "Elite of Thinkers," ought to enter the university forum (1949b, 36–37), to reverse the "devaluation of that high faculty whereby man is capable of God and of Grace," to turn back the narrowing of "the field of reality and the scope of intelligence" (1949b, 39). The task for educated laymen is to enter the secular academic forum with a full notion of the range of human intelligence. Even here, however, he alluded to the Roman Catholic "temptation of Thabor" (1949b, 40), the temptation to become a "self-enclosed spiritual monad or a citadel, a fortress of defense, or an asylum of escape." Similarly, he called on Catholic lawyers to break from the sheer adversarial definitions of their profession, to recall the "Golden Age of American jurisprudence" (1956i, 218), when the major architects of the American political consensus were lawyers who based their notions of law within the Western liberal tradition. Beyond simple advocacy, each lawyer, as an "officer of the court," has the obligation to examine the justice of each case, to bring his own "theory of the case within the tradition of American law, as this tradition is itself sustained by the broad tenets of the public philosophy" (1956i,

220). The lawyer is to be the agent of, and the advocate of, both the legal theory and the moral attitudes which are part of the American heritage of law, not simply a technician of that law.

However, Murray's fears for his own community deepened. In 1955, he began an article with the affirmation "we are established ... we belong" (1955a, 36), thus we have overcome one of the challenges that had faced Catholicism. We have nothing to fear from even the new nativisms, such as that of Blanshard. But, he continued, one of the dangers facing the American church is a settling into a middle class ethos, the possibility that Catholics may "consider their Catholicism as conventional." As "conventional," Catholics would not then be able to challenge the decayed American public consensus to regain its true foundational convictions.

In a second article, Murray continued his critique of Catholic self-awareness into the realm of the sociological. There is presently a danger that Catholicism will become simply a group-consciousness, a sense of itself as

> ...a separate social group, closed upon itself, exclusive, defensive, obliged to be aggressive in defining not only its domestic faith but also its place in society among other social groups. This consciousness of the group is not the true sense of the church any more than sociology is theology (1955b; 1960a, 145).

Typical of this group-sense is a refusal to admit the good of anything that originates outside of the group, as demonstrated in the strong, if limited, Catholic hostility to the United Nations. The United Nations is an attempt to establish an international order of law, of mutually recognized rights and values, for which Catholics should have sympathy. Murray further linked this hostility toward the foreign to a present anti-intellectualism rampant within the American scene. A destruction of the tradition of civility necessarily implies a denial of the moral worth of the other. And "it has been said that love of intelligence still stands too far down the list of American Catholic loves; the list needs to be revised."

In his 1953 "Christian Humanism in America," Murray admitted the equal abstract validity of what he called an "eschatological humanism" and an "incarnational humanism" (1953b). Eschatological humanism judges all human social constructs to be sinful; its hope rests solely in the future intervention of God, allowing no moral significance to action for justice in the present public arena. This "integrist" or "American Catholic Right" movement has been growing in the United States.

The Catholic "Incarnational Humanist" believes that the Catholic offer of redemption is indeed catholic in scope (1957b, 1960a, 189). Not only is salvation offered to all men and women, the temporal order itself (i.e., human social nature) is to participate in that order of grace. God is a God of both creation and redemption; the spirit of the Logos, eternal reason, is active within history. The spirit is "there [within history] to do a work of reason—that work of reason which is justice, and the work of pacification which is in turn the work of justice" (1960a, 191). The hope for a more just temporal order "has been a humanistic aspiration connatural to the Christian heart" (1960a, 192), resting ultimately on the belief in the power and goodness of God, in his dominion over all orders of creation.

In this 1953 article, Murray considered both alternatives as valid Christian responses to the contemporary world. By 1955 and particularly by 1957, however, Murray had explicitly chosen sides regarding which of these two Christian humanisms better represents the Roman Catholic tradition. After a rather detailed study of Origen's Christian humanism, Murray then went on to outline where present scholarly effort should be devoted in order to unite contemporary forms of knowing, particularly science, morals, and religious faith. More important here is his insistence, echoing Maritain, that "intelligence lies at the root of Christianity," that "the civilization of intelligence itself [is] a Christian task *imposed by faith itself*" (1957a, 199-200). A Christian, because of his or her faith, is obliged to develop the tradition of civility, as well as the total intellectual vision of the unity of truth—those civil virtues and truths which make us politically one and those revealed truths which can make us spiritually one.

Murray's impassioned argument for the unity of faith and reason reflected his growing conviction that a shallow emotional sentimentalism was at the core of the religious revival of his day. In an address given at St. Joseph's College in 1959, he condemned the contemporary devaluation of intelligence, with the "consequent contraction of the dimensions of reality" (1959a, 1). The fields of philosophy, religion, and law all suffer under this climate of devaluation. Religion has become a matter of "experience," not of knowledge, a matter of blind choice, not of understanding. The sole warrant for the validity of religion is presently held to be the fact that it "helps" this particular individual. While it is true that the church fought against nineteenth century rationalism, the church has been "the champion of rationality, the defender of reason's true autonomy" (1959a, 7). Further,

Faith supposes reason as grace supposes nature. If the genuine powers of reason are destroyed or undermined, the true notion of Christian faith suffers the same fate. Faith becomes irrational, unintelligible, indefensible—and unworthy of a man. Thus the destinies of Christian faith are linked to those of human reason (1959a, 8).

And, finally,

> Not even religion will supply the lack, if reason fails in its functions; for religion cannot form a civilization except as its truths and precepts are mediated to the temporal order through a rational philosophy (1959a, 10).

Thus concluded Murray's confrontation with an American Catholicism which, for him, had substituted a sociological, emotional sense of belonging for a spirit of inquiry and understanding, in the realm of faith and conjointly in the realm of polity. In one perspective, this social "groupism" was both an afterglow of the immigrant Catholic battle for a recognized, distinct place in Protestant America, and also a residual drive to remain isolated from mainstream American culture. But in another perspective, this groupism was a conformity to the practical spirit which had always dominated the American people. In this argument, America's practical sense served the same social disfunction as did the "scientism" of the academic establishment debate. Both kept their respective arenas free of those theoretical reflections which Murray considered essential to American social and Catholic religious living. In both, the tradition of reason was offered as a corrective to theoretical or practical limitations, based on reason's drive toward a universality of subject matter and valuation. In his confrontation with American Catholicism, the person of thought and the person of faith were rejoined; reason was no longer a faculty reserved for the temporal order, with faith a near-faculty for dealing in the spiritual order. Murray also moved toward a notion of necessary predispositions or commitments to reasonable discourse common to both the civil and the religious realms, and at least incidentally acknowledged the impact that a faith/reason stance can have on one's approach to civil society. The disposition toward reasonable discussion was as much a social requirement for the American people as was the Constitutional demand for free access and expression in social, moral determination. Both are requirements for an ethical, American democratic polity. But Murray was not sure that the disposition could arise from beneath the social irrationalisms that tore through his American society.

By 1960, Murray did not even bother to be consistent in his analysis of the consensus or lack of it at the heart of the American polity. I have already noted his appeal to Berle's phenomenology of social justification and consensus as a support for his own notion of social, moral justification—which he wrote at the same time he was despairingly faulting American Catholic ghettoism. In one last article to be considered here, he simultaneously worked with the premise that America was naively but good naturedly committed to techno-logical fixes, and with Voeglin's assertion that the Western tradition of civility is only skin deep, that at the heart of the West is an ongoing state of war. But at this point, the choice between any one of these starting analyses was immaterial. Murray was now fully an actor. He was arguing that there ought to be a public discussion of values, if America was to have a future; he acted as if he were engaged in a battle over the soul of modern society.

So he appealed once again to the historical convictions of American society, but recognized that those roots must be differently established. Granted that the notion of a free society was once self-evident, we must find "other, more reasoned grounds" for our self-definition as a free people (1960a, 5). A civil society is one that is committed to truth, but more basically civilization becomes a reality only if "men are locked together in argument." We have ceased to "live together, to talk together, i.e., to conspire together." We must recognize that there are laws of public argument that spell the difference between civilization and barbarism (1960a, 14). By admission of those laws, we can "limit our warfare and enlarge the dialogue" (1960a, 23). We could achieve a real pluralism through clarification, and "then, amid the pluralism, a genuine unity would be discernible—the unity of orderly conversation" (1960a, 24).

In this Murray's later understanding, neither the advocacy of procedural rules nor a disposition to argument are purely procedural or empty. To participate in social reasoning requires in a sense a submission to reason and morality itself. And Murray's present understanding of the "laws of argument" is still deeply entrenched in his broad definition of human reason, as the following description of violations of those laws demonstrates.

> Argument ceases to be civil when it is dominated by passion and prejudice; when its vocabulary becomes solipsist, premised on the theory that my insight is mine alone and cannot be shared; when dialogue gives way to a series of monologues; when the parties to the conversation cease to listen to one another, or hear only what they want to hear, or see the other's argument only through the screen of their own categories; when defiance is flung to the basic ontological principle of all ordered discourse, which asserts that Reality is an analogical structure, within which there are variant modes of reality, to each of which there corresponds a distinctive method of thought that imposes on argument its own special

rules. When things like this happen, men cannot be locked together in argument. Conversation becomes merely quarrelsome or querulous. Civility dies with the death of dialogue (1960a, 14).

Ethical and epistemological requirements for civility are inseparably intertwined. The granting of an analogical structure of "Reality" is both a moral presupposition for public discussion and a cognitive means by which the ethical dimensions of social living are discovered.

In 1961, Murray summed up his most pessimistic judgment of the contemporary American theological, ethical, social, and technological currents in an image. In "The Return to Tribalism" (1961c), he claimed that whatever consensus existed in American society was based on the emotions which are more properly the preserve of the tribe, defined by hatreds of what is foreign and by a drive for security which is sheer solidarity. The members of the tribe "tend to huddle, to get close together, to close up, to close ranks" (1961c, 6). The real danger to America is not the communist, but the "idiot," the person who does not possess a public philosophy, and therefore the person who will fall back on the ethics of the tribe. And the tribe is essentially a war-making group (1961c, 6). What is needed is a return to the tradition of reason, with its fourfold division of rationality (1961c, 10–11). There is moral reasoning by which we set the goals of our action as a people, and political reasoning by which the collective will directs the achievement of those common goods not reducible to individual interests, and legal reasoning by which an arena of freedom is created. But, behind all of these, is pedagogical reasoning, the task of teaching others not truths directly, but rather how to think in the public forum. Reasoning as a social activity is the key to civilized and civilizing living.

In one more image, Murray even questioned the possibility of American society existing without a religious consensus. If there is no consensus as to the core direction and meaning of humanity, and no public discussion of that reality, then "society is founded on a vacuum; and society, like nature itself, abhors a vacuum and cannot tolerate it" (1961c, 8). America seems to be attempting an "impossible experiment": finding its only source of unity in highly developed technology, while below that rests only "moral confusion," and below that confusion a "spiritual void." The void must cave in on itself. Can society live without a public religion? "The historical evidence would seem to argue for a negative answer." It may be possible "that an individual can live without religion, but a society cannot." And, finally, after years of defending the adequacy of natural law religious discourse, and years of frustrating attempts to do so, Murray even suggested, or more properly cried out, that perhaps an explicitly

Christian religious public discourse is necessary for social survival. Quoting John of Salisbury, Murray closed with the question "Whether or not civilization, that is civil order, civil unity, civil peace, is possible without what [John] calls in a beautiful phrase 'the sweet and fruitful marriage of Reason and the Word of God'" (1961c, 12). In 1957, Murray had argued that the Western notions of freedom were directly dependent on Christian social dualism (1957b; 1960a, 197–217), and that no other Western force of intellectual or institutional merit was capable of maintaining the necessary structure or transcendental referencing within the realm of thought necessary for that freedom. Here he suggested that the very freedoms which are at the heart of the American moral authorization principle are, then, in danger of collapse without a public consciousness of at least this aspect of the revealed Word of God.

So ended Murray's American arguments. His reliance on the authorization principle for his specific arguments gradually deepened. But more than that, he relied on the principle as a guiding maxim for his own approach to social action. Yet, the totalitarian truth claims of scientism, the cognitional presuppositions arising from Neo-Orthodoxy, the groupism and jingoism of the Catholic community, the American fixation with technical reasoning, all left him dispirited, to the point that he appears to entertain the notion that explicitly theological concepts must be brought into the public forum.

The questions of whether or not, or to what degree, Murray's notions of rationality have any imperative validity for American democratic theory must be deferred until a later chapter. Suffice it here to point out the intellectual and moral importance of the authorization principle for him, and the conflicts that he experienced in using and practicing it. By way of conclusion I will briefly review the material presented here, and suggest one minor analytic tool that might have helped in Murray's search for an ethical center of a democratic society.

IV. CONCLUSION: WHO ARE THE WISE? THE HISTORICISM PROBLEM.

Throughout his various American discussions, Murray repeatedly fell back on two distinct concepts: the American form of the authorization principle and the laws of reason. Authorization or consent was the basis for his appeal to the three-part American religious self definition (Catholic, Protestant, Jew) in his proposed solution to the school aid issue. Then that three-part understanding was used in his appeal for religious instruction within the American secular universities. And finally, the authorization principle itself ethically grounded the procedural freedoms of access and expression within the educational establishment—freedoms with which Murray could then be comfortable. All three of these issues rested on the authorization principle or its application to religiously (and morally) pluralistic America.

Murray's appeals to reason or the laws of reason usually focused on two distinct aspects of reason. The first concerned problem solving—the arena of prudential determination, of judgments within complex value situations, as highlighted in the censorship and foreign policy arguments.[30] In both those arguments, however, Murray's deeper concern seems to have been with the general social attitudes toward problem solving: a people could choose between the methods of irrational force or the methods of rational discernment and persuasion. Only the methods of freedom or persuasion could sustain the American claim that the people shape the moral directions of American policy. Reason as prudential determination and as a commitment to such determination, then, was in Murray's view an ethical requirement for democratic society.

Second, Murray also appealed to reason as the perception of the broader realities by which a people define themselves. Through much of the 1950s, his appeal entailed some content: an explicitly theistic reference, and also an order of justice by which all social constructions were to be measured. But, also during this period Murray gradually moved toward a notion of reason as operating, in the sense used before, as directive principles—a notion of reason defined in terms of the human person's intentionality. This notion first showed up in his argument against scientific monism, then in his appeal for Catholics to follow reason beyond the narrow confines of their own ghetto, or solidarity group, or irrational jingoism. And, in Murray's discussion of the social role of lawyers, he posited reason as the reality which would direct lawyers beyond the narrow role of simple advocacy to the dispassionate realm of justice (a form of practice as well as a content). That is, the intentionalities of reason, not simply its content, became an increasingly important factor in Murray's understanding of social living. But why the gradual change in his understanding of the more general levels of human reason?

First, Murray was of course defending as valid America's specification of the authorization principle. There could be no adherence to the truth of social authorization if there was not a commitment to, and a social understanding of, the nature of human moral judgment. Faith in the efficacy of discussion was the heart of the ongoing moral authorization in the social and juridical orders.

However, Murray encountered a second, more important problem. Within his censorship and foreign policy discussions, a sole appeal to authorization and to prudential determination would result in a social relativism or historicism. The people authorize the moral content of law, through rational weighing and balancing of the values as they determine/perceive them. So far, so good. But to make the legal imposition of "general morality" norms contingent on the effect such impositions might have on "public peace" (in the censorship debate) was to place the moral evaluations which might enter the legal order within a civil society which was itself open to growth and decay, moral insight and moral blindness. Even within Murray's notion of the limits of law, certain general moral norms ought indeed to reach legal expression, but might not—due to the deteriorating condition of social moral consciousness.

Murray's concern with ethical relativism went back to his original discussions on the impact of scientism on American culture. The problem of historical relativism, I believe, was the reason that the last item of the three indices for the application of law, namely, justice, was kept separate from the peace and general morality indices, particularly after his submission of general morality to public order in the censorship debate. In Murray's communism and just war arguments, he repeatedly appealed to an order of justice which was not tied to changes in historical, social consciousness. And, even in the school aid issue, he claimed that no aid to parochial schools was always unjust, even if understandable in terms of the American self-understanding or consensus.

So, Murray's appeals to an independent order of justice can be understood as an attempt to escape the relativism which could result from his increasing use of the social authorization principle. But, in the last article written for *We Hold These Truths* ("The Origins and Authority of the Public Consensus"), Murray granted that one of the roles of the wise is the ever renewed determination of the third and fourth levels of even the justice principles (1960a, 122). In each age the wise must rethink those principles which are to govern determinations of the justice of laws and social institutions. This conception in effect submitted the third element of the triple indices to a historical flow, relativizing what he had treated for much of the decade as a clear, nonhistorical given. If the remote principles of justice can be discovered (and must be discovered) with new institutions and patterns of social interaction, they can be lost and forgotten, or never developed at all, never entering into historical consciousness. If this had been Murray's final word on the grounding of social ethical principles, then justice would take on the status of an empty, voluntaristic concept.

Murray would not, of course, settle for a historical relativism. His ongoing appeal to reason as intentionality (the mind reaching for God, for a moral order including justice, for a social reality which proceeds by its own dynamisms) was an attempt to ground the truths which we as a people claim, and to ground the certitude of those truths with the same conviction with which we at least once asserted them (although differently based). Now, as Murray situated more and more of the remote principles of social ethics, including the justice principles, within a field of historical development and decline, the problem of relativism, I believe, forced him toward a stronger emphasis on the role of the wise within democratic society. And, after his historical and contemporary studies in search of a center of society's "cutting edge" (the *studium* or the educational establishment, lawyers, Catholics, etc.), the problem of historical flux did not permit him finally to locate those "wise" in any particular, identifiable social group. *Even* American Catholicism demonstrated its own susceptibility to moral ill-will and sociological blindness, falling away from "our tradition."

If the historical flux of general society necessitated an appeal to the wise, and if that same flux did not permit an institutional identification of them, then where could Murray anchor the ultimate noncontingency which he required for a nonrelativistic democratic ethical theory? In his most serenely theoretical "Origins and Authority" (1960a, 97–123), Murray's final appeal was to reason itself. The wise are those who are "reasonable," and this in at least three senses. The wise are those who allow reason to reach out to all that is real; they do not place *a priori* restrictions on human inquiry. But more to the point, they are disposed to argument, to the rational discussion of issues and of the evidence by which one argues issues. But, finally, the "wise" persons are the ones who can reasonably argue in the public forum for their own judgments. And this notion of rationally supported judgment, following on experience and understanding, Murray eventually tagged as the "non-contingent element" of the ongoing discernment of the remote principles of justice. Those who practice, and in a sense submit to, the public, prudential processes of coming to truth are the wise of society.

As I will begin to argue in the next chapter, by his adoption of Lonergan's cognitional theory and its appeal to noncontingent operations, Murray thought he had indeed escaped a sheer historicism. But there is in all but the most empiricist democratic social theories the constant problem of the gap between the reasonable judgments of the wise and the adoption of those insights and judgments by society itself. Clarity of thought for an individual or a small minority is itself difficult. But the need to position one's argument within the general public forum, and to argue by the methods of persuasion for the adoption of particular policy (much less for a general principle), creates an uneasy tension between an affirmation of the consent principle and the pursuit of social truth. In the search for truth there will always be leaders with special analytic and judgmental abilities and those who follow their recommendations. As Murray anchored his "non-contingent element" increasingly in the more difficult realms of reason (remote social principles), he began dialectically to interrelate the people as the deposit of a society's sense of justice with the elite who could continue the ongoing pursuit of truth. And yet he did not actually consider at any length the cognitional elements governing the interaction between the two. (I will return to this problem in chapter 6.)

His final appeal to an elite or the wise, however, never dissolved Murray's primacy of the consent or authorization principle. His religious liberty, censorship, and foreign policy arguments rested too heavily on the *people's* abiding sense of justice. It is the people, not the wise, who directly validate the moral content of legislation and other social institutions. The wise are to have direct access to the people, only indirect influence on government and the order of civil law. For this reason, I believe, even with his final appeal to the wise and his frustration with America, Murray still maintained a notion of society as a community of moral discourse. The people who cannot completely follow the subtleties of the elite's arguments, must still be able to discern the reasonableness of those arguments. It is the people, not the wise, who are the ultimate judges of the ethical valuations for any particular democratic society. The people themselves must proceed to specific determinations reasonably. Society itself is a field of ongoing moral argument.

Within a natural law, democratic social theory, who, then, are ultimately the wise who direct the achievement of the common good? One can answer again that they are the "reasonable" people of that society. Further, adherence to the intentionalities and to the methods of reason constitutes moral wisdom. How again could Murray understand the people's assumption of the mantle of reason, if he was to preserve the ultimacy of his authorization principle, especially given the complexity of economic and social issues that are beyond the methods of most common discourse? If one distinguished between the intentionalities and the methods of the discourse of the wise, then perhaps a mid-ground between the wisdom of the elite and the wisdom of the people could be found. The people might not be able to follow the complex methods of social argument, but they, as reasonable, could be understood to intend the social reality and the social good that is discussed by the elite. The intending of all that is real, including (1) a distinct social object which proceeds by its own rules and toward its own distinct ends, and (2) forms of cognition that reach beyond everyday languages, is a conception which might be applicable to the people at large. This common point in the intending of social reality and the cognitional manners in which it is constituted still leaves open the question of the intellectual methods by which the people follow the arguments of the elite, but it would appear to offer a foundational grounding for his claim of the ultimacy of the authorization principle for democratic society.

But what type of reason, then, was Murray reaching for? It is, at the very least, a "great act of faith in the moral sense of the people" which is communally held, a faith distinguished by a special type of discourse and reality to which all citizens are called. The citizen must at times speak the languages of the family, of the psyche, at other times the languages of economics, politics, of the juridical and even the religious. But the one language which cannot be left behind without all other particular goods collapsing is that which encompasses the social-moral, at least in a democratic society. This distinct language is by definition concerned with the common good which establishes the very conditions in which particular goods can be pursued. Other more immediate arenas of activity also include valuation and choice, and are thus fields of morality. But the moral role suggested here is a realm of morality distinct from the others and, within a democratically organized society, foundational for those others. Even the ordinary citizen must assume the attitude of "'care,' but ... not [be] 'interested parties' (in the usual sense of the latter term)," when cooperatively shaping larger social realities. Without the assumption of reason, those larger social realities collapse upon themselves, carrying with them to some degree the other moral spheres of human existence. The people's "care," then, is a will toward, or an intention of, the common social good. Even if their understanding of the analytic methods of elite argument are inchoate, their intentionality of that social good relates them ethically to those arguments and conclusions of the wise.

But what is Murray calling for here? Even his language suggests that a somewhat more adequate (if less publicly acceptable) term for that type of intentionality is "love." But then one must attempt a definition of love, and a Christian has (revealed) sources for such a definition that perhaps cannot be separated from the definitions themselves. Murray loved American society, consciously struggled over its future, found himself against a wall that resisted "sweet reason." All this will lead him haltingly to advance *theological* discourse within that society.

Here Murray has been arguing within American history and within American value commitments, as he understood them. He has not questioned the theoretical validity of the authorization principle, even if he has run against its practical validation. Murray's eventual acceptance of procedural freedoms, his discussions of censorship, public peace, and the methods of persuasion, all revolve around the concern for society as a field of ethical discrimination. They are all means of protecting reasonable public discussion from irrational limitations and from the irrational forces of social disintegration. Civil society, he maintained, must for its very existence adhere to the intentionalities and method of public reasoning.

And then there is the church. In the public discussion of religious liberty, Murray's own access and expression had been, since 1954, coercively restrained. In the next chapter I will examine his reentry into that discussion and the reshaping of the discussion in light of his democratic social theory.

Chapter Four

JUSTIFYING RELIGIOUS LIBERTY:

Moral Agency within Historical Societies

In this chapter I rejoin Murray's argument for the church's affirmation of religious freedom, as he himself rejoined the argument during the Second Vatican Council. With perhaps a sardonic touch, Murray termed the battle over such an issue to be an "intramural exercise" within the church. Recognition of the rightfulness of civil religious liberty has reached international proportions, to the point that even Russia must give at least lip-service to the right of religious freedom. The church itself must now unambiguously affirm this internationally recognized right.

But, despite Murray's diminutive evaluation of *Dignitatis Humanae*, the social processes behind the final decree did much to stimulate his own thinking. From 1960 through 1967, Murray advanced two distinct arguments for the church's endorsement of religious freedom. The first, "conciliar" argument can be distinguished initially by the target of that argument, namely, those who held that civil religious freedom can at best be supported as a lesser of two evils—the toleration view. A second distinction concerns Murray's starting premises. In this conciliar argument he will argue within the principle of Christian dualism, and its corollary of the rightful autonomy of the civil order. Just as, in his American debates, he had argued within and for the authorization principle, attempting to defend that great act of faith in the people and its concomitant commitment to the social methods of freedom, likewise here he will presume the validity of American specifications of the authorization principle. Without much examination of their validity, he will argue that those civil secular commitments and specifications can and ought to be conjoined through explicit affirmations with the church's own independently based concerns, i.e., with the church's own freedom to preach the gospel. This argument within the dualism principle and its logical and historical corollaries, then, is much like his 1950s religious liberty arguments. It is theological in that it is based on the premise of social dualism. However, the argument is now augmented by Lonergan's notions of emerging insight,[1] "historical consciousness," and the social nature of all human cognition, including the theological. This argument will be the subject of section I.

After the council, Murray struck out in a somewhat different direction in an attempt to justify the church's now accomplished affirmation. His own concerns then shifted to what he considered inadequate justifications of civil religious liberty, the arguments of those who attempted to base religious liberty on interpersonal or individualistic cognitional theories. This postconciliar discussion forced Murray to reach *behind* his appeal to emerging moral insight in the temporal order to the moral forces that generate such insights. Central to the move between these arguments will be Murray's repositioning within his argument of what he called the jurisprudential principle (or in the second argument, the "free society" principle): as much freedom as possible, as much coercion as necessary. In the conciliar argument, the principle is a rightful insight emerging out of Anglo-American political tradition, and as such required affirmation by the church. In his postconciliar argument, it is more deeply and clearly situated as an exigency for the people's constructive moral response to changing social situations. With this concentration on human agency, as applicable to the realms of both civil and religious meaning, the second argument is less dependent on the principle of social dualism, and, therefore, more "philosophical" in Murray's present understanding of the term. Further, in the process of this argument, Murray himself had to break out of the definition of rights as simple immunities, to an ethically based notion of rights as empowerments to participate in the active reconstruction of one's social environment. And this notion of active, positive human agency in the ongoing definitions of social realities can be transferred at least in part to the church as a people, as a society likewise in need of such ongoing redefinition (as will be seen in the next chapter). Murray was here reaching for the roots of his authorization principle. And once again the pivot by which he did "step behind" that principle was Lonergan's cognitional theory.

In the conclusion to this chapter, I will attempt to point out that Murray's postconciliar argument was simply a clarification of the basis of religious freedom as somewhat hazily developed in his conciliar discussion. His understanding of society as historical and as defined by commonly affirmed meaning was consistent with his later emphasis on the ethical responsibilities that individuals and institutions (including the church) have toward the development of that meaning, and that reality.

But first it will be helpful to present two occasions or viewpoints which structured Murray's own concerns from 1960 to his death in

1967. To begin with, there were the events, texts, and dynamics of the Council itself. A brief reference to the historical events of the Council and the various texts that developed in the course of the Council will situate and structure some of the shifts in Murray's own argument. There is some debate, or at least confusion, over just how much of Murray's perspectives guided the argument of *Dignitatis Humanae*. Therefore, along with the conciliar events I will also outline Murray's absences from, as well as participation in, the conciliar discussions. Second, some introductory mention should be made concerning Bernard Lonergan's influence on Murray during this period. Throughout his argument (and in those which I will take up in the next chapter), Murray did make extensive appeal to Lonergan's epistemological theory as presented in *Insight*, and to those notions of "historical consciousness," "dialectics," and society as "constituted by meaning," all of which Lonergan himself was developing during this period. Of immediate concern is not the accuracy of Murray's Lonergan interpretations, but his own use and adaptation of such concepts for his own argument.

A. The Second Vatican Council.   Prior to the Council, in December 1960, the topic of religious liberty was taken up by Augustin Cardinal Bea's Secretariat for Christian Unity, to be discussed in the context of the broader topic of ecumenism.[2] After a jurisdictional battle with Cardinal Ottaviani's Pontifical Theological Commission and during the Council's first session (October to December, 1962), Bea's Secretariat developed two different statements on religious liberty, to be appendices to an ecumenism decree (the "first" and "second" texts). Murray did not participate in any of these discussions, nor in the drafting of the texts. As he himself stated, he had been "dis-invited" from participation as a *peritus* in that first session.

In April 1963, under the patronage of Cardinal Spellman, Murray was reinvited as counsel to Bea's Secretariat. During the second session (September to December, 1963) Murray spearheaded a move by the American bishops to place the religious liberty issue on the Council's agenda, then helped formulate a series of criticisms of the first two texts (e.g. 1963a, 1963b). Between the second and third sessions Murray proceeded to produce for conciliar distribution his rather extensive article, "The Problem of Religious Freedom" (1964f), which attempted to present the "conservative" and "liberal" positions on the issue (the difference between religious tolerance and religious freedom). The liberal position which he presented was, of course, his own. The third conciliar session (September to November, 1964) began with a full conciliar debate on the second Secretariat text. Many of the American bishops' interventions were written by Murray. After this public debate, the drafting of the third text, the *textus emendatus*, was handed over to a commission, with Murray as the "first scribe." The text was distributed on November 17, but political maneuvering and printing delays put off debate until the fourth session.

During the interim between the third and fourth sessions, Murray received written interventions on his, the third text, and worked them into a fourth text, the *textus re-emendatus*. The fourth text was publicly debated during the first week of this session (September to December, 1965), and voted as the established conciliar text. It was, however, still open to further oral and written interventions.

A final text, the *textus recognitus*, was drafted by a commission of bishops, presented to the Council on October 25, 1965, and approved the following day. Several minor revisions were then added, and the decree was finally approved and promulgated on December 7. It should be noted that on October 5, having suffered a collapsed lung, Murray was removed from the drafting of the fifth text.

In the discussion that follows, the two most significant periods are the second interim session, with the publication of Murray's "The Problem of Religious Freedom," and both phases of the *textus recognitus* formation: first, the interval of its major drafting between October 5 and October 25, 1965 and, second, the period after October 25 during which minor revisions were added.

B. Murray's Reliance on Lonergan.   At points throughout the last chapter I cited several instances in Murray's writings that suggested some contact with those of Bernard Lonergan. About the same time as the publication of Lonergan's *Insight* (1957), Murray shifted over to Lonergan's three rational operations (experiencing, understanding, judging) to ground his notion of the interaction of an elite and the people within democratic, civil society. With these three operations, he then admitted the contingent nature of even the tertiary principles of justice, thereby positioning the three elements of public order within the historical development and decline of society. Although Murray, as editor of *Theological Studies,* had encouraged and facilitated the publishing of Lonergan's dissertation on the Thomistic notion of *Gratia operans* (Lonergan 1941), there is little evidence of this first exposure having had much effect on Murray. Those who studied and worked with Murray claim that little if any reference was made to Lonergan in Murray's pre-1959 Trinitarian courses, while those who studied with him after 1959 remember his course as entirely based on Lonergan's notion of Trinitarian development. In that pivotal year, 1959, Murray had organized a special Jesuit meeting in conjunction with the annual Catholic Theological Society of America Convention,[3] the topic under discussion being Lonergan's Trinitarian theology and the impact of *Insight* on the notion of the development of Trinitarian doctrine. By 1962, Murray offered a course entitled "Method in Theology" which was based on seven Lonergan publications.[4]

It would appear, then, that immediately before the Council Murray was well exposed to Lonergan's Trinitarian theology and to the epistemological theory of *Insight*. Further, in 1966, Lonergan sent Murray a requested copy of a paper entitled "The Transition from a Classicist World-View to Historical Mindedness,"[5] a distinction or differentiation of human consciousness to which Murray made appeal in 1964, although the late date of Murray's acquisition of that paper should be noted. And, finally, shortly before Murray's death, Murray and Lonergan exchanged a series of letters on the difference between dialectic as a form of logic and dialectics as a means of "escape from classicism" into an analysis of "historical process."[6] During this period Murray appealed to a type of dialectical process for understanding the development of the church's doctrine.

Throughout this chapter, then, I will indicate some of the key Lonergan themes and concepts that Murray adopted, and the forces within the religious freedom discussions that occasioned the adoption and adaptation (and perhaps distortion) of those themes and concepts. Given the limited focus of this chapter on the religious liberty debate, however, the full impact of Lonergan's influence will become visible only in the next two chapters, when Murray returns his attention to the constitution of the church and of society at large. There, Murray will more clearly work with a notion of civil and religious societies as constituted by forms of dialogue, as distinct human realities constituted by meaning. The turn to moral agency which is outlined here will be found in chapters 5 and 6 to be based on a general theory of social meaning, akin to Lonergan's ethical emphasis in the latter's later work, *Method in Theology* (Lonergan 1972). Whatever reference is made to Lonergan's influence, therefore, like the topic of religious liberty itself, will be correlated with the discussion in the remaining two chapters.

I. THE THEOLOGICAL DOCTRINE OF RELIGIOUS FREEDOM: A COMPLEX JUDGMENT WITHIN HISTORICALLY DEVELOPING SOCIETIES.   By the beginning of the Council, Murray had been effectively silenced, since 1954, at the insistence of Ottaviani and the American conservative faction. He had not, of course, stopped thinking about religious liberty. Nor did he cease writing on the issue. We have two articles written in the late 1950s which can serve as introductions to his conciliar writings, highlighting the novel elements of the latter and indicating just how reliant was Murray on Anglo-American political theory. It should be remembered that 1959 appears to be the pivotal date in Murray's dependence on Lonergan and, particularly, for our purposes here, on *Insight*. After these preliminaries, the major portion of this section will focus on Murray's 1964 argument (1964f), and will follow that argument as it evolved through one more article on the development of doctrine (1967b). But first I will pick up the threads of his argument as they appeared in the late-1950s.

A. One More Argument That Failed.   In 1954, Murray had increasingly based his case for religious freedom on the ethical self-development of civil society, which entailed the consensual affirmation of the con-joined civil rights, including religious freedom. This was an ethical reality and an affirmation to which the church had to be attentive, if the church was to deal in a responsible manner within its valid concern for the temporal common good. Further, there was the strong suggestion that the church must be attentive to developments in political philosophies, as these occurred within secular society. The church had inadequately based its own judgments concerning the common good on outdated understandings of political facts and on equally dated theoretical conceptions of political reality.

   In 1958 and 1959, Murray again submitted two articles on church-state relations to his Roman censors, and both were again rejected.[7] The articles are interesting in that Murray tried to suppress his previously stated thesis of the church's dependence on moral and philosophical sources beyond its own institutional boundaries. Both are attempts at what appears to be, at first sight, theological deductionism, a conclusion to religious freedom from exclusively theological premises (without, however, prescinding from the non-ideal, contingent nature of all forms of legal determination).

   Murray again contrasted two theories of Catholic church-state relations which now he called "disjunctive" and "unitary." The disjunctive theory begins with the theological premise that the Catholic Church is the one true church and deduces immediately the juridical conclusion of establishment.

> The conclusion is presented as Catholic doctrine in the field of Church-state relations. It is a statement of what is true and necessary in principle, in abstract, in the order of the ideal (1958a, 7–8).

Further, the disjunctive theory starts again from the ethical premise, "error has no rights," and concludes to legal intolerance of non-

Catholic public expression. "Because error has no right not to be suppressed, it follows that error ought to be suppressed, wherever and whenever the possibility of suppressing it exists" (1958a, 8–9). But for Murray the second ethical premise was "unnecessary." To conclude to a human law of establishment from a theological premise entails acceptance of coercive restraint, since by definition human law is essentially coercive. The legal establishment of one religion, as the disjunctive theory affirms it, logically implies intolerance or coercive restraint (1959a, 1).[8] A noncoercive expression of a common national faith, even if carried out through governmental apparatus, would not be human legal establishment in the sense of the disjunctive theory.

The disjunctive theory does allow for a conclusion to nonestablishment under the index of public peace: the minimal level of social cohesion necessary for the avoidance of sheer public disintegration. The theory is, however, disjunctive in that it sets up two levels of moral evaluation, the first at the level of (timeless) theory (the theoretical preference for establishment over nonestablishment) and the second at the level of fact (the purely quantitative measure of a nation's Catholicity as an index of the possibility or impossibility of establishment) (1958a, 11–13). Its governing norm for human law in the service of religion is "the possibility of coercion," or "as much coercion as possible, as much freedom as necessary."

The basis of Murray's criticism of the disjunctive theory was his concept of religious liberty as a human law. As a human law, a judgment for establishment is a temporal construct oriented to a particular (transitory) common good (1958a, 15). As such, no theoretically timeless preference can be given to establishment, and therefore no permanent bias for intolerance or for the principle of "as much coercion as possible" can be given to the church's argument. Judgments of human law are always shaped within the historical facts of a particular society at a particular time. As human law, establishment is morally validated by its service to the temporal order, not immediately to some theoretical order of truth.

Murray's own "unitary" theory also began with theological premises. The first is the premise that it is God's will that Catholicism is the religion of civil society (1958a, 15–16). But immediately, prior to judgments of value, the "theological fact" of religious pluralism presents itself. This fact of religious pluralism is not simply a fact of the human, temporal order. Religious pluralism has been theologically defined as a permanent condition of the temporal order, as witnessed to and predicted by the Scriptures (1959a, 8). As a theological, permanent truth concerning that order, any argument concerning the human institutionalization of church-state relations must take account of that fact.[9]

Second, the church also proceeds out of the premise of Christian constitutionalism (1958a, 18–20; 1959a, 17). The world as presented to us in revelation is "ontologically" constituted as divided between two societies, two authorities, two laws. The church as a separate society is governed in its own considerations only by the criteria of moral and religious truth. It is "uncompromised" by any temporal considerations. Although the state itself must stand under the judgment of religious and moral truth, the primary concern of the state is with the order of public peace (1959a, 10–11,13). The action of government is limited to social goods (not private goods), under the index of public peace (not the entire social common good), and within the limits of law (to external acts). In the civil order, the statesman is the ultimate judge of the moral worth of a law, as that moral worth is defined by the limited temporal ends of civil law (and according to the nature of prudential determination) (1959a, 20). Therefore the problem of establishment and intolerance is governed, even for the Catholic layman, by temporal conditions of fact; there is no priorized or hierarchical relationship between establishment and separation of church and state.

Murray's principal target throughout these articles was a theoretical value priority given to establishment over nonestablishment. His means for dissolving this theoretical priority was to situate all legal institutionalizations of church-state relations within civil society as a civil reality, i.e., as nonpermanent, temporal. But he apparently felt some obligation to confront the initial starting premise of the disjunctive theory. The result was something of an attempt at, again, a theological deductionism. His "theological fact" of religious pluralism was little more than a rather simple application of a biblical proof-text methodology.[10] But he also included the parallel, nonderivative, yet theological notion of Christian constitutionalism which set up a clear, second, independent basis for his argument. Still, although his theological principle of Christian social dualism does support the conclusion of the freedom of the church and even possibly an unspecified notion of the relative autonomy of the temporal order, it does not in itself establish a society-state distinction with the correlative limitations of state competence (public peace) and instrumentality (law). Even more basically, Murray's two distinct theological premises (pluralism and dualism) do not in any obvious or logical manner lead to the social norm of "as much freedom as possible, as much coercion as necessary," which was the actual point of contention between theories of tolerance and his own theory of religious freedom. Without direct appeal to contemporary notions of religious freedom and to contemporary, autonomous notions of political and social theory, much of his argument (using one of his favorite images) remained suspended in mid-air.

Finally, three conceptual issues were only tangentially touched in these articles—issues that would return to dominance during the Vatican Council, once the ecclesiastical fetters were removed. First of all, Murray asserted that the church's freedom included "her shared right to regulate the *res sacra in temporalibus*" (1958a, 2), implying but not specifying some principle of limitation. Second, he distinguished the church as (a) an institution with access to civil society and (b) a "community of faithful" with access to the institutional magisterium (1958a, 1), establishing at least a partial ecclesiastical parallel to the state-society distinction. And, third, he asserted that Christian constitutionalism is a composite notion, made up of three distinct *doctrines*: "a theology of the church, a philosophy of the state, and a philosophy of society." Here the term "doctrine"[11] is used in a sense similar or analogous to the judgments of the wise concerning the remote principles of justice, as at least partially developed in the third chapter of *We Hold These Truths,* opening the door to a discussion of the development of even a theological "doctrine" in terms of emerging insight.

However, without a direct appeal to Anglo-American political theory and the imperatives that the theory might place on the church's own understandings and judgments, Murray's priority of freedom remained ungrounded. This was the best he could do without an appeal to the political and moral realities and theories arising outside the boundaries of the church.

B. The 1964 Argument: Shifts in Governing Questions and Convergences. As mentioned above, Murray's public unshackling took place in April 1963, at the insistence of Francis Cardinal Spellman. April was a good month for Murray. Not only did he gain access to the public discussion of the Council, he also received substantial support for his religious liberty argument in the April 11 promulgation of John XXIII's encyclical *Pacem in Terris.* Two central features of that encyclical will serve as introductions to Murray's 1964 "On the Problem of Religious Freedom," features or themes which expose the "coequal" bases for his argument. The first theme is that of the contemporary juridical conception of the state, its definition and affirmation by John. This would lead Murray to an extension of his study of the "tradition" in the second part of the 1964 article. The second theme is the concept of the "dignity of the human person," a notion which became a grounding for, and the title of, the Declaration on Religious Freedom. (Consideration of a third theme, the centrality of freedom for civil society, will enter into my discussion in the second section of this chapter.)

Murray quickly responded to *Pacem in Terris* with an article in *America* (1963f), his first in two years. His endorsement of the encyclical focused primarily on the concept of the state which served as the basis for John's reflections on international society. John "leaves behind the predominantly ethical concept of society-state which was characteristic of Leo XIII," adopting the "more juridical conception of the state that was characteristic of Pius XII" (1963f, 612). He accepts a society-state distinction with the three subsequent political principles of "society as a sphere of freedom, the state as constitutionally limited, even by a written constitution, and the principle of public participation in the public administration" (1963f, 612).

Remarkably, Murray's analysis of *Pacem in Terris* did not make mention of religious freedom, although Murray had just been named a *peritus*. Over a year later, during the Council's second interim, he published through the Council's documentation service a three-part article on "the state of the question," ostensibly an attempt to present the counter positions on the issue "fairly and fully." He again tried to place the present argument between conservatives and liberals (or, in neutral terms, between the "first view" and the "second view") within a history of Western political and religious thought. The point of difference between the first and second views concerns an answer to the age-old question of the public care of religion (1964f, 47). This question has undergone many changes. The problem itself is pre-Christian. Even in the Roman Empire, "the citizen was permitted his freedom of conscience but was compelled to offer sacrifice to the Empire." That is, public power recognized the inviolability of the individual conscience, but did not recognize freedom in the public expression of religion. This question was taken up and modified by Augustine in his insistence on the "necessary freedom of the Christian act of faith," while he consented to "the use of the imperial power to take coercive care of the Donatists." Not even the first view presently argues that coercion is a proper or even a practical means of affecting Catholic religious commitment within the individual or within his immediate personal environment. The "state of the question" has changed.

Within the dualism premise of Gelasius, Gregory the Great extended the zone of religious immunity from state intervention. For Gregory, "the first imperial care of religion was to be a care for the freedom of the church, a respect for the immunity of the church from imperial intervention in her internal affairs and in her apostolic office" (1964f, 48). Therefore, as a consequence of the emergence of Christian dualism, the freedom of the church as an institution and as a religious community was situated as the principal concern of the state in its "care for Catholicism." That is, the state's public care function was defined as primarily juridical, the recognition of public immunity from coercion for the Christian peoples and society.

The question of public care was again shifted by another historical flow of political and religious events. In the Middle Ages, Catholic religious adherence became a primary requirement for political unity, so the state could and would publicly care for religious unity by coercive means for the sake of its own temporal unity (1964f, 49). Then, with the Reformation and the rise of monarchical absolutism, the classical, ethical conception of the king and of the state reemerged. The Christendom notion blurred the notion of social dualism, while the ethical and paternalistic notion of political sovereignty likewise submerged the conception of juridical protection as the primary element in the public care of Catholicism. Within the historical process, then, two key social and political principles, based in Christian faith, were lost from view.

The historical shift from monarchical to atheistic state absolutism again altered the state of the question (1964f, 53). With Leo XIII the principle of dualism, with its recognition of two relatively autonomous societies, and the principle of the freedom of the church as an institution and as a people, began to reemerge into central focus. Leo himself, however, was still caught within an ethical conception of the state, as this had been augmented by the Reformation and Counter-Reformation notion of the confessional state (1964f, 55). The total care of the common good was committed to the government, dissolving any distinction between society and state. Similarly, Leo cast the ruler in the model of the primary social servant of God, "the architect of the social order, the supreme agent responsible for the Christian quality of social life" (1964f, 56). Third, given the political and religious immaturity of the people, government was viewed as paternal, as protective of a people who were not capable of defending themselves.

This ethical conception of government was itself challenged by the historical flow of political events. With the rise of Nazi and Communist totalitarianism, Pius XI, Pius XII, and John XXIII gradually "bid adieu" to that ethical notion, and adopted a juridical notion of government (1964f, 65–66).[12] This was not done unambiguously; the old ethical conception dies slowly. But the movement in the development of the church's doctrine has been toward a juridical conception of the state, and a limitation of the public care of the Catholic church within that juridical conception. Since Leo XIII, however, the principles of social dualism and of the freedom of the church have dominated all church-state considerations. The present state of the public care question is framed within these two principles.

Noteworthy in this historical analysis is Murray's new insistence that even the primary principles of dualism and freedom of the church depend on the historical flow of events for their emergence, disappearance, and reemergence. He made no apologetic attempt to demonstrate the permanence of those principles in church thought or in the church's social dealings. The question of the public care of the church remains constant; the principles of its solution, much less the actual solutions themselves, do or did not.

So far, I have presented only one of the two bases which Murray offers for the church's affirmation of religious liberty: the changing statement of the public care question. He also offered a second, independent leg for his argument.

It is likewise within the historical process of emerging insight, now within the secular order, that the Vatican Council must find a second basis for its own contemporary statement concerning the public care of religion. And the primary datum governing the present statement of that problem is the current growth in personal and political consciousness of the people. Somewhat remarkably, in the 1963 article on *Pacem in Terris,* Murray made no reference to John's term "dignity of the human person," a term which occurs over thirty times throughout the encyclical. In his 1964 article, however, the term has been shifted into central position.[13] According to Murray, John recognized that the new element of the present social situation was a "rising social sense of the dignity of the human person" (1964f, 17–19, 64). For Murray, this contemporary affirmation of human dignity has two dimensions. It is a "personal and political consciousness." As a personal consciousness, it is an affirmation of the value of the individual person, with the correlative claim of immunity from coercion for individuals and social subgroups. Since the human person is recognized as valuable, the state is juridically defined as limited to the good of public order, i.e., as restricted from control over the attainment of private goods (the "juridical principle"). As a political consciousness, this contemporary sense of human dignity lays claim to popular constitutionalism, that is, that the people, not the state, are the main agents of the ethical direction of society, including the definition of the proper constitutionally limited role of government (the "political principle"). "Dignity," therefore, has for Murray an individual and a social reference. The juridical principle has as its primary reference the human person. The political principle primarily refers to a people, a social body. Both of these references are for Murray essential (coequal and independently developed) aspects of the present affirmation of human dignity, and both principles are essential for a correct judgment concerning religious liberty.

Murray made no attempt to derive the contemporary affirmation of human dignity, with its correlative political and juridical principles, either logically or historically from Christian theological or moral principles. He did not try to demonstrate that "your political theory is really our own," as he had done in his American debate. Since the reign of Pius IX, the church has brought to the fore the two theological principles of dualism and church freedom. During that same period, confronting much the same enemies, the peoples of the political order have likewise developed the political principle of social control over the state and the juridical principle of immunity. The development of modern social consciousness has had an autonomous upbringing.

Now, if the church's nineteenth century confrontation with totalitarian democracy led to the (re)emergence of the two theological principles as the norms governing the restatement of the question of the public care of the Catholic Church, then how has the twentieth century question of public care been altered by the development in personal and political consciousness? "The question today," Murray asserted, "is whether public care of religion is not only limited *by* a necessary care for the freedom of the Church, but also limited *to* a care for the religious freedom of the Church together with a care for religious freedom of all peoples and all men" (1964f, 48). The differences between the responses to this new question by those of the first and of the second views revolve around a subsequent "conceptual question" (*quid sit?*) and a "question of judgment" (*an sit?*) (1964f, 22).

The conceptual question is simply, what is meant by religious liberty today? According to Murray, the modern consensus affirms religious liberty as an immunity from coercion in religious matters, that is, as a juridical right. This juridical right entails both "freedom of conscience" and "free exercise of religion" within the public forum. The free exercise of religion is held to be composed of two immunities—freedom from being forced to act against one's conscience and freedom from being forced not to act according to one's conscience (1964f, 25). This complex notion of religious freedom entails also a "second conceptual question: what is constitutional government?" (1964f, 28-29).[14] The answer to this question is based on three distinctions between (1) the sacred and the secular, (2) society and state, and (3) the common good and public order. Again, for Murray, a proper definition of religious liberty must include individual and social or political aspects.

The questions for judgment which confront the Council concern "junctures" or "convergences" (1) within the modern consensus concerning juridically and politically defined freedoms and (2) between those secular conceptions and the theologically based conclusions of the church's own argument.

First, the present temporal consensus concerning religious liberty affirms an indissoluble link between freedom of conscience and freedom of religious expression. "Both freedoms are given in the same one instance; they are coequal and coordinate, inseparable, equally constitutive of the dignity and integrity of man" (1964f, 38–39). The basis for this secular judgment has been the recognition of the truly social nature of the human person, that freedom of conscience is itself weakened when the human person is denied freedom of public expression. Second, it is also based on the further recognition that the state as a temporal body has no authority in religious matters, as religious expression arises either in the private or in the public forum. This judgment of linkage is, like the definition of religious freedom itself, based simultaneously in personal and social (political) realities.

This affirmation of a link between the freedoms of conscience and of expression parallels a link by the church between its own "internal freedom to self-governance" and its "external freedom to fulfill her apostolic office" (1964f, 36), that is, the church's freedom of access and voice within civil society. Just as civil society affirms the link between the internal and external freedoms of the human person, so the church affirms a link between its own freedoms within the private and public forums. There is a parallel between the church's affirmation (judgment) concerning her own freedoms and the people's affirmation concerning theirs.

To parallel the two affirmations within two distinct societies does not, of course, establish the church's acceptance of modern civil religious freedom. So far in his argument, Murray's principal target was a dichotomizing of the personal and public arenas, a "sort of Kantianism" that would deny the necessary social aspects of faith (1964f, 38). It does, however, indicate the extent to which Murray was still dealing with two independent realms of meaning, each of which proceeds toward judgments of fact and value within distinct starting premises. His problem was now how to tie together the judgments made independently within the two, without reducing one society to the other.

In his earlier argument with the thesis-hypothesis school, Murray had argued that Pius XII's adoption of a juridical notion of the state implied that all forms of church-state institutionalization must be understood as contingent judgments—as tied to particular historical circumstances and as admitting no ideal solution. Now he argued that Pius' adoption of the juridical notion began the process of conjoining the church's argument for its own freedom with modern political consciousness. Pius looked to the modern juridical state to provide the church with "a stable condition in law and in fact and full freedom in the fulfilment of her spiritual mission" (1964f, 98). In other words, juridical, constitutional government was understood to be the proper modern method for insuring both the internal and the external freedom of the church. With Pius, a "juncture" had been formed between the secular juridical definition of government and the project of the church's freedom. The theological issue of ecclesiological freedom has been judged compatible with, and presently best guaranteed by, a juridical notion of government. This is the first "juncture" required by the church.

If this first "juncture" tied together the church's spiritual mission with the political aspects of contemporary consciousness, the next juncture would unite the church's temporal concern for the common good with the personal or immunity aspect of modern consciousness. Murray had earlier argued with Sturzo that, within contemporary consciousness, all civil freedoms are thought to make up a whole cloth, that the fate of the individual democratic rights is interrelated and interdependent. Here he argues that John XXIII, working also within a juridical understanding of government, recognized and affirmed the conjoining of the church's freedom to exercise its rightful concern for the common good with the people's (immunity) freedoms. "The two freedoms are inseparable—in fact, they are identical. They stand or fall together" (1964f, 81). John found that both freedoms are necessary for society. The tradition had always asserted that the freedom of the church was a requirement for the human quality of society. Now John recognized that the freedom of the people was likewise a requirement for a human and humane society (1964f, 82). On this basis of the temporal, social good, the joining of these two sets of freedoms has been effected.

Now, if Pius did link the constitutional notion of government with the freedom of the church, and if John linked modern democratic freedoms with the church's legitimate concern for the common good, they did not unambiguously forge such links. What is pastorally required of the Council is an unambiguous affirmation of these two "junctures," an affirmation required for ecumenical interaction and for a defense of both the church's freedom and the people's freedom in the face of modern totalitarianisms. "What the pastoral solicitude of the church today demands, the doctrine of the church likewise proclaims and authorizes, namely, a universal care for religious freedom in society and state" (1964f, 70–71). The primary responsibility of the Council, therefore, is an affirmation of the relationship between elements within contemporary social self-understanding and its own theologically based spiritual and temporal mission.

Murray's principal argument for the church's affirmation of religious liberty was based on a distinction between understanding and judgment, as this notion of intellectual operations was applied to two distinct orders of human activity, or, one might say, as it was applied to two distinct societies. The church has its own notion of freedom, the freedom of the (Catholic) peoples in the face of changing political forms. The secular order has developed its own notions of freedom, both individual and social, particularly in the face of modern totalitarian governmental forms. Various judgments within those two distinct societies have, in a parallel fashion, linked freedoms (primarily as immunities) between the internal and external forums. The church is now called to unambiguously link its notion of ecclesiastical freedom with the temporal notion of juridical government. It is further called upon to link its own freedom with all civil freedoms, born out of a care for the temporal common good and out of concern for its own mission to the peoples.

The notion of judgment or affirmation forging "junctures" between the goods and structures of the dual societies appears to be the underlying conceptual frame for Murray's claimed emerging "convergences" between five principles which must govern the church's affirmation. These principles are:

> ...(1) the theological principles—the dyarchy, the freedom of the Church, the freedom of the act of faith; (2) the ethical principles—religious freedom as the rightful exigence of the contemporary personal and political consciousness; the insight that the free man, bound by duties and endowed with rights, is the origin and end of the social order; (3) the political principles—that the public power is not the judge of religious truth or of the secrets of conscience; that the primary function of the public powers is the vindication of the juridical order of human and civil rights, i.e, the fostering of the freedom of the people; (4) the juridical principle—that the criterion for public restriction of religious freedom is some necessary requirement of public order; (5) the jurisprudential principle—that necessity, not possibility, is the further criterion for coercive inhibition of the free exercise of religion (1964f, 76, 6).

The theological principles are unique to the church, and a primary, but not exclusive, focus in its own judgments concerning juridical institutionalizations. But the political and juridical have arisen autonomously in the temporal order and have been, and must be, adopted by the church. It is "history, not logic" which has brought these three sets of principles together, out of which a judgment must be made (1964f, 100).

The convergence of the two remaining sets of principles offers some slight problems. The ethical principles (religious freedom as the rightful exigence of the contemporary personal and political consciousness; etc.) are thought by Murray to be merely an exposition of the content of the contemporary consensus concerning the "dignity of the human person." As such, it is an ethical affirmation which has arisen in secular society, but concerns a moral or spiritual reality over which the church has a *shared* right of regulation, even though the church has had little role in its development. This again can be understood in terms of social dualism.

The jurisprudential principle (that necessity, not possibility, is the further criterion for coercive inhibition of the free exercise of religion) can likewise be understood in terms of social dualism: it is a social "bias" particular to Anglo-American forms of constitutional government. In the present argument, Murray appeared satisfied to claim that this bias, which is actually the basis of the disagreement between the first and second views, is merely a rightful affirmation of contemporary secular ethical consciousness. Murray will later be forced to link this jurisprudential principle not only with contemporary moral consciousness, but also with the dynamic search for the fulfillment of any moral responsibilities. That is, he will not be allowed to affirm the principle solely or even principally because it has been affirmed within the Anglo-American tradition. But, Murray will still situate the development of this principle within the historical emergence of insight and judgment, as already described.

In the final section of his 1964 article, Murray attempted to spell out the differences between the first and second views by reference to the type of argumentation used by each and the points at which some dialogue might occur. He in fact asserted that there was no mutual communication between the positions—they were not talking about the same things. (The tone of his presentation of the counter arguments is similar to the latter phase of his exchange with MacIver—"our minds are not meeting—in the sense, I mean, that they are not even clashing.") In the present conciliar debate, Murray attributed the lack of engagement to "the contemporary clash between classicism and historical consciousness" (1964f, 89). Although he professed that such a fundamental difference in perspective was beyond the scope of this 1964 article, he did put forth a few clues as to what he himself meant by this classicism-historical consciousness differentiation.

The classicism-historical consciousness distinction is at least partially exposed in the type of objections advanced by each of the views toward the other. The first view claims that the second is in theological error; the second accuses the first of theological fallacies (1964f, 89).[15] The first view appeals to a specific set of ecclesiastical affirmations concerning the political order and absolutizes those affirmations as "ideal" or as the final word on the Catholic view of church-state relations. It allows no theoretical significance to recent social-historical developments; such developments only condition the question of the application of the ideal. Those who profess the contemporary state of the question or the valid answer to the question of public care to be other than that present in the nineteenth century ecclesiastical solution of the problem, i.e., those who disagree with those religiously authoritative sources, are in religious and theological error.

The second view accuses the first of theological fallacies of two different varieties: archaism and anachronism (1964f, 89–91). To miss the modern developments in the state of the question, primarily the development of personal and political consciousness, entails an archaic return to a situation which is no longer existent or definitive. Murray here compared this change of the question to that which led to the Nicene Christological definitions. Eusebius of Caesarea was the first victim of the archaism fallacy. He and others "refused to consider the fact that Arius had asked a new question which could not be answered, without ambiguity, in the scriptural formulas" (1964f, 90; cf. also 1966f). Similarly, "the First View is archaistic after the growth of the personal and political consciousness in the twentieth-century. With this growth in man's understanding of himself as a free person in a free society, Catholic doctrine on religious freedom must likewise grow in its understanding of itself" (1964f, 90). Further, any attempt to read back into Leo XIII the second view would be anachronistic (1964f, 100). Again, the development of twentieth century personal and political consciousness has presented a new question, which must be answered in light of all the significant contemporary factors which inform the question.

Murray was attempting to draw a parallel between the Lonergan notion of the development of theoretical consciousness in the Nicene question and the notion of the development of contemporary personal and political consciousness. The basis of his comparison seems to be his assertion that insight concerning the church's own sociopolitical situation emerges from the general sociopolitical situation of the time. He can therefore say:

The link between religious freedom and limited constitutional government, and the link between the freedom of the church and the freedom of the people—these were not nineteenth-century theological political insights. They became available only within twentieth century perspectives, created by the "signs of the times." The two links were not forged by abstract deductive logic but by history, by the historical advance of totalitarian government, and by the corresponding new appreciation of man's dignity in society (1964f, 100).

Three levels of what might be called "contingency" are suggested here. First, since Murray had already and consistently defined establishment-intolerance to be a problem in the temporal, political and juridical order, he could claim that the church's judgments of new forms of church-state legal relations *must* in every age take account of the new political and social realities, as these latter arise through insight and judgment within a society distinct from the church. This would be simply the need to recast civil laws as particular determinations within each historical age, a requirement based on the notion of the prudential nature of all temporal, civil law. Further, however, Murray now insisted that a solution to the twentieth century public care question was itself dependent on new insights and judgments within the church itself, those "truths" involved in the two links or junctures, but also in the affirmation of social dualism and the freedom of the church. This goes beyond his notion of civil law as particular determination to a broader notion of the contingent nature of all historical judgments or affirmations, as adopted from *Insight*. But, third, Murray has hinted at, and partially appealed to, another level of historical development. If it is to deal with the new statement of the public care question in an adequate manner, the church must confront its own past and understand that past for what it was, a complex dialogic relationship with the temporal order that yielded judgments which are no longer relevant. A direct challenge has been presented to the modern church, to shift from one perspective to another concerning the attitude the church takes toward its own historical truth claims. Just as the perspectival shift in the personal and political consciousness of the people has transformed the sociopolitical order, so the shift to historical consciousness will transform the church's understanding of itself and, therefore, its own reality.

I will note further on than Murray was unsure of this last "level of contingency"—the classicist and the historical consciousness perspectives toward the meaning by which the church is constituted. But he was quite clear about the proper fate of religious intolerance in the modern world. "The institution cannot be tolerated today even as a harmless archaism" (1964f, 103). Religious freedom as a juridical immunity should be affirmed unambiguously and universally by the Council.

C. The Development of Doctrine: The Dynamics of Thought.   Murray's 1964 argument for a change in the church's understanding and judgment was, then, based on a conception of the "relativities of human history," that is, on the emergence of insights and judgments within both civil and ecclesiastical societies. Changing historical social situations have led to novel conceptions of religious liberty and to the "junctures" between those conceptions and the church's concern for its own freedom and mission.

In a 1967 article entitled "Vers une intelligence du développement de la doctrine de l'église sur la liberté religieuse" (1967b), Murray worked out a notion of the development of doctrine as based also on "the dynamisms of thought." After highlighting the differences between the Leonine theory of tolerance and *Dignitatis Humanae's* theory of religious liberty, he spelled out three such rational dynamisms.

> There is (1), for instance, the generic movement noted in *Humani Generis*—"toward the elucidation and detailed formulation of matters contained in the deposit of faith only obscurely and in some implicit fashion." This movement is often accomplished by passing from undifferentiated to the differentiated concept—in the technical Scholastic vocabulary, from the "confused" to the "distinct" concept. Thus in the undifferentiated concept of John, that the Son is "from the Father" (16:28), the distinction was later made between the eternal procession and the temporal mission, and an earlier theology of the Son's mission was relieved of any suggestion of subordinationism. Again (2), development may involve a dialectical process whereby earlier understandings of an affirmation, which were inconsistent with the original sense of the affirmation itself are perceived and corrected. Bernard Lonergan has shown this dialectic at work in the series of ante-Nicene writers, in the process that led to the homoousion. Further, (3) a change of perspective may bring to light a truth which had not been clearly seen or stated before. Thus the dogma of Filioque came into view when the perspective of Gregory of Nyssa, set by the Origenist emphasis on the distinction and order of the divine persons, was altered by Augustine to a new perspective set by his focus on "Deus Trinitas." These factors of development are well known. And they may be looked for in the development of the concept of religious liberty (1967b, 114).[16]

The remainder of the article is an attempt to understand the movement from Leo XIII to *Dignitatis* in terms of these rational dynamisms.

First, Murray noted the shift between Pius IX and Leo XIII in the reemergence of the principles of dualism and the freedom of the church as central to the church's argument. He did not attempt to demonstrate that this reemergence was due to any of the three rational dynamisms mentioned above. Both Pius and Leo confronted the theological claims of Continental monism; and Pius IX was simply thoroughly blinded by the polemical tone of the argument (1967b, 113).[17]

With Leo as a starting point, Murray then argued that there were two levels of doctrine within Leo's teaching. The first and most fundamental were the principles of dualism and freedom (1967b, 115–18). And within these principles one must conclude to the rightful autonomy of the political order and the incompetence of government in religious matters. However, "there is another level to the doctrine of Leo XIII, on which he defends the confessional state on the classic model, and concedes to it a religious prerogative—a power of judgment with regard to religious truth and a consequent power to decide whether to be tolerant or intolerant of religious error" (1967b, 126). Once again, then, Murray appealed to the dualism of theological truth and political reality, or the premises of revelation and those of the natural, rational understanding of the state. And it is the latter that caused Leo to opt for simple toleration in the question of religious liberty.

Murray now suggested, however, that the last century of church thinking represents a dialectical removal of the inconsistencies between the principle of governmental incompetence and the conferral of such competence within the confessional state model. The key factors in such a dialectic have been the (re)discovery of the juridical notion of the state, primarily conducted by Pius XII, and the affirmation of human dignity by John XXIII.

Further, Murray attempted to point out that these two notions of juridical limitation and human dignity had some (minor) position within Leo's own thought, particularly in *Rerum Novarum* and in his attempts to educate the Catholic peoples (1967b, 122–26). Therefore, *Dignitatis Humanae* can be understood as making clear principles which were only haltingly present in Leo's writings.

But the dialectical removal of inconsistencies and the retrieval of unclear concepts had to await a change of perspective (1967b, 126–27). The change was again brought about by the rising consciousness of the people and the juridical notion of the state. But, since Leo wrote within the perspectives of the confessional state, he was himself incapable of such dialectical thinking. His own perspectives "were set by historical factors in the culture of his own day. And within them his theory of tolerance, with its political promise, came naturally to his pen" (1967b, 126).

Murray therefore understood the development between *Libertas* (Leo XIII, 1888) and *Dignitatis* to be a dialectical removal of inconsistencies, conditioned on the emergence of insights and judgments and their adoption by the church. He could claim that "this raises no difficulty from the standpoint of a theology of the magisterium," for Leo was defending "a political proposition, not a truth of faith nor a truth connected with faith" (1967b, 127). One must note, however, that Murray has not explained, within the three notions of development presented above, the emergence of dualism and freedom of the church with Leo, certainly principles which are "connected with faith." He could possibly have discussed the nature of Pius IX's polemic in terms of historical (and personal) factors which blocked the recognition of such theological principles, but even in 1967 (or at least in this article), he was still hesitant to view the development of "theological truth" within the church as itself submerged within the historical processes of emerging understanding and judgment.

In this article, the suggestion of "inconsistencies" between conclusions as they arise from theological and political principles raises the possibility that, all things being equal, a particular political theory might be more compatible with the theological principles of dualism and freedom than might be another political theory. There is, however, no suggestion that such a political theory derives logically from theological principles. The compatibility is recognized only within a shift in perspective which is more akin to a shift of horizon than to any form of logical derivation or inference.[18] The inconsistencies between theological principles and political philosophies are removed always in interaction with historical realities, not the least of which is the ethical configuration of the people's self-consciousness.

Thus Murray attempted to advance his argument for religious liberty somewhat within the premises of Lonergan's notion of historical consciousness. That Murray did not have complete control over such a notion can be demonstrated by his claim that Leo XIII was a man of "historical consciousness" (1967b, 134), meaning by the term that Leo was quite aware of the illiterate Catholic masses and of the totalitarian claims of Continental democracy. There is here little indication of Lonergan's notion of historical consciousness as a specific differentiation of human consciousness.[19] Murray used the concept to enforce his own appeal to historical facts, thereby discounting the possibility of an "ideal" solution to church-state relations, as advanced by the "first" view. In this again, his argument is close to the notions of the contingency of all human judgments as presented in *Insight*.

Murray's historical justification of religious liberty was bound to run into trouble at the Council. As it turned out, the disjunctive or tolerance view was held by a small, if vocal, minority. The conciliar fathers were, much to the surprise of many, prepared to affirm the modern notion of civil religious liberty. The problem then became a conflict between various justifications or explanations of that affirmation. In the remainder of this chapter, I will follow Murray's own attempt to reach behind the authorization (which emerged in modern political thought) to the necessary moral requirements for the emergence of all moral judgments and commitments.

II. PHILOSOPHICAL JUSTIFICATIONS OF THE RELIGIOUS FREEDOM DOCTRINE.   As reported by Pelotte, even during the first session and at a distance, Murray suggested that any affirmation of religious freedom by the Council must be accompanied by an argument for that affirmation (Pelotte 1980, 79). The reason given at the time was the pastoral necessity of demonstrating that the church was not simply affirming religious liberty out of some type of expediency, a concession to the imperfect state of the modern world. In 1966, he added a second reason for such an argument. Given that religious liberty has been, historically, the conclusion from premises of "skepticism with regard to religious truth, or of moral relativism, or of religious indifferentism, or of laicist or secularistic conceptions of the functions of government" (1966a, 570), it was necessary that the church demonstrate that an affirmation of religious liberty can be made out of rational and Christian principles. The argument must be recognized as reasonable, without an implied or suggested affirmation of those ideologies which the church has rightfully opposed.

This being said, the problem then shifts from the doctrinal affirmation of religious freedom to the reasons advanced for that affirmation. The full church argument will and must take account of the church's own theological premises, and must clearly state that argument. However, the need to present a *public* argument for the doctrinal affirmation also offers some constraint on the main type of argument which can be advanced in that forum. *Dignitatis*, according to Murray, was directed to all peoples, not simply to Catholics or Christians, and it affirmed the right to religious freedom of all peoples. Therefore, the argument for that right must be based on premises acceptable to the pluralistic world of all men and women of good will.[20] That is, the main argument must be philosophical in Murray's sense. Both the third draft and the final draft of *Dignitatis*, therefore, did base their arguments on reason, with only secondary appeal to theological or revelational premises.

In this section I will examine Murray's reaction to three distinct attempts at grounding religious liberty (1) in human conscience, (2) in more individualistic theological principles such as the freedom of the act of faith, and (3) in the moral obligation to search for the truth. In

these considerations Murray's individual/social and theological/phil-
osophical distinctions will again be at work, defining the shape of the
universe within which his own argument was advanced. Finally, I will
examine his attempt to found religious liberty (4) in the moral agency
of the individual and of society at large. Tied up in his argument was
the attempt to situate the jurisprudential principle ("as much freedom
as possible . . . ") as a requirement for ongoing moral discernment and
behavior.

A. The Argument from the Exigencies of Human Conscience.   The first two
conciliar texts on religious liberty attempted to found the right to
religious freedom on human conscience. In a conciliar publication,
Murray countered that the modern notion of religious freedom which
the church was to affirm was "broader than freedom of conscience
(scil., freedom of personal internal religious and moral decision)"
(1963a, 2). In question is the notion of the free exercise of religion, that
is, "all external and public manifestations of religious faith, in worship,
observance, witness, and teaching." One cannot derive freedom in the
external realm of expression from the internal realm of conscience.
Both realms have to be given as "immediate data" in the notion
affirmed. A limited, individualistic understanding of religious freedom
(as based on conscience, on the freedom of the act of faith, or on
"dignity" simply as predicated of an internal sense of personal
integrity) does not constitute a right in the external, juridical forum, at
least not immediately or by logical necessity.

Although Murray's 1964 article was primarily directed against
the conservative, "tolerance" position, he did make a brief comment on
this first attempt to found religious freedom. His argument was
slightly different from, but correlative with, the internal-external
distinction. Murray argued that one cannot start in the realm of the
theological-ethical and derive from that realm the juridical-political.
The danger of the rights of conscience argument is that it misses an
essential component of what is presently meant by religious liberty.
The juridical-political argument is "coordinate" with the theological-
ethical. It arises with equal immediacy as an exigence of contemporary
moral (personal and political) consciousness. The "conscience" view is
"vulnerable, in that it seems to divorce the issue of the rights of the
human person from its necessary social-historical context" (1964f,
21). That is, it appears to be as abstract as is the conservative view.
Without a clear conception of the juridical-political, and a situating of
religious freedom within that context, the "conscience" view "risks
setting afoot a futile argument about the rights of the erroneous
conscience" (1964f, 22). By its positioning of the right within the

juridical-political universe, Murray's view avoids any discussion of rights as predicated on the internal correctness of the individual conscience. This argument is parallel to the argument which Murray brought against the conservative position itself.

The internal/external and theological-ethical/juridical-political distinctions were brought together within a spatial image in 1966. In "The Declaration on Religious Freedom: A Moment in Its Legislative History" (1966c), Murray focused on the transition from the argument of the first two schemas to that of the third, his own argument. He again objected that the first two schemas did not advance from the world of the interpersonal to that of the social or political. Any argument from theological principles or from individual moral dynamisms (in the sense of conscience as a human rational faculty) concerns only man's "upward" relationship to an order of truth (1966c, 24). But the contemporary notion of religious liberty concerns one's "outward" relationships with other men and women. Rights are urged against others, not against an order of truth. Religious liberty is defined solely in terms of outward immunity, as are all civil rights, and are not even claimed as positive empowerments, as are socioeconomic rights. And this immunity is again defined as a freedom from constraint and from restraint in the public forum (1966c, 30). To affirm particularly this immunity from restraint, the Council needs to get beyond a simple "upward" theological-ethical argument to the "outward," the political. And the political is "decisive." It entails the notion of limited government which is not derivative from those aspects of man's "upward" relationship to the order of religious and moral truth.

Against the conservative position, Murray did defend the limited validity of the conscience argument, but attempted to situate it within a larger ethical context. The conservative view

> ...overlooks the principle that objective truth becomes a norm of action only in the internal forum of conscience, as conscience itself apprehends the truth and its imperative character...the laws of conscience are themselves elements of the objective moral order (1966c, 23).

Any discussion of the ethical direction of society must therefore take account of the appropriation of ethical knowledge and of the duties which follow from conscience as the proximate source of ethical obligation. The problem with the freedom of conscience argument is that this argument itself, like the conservative argument, does not appeal to the full range of elements within the moral universe which must enter into a definition of religious liberty. It ignores the essentially social character of modern rights claims, as well as the juridical-political environment in which the notion of rights has, historically, gained its definition.

Murray's understanding of the conscience argument and his critique of it reflects his criticism of his own 1946 argument for religious liberty. In that argument he attempted to move from a faculty psychology definition of conscience to a political right. In this present liberal argument from conscience, he apparently perceived the same fundamentally individualistic cognitive theory. Consistent with the 1946 argument, however, is the insistence that an argument for religious liberty be situated within a definition of the ethical universe, an aspect of which is distinctively and originally social. But now the definition of government and the people's self-understanding are historically given, independently and autonomously, within a secular, political society. At one level, then, his criticism of the conscience argument is "natural" or philosophical, that is, it is a criticism of an inadequate foundational epistemology. At a deeper level, however, there is a criticism which appears to be based on the principle of secular society's rightful autonomy, a principle which was generated in Murray's own thinking by the theological principle of social dualism. That there might be within Murray's own thought, further grounds for the social autonomy of the people is not immediately apparent from any of his 1964 writings.[21]

B. The Argument from Christian Faith.   The autonomous development of the civil order was the basis for Murray's critique of another conciliar attempt to "radicate religious freedom in religion itself— concretely, in the Scriptures, and in the traditional doctrine of the necessary freedom of Christian faith" (1965c, 139). The attempt here was again to proceed from the theological order to the juridical order, even though it is in the juridical order that modern religious freedom is defined. Some of the conciliar fathers wanted simply to "quote and argue" from Scriptures to juridical freedom. Others wanted a more historical argument. They would assert that "the slow movement of mankind to a sense of human dignity and freedom, and to institutional expressions of this sense, has been due not least to the hidden spiritual power of the Gospel's message of liberation" (1965c, 140). These theological attempts to ground religious liberty, which Murray called the "French" view, considered the third (Murray's) schema to be "superficial" (1965d, 42).

Murray's own critique of the French theological attempt, however, is again immersed in his premise of dualism, this time with an historical critical edge. The church itself had little to do with the development of the modern affirmation of religious liberty (1964b, 2–3). In agreement with Pavan, Murray claimed that the church came to an affirmation of political rights (one of which is religious liberty) and of socioeconomic rights in an "inverse fashion" from the general political order. Only with *Rerum Novarum* did the papacy begin to affirm one aspect of those rights (the socioeconomic) which constitute the notion of the dignity of the human person. And only in Vatican II did the church face up to, and affirm, civil or political rights. In the modern world, however, the recognition of civil or political rights as immunities came first; then socioeconomic rights were recognized and affirmed well before even *Rerum Novarum*. The church had little to do with the development of either set of rights. "Hence the Church is in the unfortunate position of coming late, with the great guns of her authority, to a war that has already been won, however many rearguard skirmishes remain to be fought" (1965d, 43). The declaration is, then, an act of humility on the part of the church (1966a, 566), a recognition that the church has learned and must learn from the moral claims made and developed independently of her own teaching authority. The attempt at scriptural or historical derivation from theological principles seemed to most of the Council fathers to be an unwarranted "triumphalism."

Murray, then, criticized both the argument from conscience and the argument from theological starting points, for ignoring the fact of the autonomous development of the juridical notions which define modern religious liberty. Further, he argued that from either of the positions it was impossible to limit but allow the curtailment of public religious expression. That is, no three-part concept of public order (i.e., public peace, general morality and justice) could be developed with which to guide the state's use of coercive force within the constraints of the state's limited public function (1966c, 23–35). Any statement on religious liberty by the church must recognize those legitimate uses of public coercion in what concerns religion, or the state is denied its own autonomy, which would place the argument back within the premises of the toleration argument.

C. The Argument from the Personal Exigence to Seek the Truth. It is generally agreed that the conscience and theological arguments were rejected as the primary theoretical justifications for *Dignitatis*. What argument for religious liberty, then, was accepted by the Council? There seems to be some disagreement over the answer to this question. In one article, Murray himself claimed that the third (his) schema represented a "new doctrinal line" which was maintained throughout the final revisions, including the declaration itself (1966c, 16). This opinion also seems to have been held by Pelotte (Pelotte 1978, 97–99).[22] But Murray also went to some lengths to discount the inclusion within the *textus recognitus* of an argument for religious freedom from the moral obligation to seek the truth (1966a, 568–70; 1966d, 680, note 7). According to the truth argument, each person must be allowed religious freedom in order to pursue and adhere to what is true. The obligation to seek the truth therefore founds the juridical right to immunity. Richard Regan appears to have more precisely understood the shift between the fourth and fifth texts. He points out that the final version of the declaration adopted the exigence to seek truth as the dominant grounding for religious liberty, reducing the arguments from the freedom of conscience and from the juridical nature of the right to ancillary positions. He notes that the initial reference in the first paragraph of the decree to a juridical conception of the state was a last minute addition to the text, after the "truth" argument had been approved by a second conciliar vote.

Regan's judgment that the final decree reduced Murray's argument to a secondary position might explain not only Murray's own ambiguous response to the decree, but also his several postconciliar attempts to develop his argument. In his annotations to the declaration, he asserted that the "doctrinal" in the decree was the affirmation of juridical religious freedom, not the argument proposed for that affirmation (1966d, 680). It is now the task of theologians to work out a more reasonable argument. The basing of human dignity in the search for truth was, in his opinion, pastorally motivated. "The concern was lest religious freedom be misunderstood to mean a freedom from the claims of truth—in particular, as these claims are declared by the Church" (1966a, 571). It indicated that some at the Council were still living "in the long shadow of the nineteenth-century." However, the exigence of the person to search for the truth "fails to yield the necessary and crucial political conclusion, namely, that government is not empowered, except in exceptional cases, to hinder men or religious communities from public witness, worship, practice, and observance in accordance with their own convictions." Once again, the political and juridical premises must be equally and independently asserted, if the case is to be sufficiently argued. An argument solely within the need to search for the truth is vulnerable to the claim by government that it itself already holds the truth, and therefore that a dissenting individual has no right to publicly challenge that truth.

D. *Murray's Argument from Individual and Social Ethical Agency.*   If Murray rejected arguments from conscience, from theology, and from the individually conceived imperative to search for truth, what argument did he accept? He actually advanced two such arguments which were only partially separated. Again, the crucial points for any such argument are (1) the limitations placed on coercive power (government) and (2) the warrants under which coercive power may be used in the curtailment of public expression. Throughout all of his presentations, the final index of governmental interference was what he in 1964 had called the "jurisprudential principle"—as much freedom as possible, as much coercion as necessary. It is this "bias" toward freedom which is the "final limit" placed on government (1966c, 36). Murray had difficulty, however, positioning this principle within his argument. The principle does not immediately derive from the political limitation of government, nor even from the empowerment of government to act within the norms of public order. Rather, this jurisprudential principle itself defines the notion of public order as a limited portion of the general common good. Given his notion of the relative moral autonomy of the civil society, Murray could and did claim this bias to be a secularly affirmed principle to which the church must be attentive (1964b, 4). After the Council, however, he, as it were, dug behind that secular affirmation, grounding the principle, on the one hand, on the moral nature of the human person and, on the other, on the ethical requirements for social, historical living. First, I will consider the argument for religious liberty and for the jurisprudential principle from the moral nature of the human person.

Perhaps in response to the claim that his theory was superficial, Murray did attempt to develop an analytic, if not "logically derivative," link between moral discourse and the juridical-political. The foundation for the right of religious liberty is again understood to be the dignity of the human person, the recognition of which occurred within modern civil society. The object of the right is negative, that is, it is an immunity from coercion. The beginning point for the argument, however, is "dignity" understood as based on the nature of the human person as a moral subject (1966c, 38–40). And this moral subject stands within a universe constituted by a vertical relationship to an order of truth and a horizontal relationship to other men and women (1966a, 571–72). Included in this notion of dignity, then, is the premise of the human theistic orientation and the further premise of the social nature of the human person. Or in Murray's earlier terms, the moral agent must be viewed as existing within a moral universe open to all that humans can intend.

Although as human, the individual can make no claims of rights against the order of religious and moral truth, yet also as a moral subject, the person is most fundamentally constituted as human in the freedom of religious choice. And, again as a moral subject, he can and must make claims for immunity from coercion in the juridical-political order (1966a, 572); he must demand the possibility, and exercise the possibility, of moral action determined and pursued in freedom. Freedom is a necessary requirement for moral agency in both the vertical and the horizontal relationships. Therefore, claimed Murray, the principle of "as much freedom as possible" follows directly from human moral nature. The human person needs a "zone of freedom" in order to be moral (1966c, 39). This personal, ethically required autonomy of the individual is an aspect of what is presently affirmed to be human dignity.[23]

In another article, Murray positioned the necessary principles for religious liberty within the initial notion of human dignity as follows. The starting point for such an argument is the dignity of the human person, a dignity which is founded on the responsibility of the person for the construction of his own nature *and* for the construction of society (1968, 569). This responsibility cannot be taken away even by God. In fact, man is held responsible by God for his life and fate. Murray called this starting point an "ontological principle," which again is an initial positioning of the moral subject within an individual, social, and religious universe. A second, "social" principle follows (*consequitur*) from the first ontological principle, namely, that "the human person is the subject, foundation and end of the whole social life," as this social principle evolved in the thought of Pius XII and John XXIII. With the dignity of the human person as the primary value for social action, the orders of morality (the vertical relationship) and the "moral-juridical" (the horizontal relationship) find their unity.

From the first, ontological principle, "taken with the social principle," there follows (*consequitur*) a third principle, the "principle of a free society": as much freedom as possible, and as much restriction as is necessary within the limited norm of the public order (1968, 570). Again, from the ontological and the social principles taken together, there follows the fourth, the juridical principle—the guarantee of equality of all citizens before the law, equality because all citizens share equally in the dignity of the person and are equally the subject, foundation, and end of society. And, finally, there follows a fifth, political principle which claims as the primary duty of government the protection of the dignity and rights of all its citizens.

These five principles, taken together, include all the essential factors involved in the question of religious liberty; out of a vision (*quasi visionem*) generated by these five principles, a decision or judgment concerning religious liberty can and must follow (thereby setting up the prudential nature of all juridical institutionalizations).

Several features of these later arguments should be noted. The first is that even here Murray has taken for his starting point the human subject as situated under a moral order which points to (as it were) the divine grounding of human life and to the historical society in which the person is situated (1968, 571). He uses the term "fundamental option" to describe the freedom of the human person under the aspect of response to the divine.[24] The moral subject is likewise situated within a social field. Both of these initial, essential elements of the moral subject are included under the term "responsibility." Even the fifth schema's moral obligation to search for and adhere to the truth appeared to Murray to be too individualistic and too unhistorical in its starting presuppositions. In its initial definition, the moral universe of the human agent must include the dialogic partners and realities involved in the exercise of moral agency.

Second, Murray's "social" principle corresponds roughly to the 1964 "political" and "juridical" principles, insofar as its intended subjects are the social institutions or social forces which act on the individual. In this reclassification, Murray has preserved his "coequal" individual and social starting points for ethical discourse. This new classification, however, is generalized beyond simply those institutions and forces which normally fall under the label of the "political," that is, those institutions which monopolize police power. All social institutions are to act under the directive of as much freedom as possible. Further, this social principle, from the perspective of institutional or social forces, implies a positive function or empowerment beyond the simple immunities which were highlighted in the 1964 political and juridical principles. This social principle locates all social forces within the moral direction suggested by the 1964 "ethical" principle, as the latter was dependent on the society-state distinction. The moral function of society in general (and of the institutional parts thereof) is the preservation and advancement of human dignity, as human dignity is understood primarily as a positive empowerment to shape one's social reality. Social institutions are to work to empower the people, so that the people can shape and reshape those institutions.[25]

Third, the jurisprudential principle—which, in the 1964 argument, was fifth in the list of important principles—is here situated within both the "ontological" and the "social" principles, as a requirement for the moral activity of the individual and the moral activity of society in general. Murray insists that this "principle of a free society" follows from both the individual-oriented "ontological" principle and from the institution-oriented "social" principle, preserving in the process his ongoing claim that individual and social aspects of historical living must be affirmed simultaneously and independently. One cannot adequately start from either pole of the moral universe and derive the other.

Finally, with the norm of "as much freedom as possible" established within the moral nature of the human person and the moral functioning of society at large, Murray could then give the political and juridical principles primarily *positive* definitions. Constitutional constraint on the governmental institutions has become the role of protecting the dignity and rights of all citizens, and immunity has become equality before the law. He could more easily discuss the positive activities of governmental power with the jurisprudential or "free society" principle previously established.

In light of his 1964 article, Murray has here made another attempt at the "conceptual question"—an exposition of the modern notion of human dignity. Further, he has tried to advance an argument for religious liberty which is not secularistic, atheistic, or positivistic. It should be noted that there is no appeal to what he understood as a theological principle. And, unless he has tremendously reversed himself, the "following" from the initial notion of dignity to the four later principles must not be understood as in any sense a logical deduction. Murray has not given up on his understanding of historical development, that is, on the conjunction of principles through emerging insight and dialectical adjustment. This argument was an attempt to situate the jurisprudential principle (1) within the contemporary notion of human dignity (the moral subject positioned within an ethical universe), and (2) within the basically positive ethical function of social institutions. The argument represents a turn to the active, socially constructive moral subject, both individual and social, as the ground for human freedoms. And for Murray it was necessary to argue independently for individual and social freedom, as the next argument will support.

The independent social grounding for the jurisprudential (free society) principle is highlighted by a second, distinct argument which Murray advanced for that principle. In nearly every article he wrote during and after the Council, and in conjunction with all those attempted arguments for religious liberty from the moral nature of the human person within an "ontological" and "social" world, Murray further appealed to the four factors which John XXIII found to be essential for any social body. In the previously discussed "Things Old and New in 'Pacem in Terris'," Murray rejoiced that John had added freedom to the list of three essential supports for the political order— truth, justice, and love (1963f, 613). The Pope asserted "that all order, if it is to be qualified as reasonable and human, must be founded on truth, built according to justice, vivified and integrated by charity and put into practice in freedom." Elsewhere, the Pope made clear that freedom is *the* method for the "realization of order in human affairs, as well as the goal of the order itself" (1963f, 613).

In his 1964 article, Murray called freedom one of the four spiritual forces which animate human society, and continued:

> Truth, justice, and love assure the stability of society; but freedom is the dynamism of social progress toward fuller humanity in communal living. The freedom of the people ranks as the political end, along with justice; it is a demand of justice itself. Freedom is also *the* political method whereby the people achieve their highest good, which is their own unity as a people (1964f, 82).

Freedom, then, was understood to be the "spiritual force" which is a requirement for the ongoing moral development of an historical society. In 1966 Murray linked the notion of freedom as a social force with moral agency, then linked freedom to truth and love, as well as with justice.

> The truth [of human dignity] therefore requires that in society there should be as much freedom as possible. Moreover, that which is primarily due in justice to the human person is his freedom—as much freedom as possible. Finally, love of the human person and love among human persons require that the freedom of each and of all should be respected as far as possible, and not curtailed except when and insofar as necessary (1966a, 574).

Further, "only by the usages of freedom in their full range can society, like the human person, make progress toward equal justice that is its goal."

Murray has grounded the first half of the jurisprudential or "free society" principle both in the modern affirmation of the dignity of the human person and in the requirements for historical, moral development of society as a social body. The second half of the jurisprudential principle is defined by the constitutional limitation placed on the state—or the norm of public order as the minimal condition necessary for public survival. Murray has related this juridical definition of the state to the modern affirmation of human dignity, insofar as that (ethical) affirmation of human dignity has arisen in a society which is distinct from the state and which is formative of the state. He has also related this juridical notion to historical process insofar as the juridical state has arisen through emerging insight and judgment in the temporal order. The second half of the jurisprudential principle, then, is tied both to the modern affirmation of human dignity and to the historical, ethical development of society as a social body.

Now, if one ignored for the moment Murray's conviction that human dignity is an aspect of secular, moral consensus and all that that implied for him, then "dignity" might appear to be an individualistic principle. Some of this individualistic connotation was perhaps inevitable. As Murray pointed out, the use of the term by John XXIII in *Pacem in Terris* was quite personalistic (1963f, 612). I have noted Murray's initial ambiguity about the term. Further, the right for which Murray was arguing, in 1964, was purely an immunity, which again might imply an individualism. As he noted, the right first clearly came to expression in American constitutionalism, and the American founding fathers were not interested in or even aware of rights as empowerments in social living (1966a, 580–81). Affirmations of rights as positive empowerments in the full sense that we affirm today arose only with the conception of socioeconomic rights.

But throughout his various writings, Murray has attempted to establish sociality as an initial defining condition even for rights as immunities. The human person is initially situated within sets of relationships and responsibilities; it is from the horizontal set that the definition of rights arises. He therefore understood rights as immunities to be primarily instrumental values, means by which moral living becomes possible for the individual and for society at large. Under the impact of his growing notion that each historical age must find the new ethical truth about itself as the social reality around it changes, Murray based freedom in a notion of social, ethical development which was somewhat more in line with the social and historical aspects of his 1964 argument. Both the individual and society require freedom if they are to act responsibly[26] toward the divine and human realities in which they are historically situated.

Murray eventually questioned even his previous claim that freedom is "the highest political goal," a claim which might be deduced from an individualistic civil rights theory. Consistent with his view that freedom is an empowerment or a force in the ongoing constitution of society, he admitted that "the duty of government [is] to supply the fullest possible measure of what Mortimer Adler, for instance, would call the freedom of self-realization, by providing a multitude of opportunities in terms of which people could pursue, through their own choice, their own higher perfection" (1966a, 581).[27] It is understood, however, that any positive action of the state toward freedom as empowerment, such as is involved in education, must be constrained and directed by the moral sense of the people. Government, as civil freedom itself, is instrumental to the moral action of the people, as such action develops through historical processes.

III. CONCLUSION: TOWARD AN ETHICS OF CONCRETE, HISTORICAL RESPONSIBILITIES.   Murray's religious liberty argument has moved about as far as it can go toward a notion of ethical development which is historically and socially aware. In the next chapter, he has more to say about such development in connection with issues other than religious liberty. But before moving on, it might be good to summarize what has developed within these two distinct arguments and to suggest a possible connection between them. Again, section I dealt with Murray's attempt to base religious liberty on the notion of emerging insight and judgment within two distinct societies; section II with his grounding of religious liberty in the notion of positive moral agency toward social meaning.

In the 1964 argument, Murray used the term "historical consciousness" to distinguish the second from the first view. As mentioned, however, Murray used the term primarily as a tag for the notions of (1) emerging insight within an historical field and (2) the contingency of all human judgments, again within an historical field. These notions are consistent with the epistemological theory presented in the 1957 *Insight*. In his development of doctrine discussions, Murray also appealed to "historical consciousness" as providing different fundamental perspectives, the basis for noncommunication between the first and second views. However, at least at that time, these different perspectives were primarily defined by different understandings of the social function of government, and, more importantly, by different evaluations of the moral abilities of the people. That is, the perspectival difference between the two views implied different attitudes toward the ethical agency of the people.

In the 1964 argument, just as Murray did not try to defend the authorization principle, likewise he simply accepted the jurisprudential principle as a given and as a good, a rightful moral-juridical principle arising within the contemporary secular moral consensus. After the Council, however, he himself understood the need to frame an argument for that jurisprudential principle which would be more than a simple recognition of a contingent social fact. As much freedom as possible was, in the final analysis, at the core of the disagreement between the first and second views. Murray then attempted to ground it in moral agency, both individual and sociohistorical, as an ongoing requirement for the moral development of the individual and of society. Valid insights might indeed emerge in almost any social setting, but individuals, institutions, and society at large bear responsibilities to facilitate such emergence. The insistence on uniquely social responsibilities suggests an ethics that is distinctly social, and that is presupposed in the resolution of any other social-ethical issue. This will become clearer in the next chapter, where Murray will define societies (including the church) as, most fundamentally, constituted, not by their institutional structures and boundaries, but rather by the collective self-understanding that groups of people develop and affirm in the face of historical change.

At first sight, these two arguments are quite distinct. But if the 1964 argument is examined more closely, there appears at its base an insistence that the church must present an argument for religious liberty that is reasonable, that is intelligible to modern peoples—a public reasonableness required for the preservation and development of the church's role in the moral direction of civil society. A note of ethical responsibility, therefore, permeated Murray's understanding of the necessity and the form of the decree. Further, however, Murray argued that the church must be responsible and reasonably responsible toward the (social) ethical realities which embody its own environment in the world. The church can and must learn from the secular, civil and political orders; it has a *shared* right in the valued aspects of human social living.

If this reading of the 1964 argument is correct, then there is obviously a similarity between it and Murray's moral agency grounding. In fact, they can be adequately understood only in relation to one another. The moral agent, whether an individual, or a church, or a government, is initially situated within a concrete set of relationships with God and with other individuals and social institutions. Out of these quite concrete relationships arise responsibilities toward all to which the human spirit is open. And, since these relationships are sunk in history, that spiritual force which leads to new ethical insights and judgments, namely, freedom, is a primary requirement for the moral health both of the individual and of society at large. The ongoing ethical reconstruction of the civil, social order demands as much freedom as possible. Even the church, as a society distinct from the civil order, must maintain its own freedom in order that it may enter into morally responsible dialogue with that civil order, if the church is to fulfill its mission to that order.

Murray's argument has, then, converged on the theme of active, creative responsibility, from both an apparently individual and a sociohistorical perspective, from the perspectives of civil society as well as ecclesiological society. The next chapter will continue this study of the Lonergan influence in this turn toward moral agency, and of how this turn substantially dented some of Murray's long-term convictions that conversation was impossible, or undesirable, particularly in regard to Protestants and even Communists. If the church itself is to behave responsibly within its own sociohistorical environment, it must enter into dialogue with the individual and social realities which constitute that environment. There will even be some suggestion that a type of social reality akin to moral conversion is necessary for social reconstruction.

Chapter Five

THE CHURCH AT THE "CUTTING-EDGE":

New Conversations among New and Old Social Differentiations

Murray understood American society to be based on a commitment to the people's social, moral primacy, and the church as committed to facilitating the moral direction of international society. However, amid his increasing calls for the exercise of moral agency, Murray continued to claim through much of his life that a *theologically* differentiated America could not, on revelational grounds, come to any functional national consensus, that America would remain theologically, radically pluralistic in the strong sense of dichotomous (there was not even a basis for "analogical conversation" among those theological differentiations). Rather, for both the national and international arenas he placed his hopes on a natural law, religious and moral content, behind which all people of good will could stand. Now, his late-1950s recognition of the radically pluralistic nature of America's moral commitments was fortuitous. It forced him, in the new articles for *We Hold These Truths*, to concentrate on the means by which social meaning and ethical directions could be formed in the face of technical and ethical, as well as theological, pluralism. Conversation, with the requirement of free access to that conversation, became an activity by which the American people could arrive at the resolution of particular public ethical issues, but conversation also became an activity within which and by which social solidarity or unity could be generated. Being locked in conversation, rather than in polemics, is the moral essence of Western civilized living. During the Council, he therefore would define "civil society" as a "form of dialogue" which "does not disguise but brings to light the differences of men" (1966h, 592).

But the main reason for breaching the walls of mutual American unintelligibility was not simply social survival—the sense of collective solidarity necessary for any group. The reasoned breaching of those walls was necessary for America if it was to live consistent with its founding "great act of faith in the moral sense of the people," the American specification of the authorization principle. And then Murray attempted to reach behind the authorization principle, to generalize his own conviction that the moral forces necessary for our modern world had to be unlocked in a manner consistent with the makeup of modern society, that is, that only through the mature exercise of public discussion could the moral direction of any modern society be initially and continually shaped. The mature moral direction of society must be formed through reasoned public debate.

It is therefore little wonder that the notions of "conversation" and "dialogue" permeated Murray's reactions to the Vatican Council and to the debate about religious liberty. In a brief eulogy for John XXIII, Murray suggested that John would be remembered as the pope who started something new in the modern church. "He started the bishops talking, not privately to Rome in terms of questions and answers, but publicly to one another in a free interchange of argument." He was not a pope of answers, but of questions, "notably the great, sprawling, ecumenical question—to which he returned no definitive answers.... The symbol for him might well be the question mark—surely a unique symbol for a Pope" (1963a, 855). John attempted to draw all the faithful into conversation, but even further, because of him "it is also not possible now to impatiently turn away from any of the voices, within or without the church, of whom it can be said that the Pope once listened to them." The Council itself was a "splendid event of freedom" and of dialogue which will forever mark and alter the church (1966i, 734).

Now, as Murray confronted civil and church members who relied on coercion for the sake of social survival, he found the fundamental disagreement between them and himself to be not simply a question that was open to empirical verification. The disagreement concerned a more fundamental cognitional reality than could be supported or denied by empirical analysis. Generally, such a reality might be called a "perspective," and in this case was an evaluation of, and commitment to, the moral possibilities of the people—that they could be socially moral and committed. At the end of his American debate he argued less that Americans are in fact moral, than that they ought to be moral; and at the end of his religious liberty debate he argued that the main task of the church was the engagement of active moral will. Those who would rely on coercive force in the public shaping of any society differed from their opponents not so much in factual matters of judgment, as in a fundamental perspectival orientation toward their fellow human beings. Such a perspective is prior to empirical verification; it rather shapes the questions and the data used in empirical arguments and verifications, as well as the methods to be used in public argument. There is, Murray found, a level of choice that has to do more with the directions of the human heart than with sweet analytic reasoning, but that is also fundamental to the formation of social reality and the meanings that constitute that reality. Perspectives can be adopted which make the moral shaping of modern society impossible; likewise, other perspectives can be adopted which facilitate the moral forces necessary for an ethical and just society.

Now, granted that modern society is, as the sociologists say, permanently differentiated: technically, culturally, socially, cognitionally, theologically. Granted further that modern society is historical: new responses are continually demanded as new questions arise out of that differentiated mix. What is required to respond morally to such diversity and social movement?

The answer that Murray now suggested was a series of perspectives, one (and the most fundamental) of which was the authorization principle. In this chapter, I will take up several other, new "perspectives" which Murray, during and after the Council, judged to be necessary for moral action between the church and civil society, as well as within both. Here, however, these new perspectives concern not so much the temporal realm as defined in his first, "essentialistic" religious liberty argument, but rather enter into the very definition of the church itself. There was much implied movement in his understanding of the church, but he became capable of explicitly exploiting these new understandings only in light of the new conciliar perspectives. And with these perspectives, Murray deepened his appreciation of both the novel problems facing the church and the differentiated or pluralistic nature of that church, thus requiring, again, communication within such a differentiated church.

The first was a "new ecumenical perspective" that, in Murray's judgment, tore at the walls which separated the various Christian churches. Murray seems to have accepted this new perspective wholesale from the Council, not expanding its theoretical ground, but only working out its implications for ecclesiology and ecclesiological action. The first section of this chapter will take up the implications of this new perspective for Murray's ecclesiology, and the shift in what he considered the major point of difference between Protestantism and Roman Catholicism. Be it also noted here that Murray now could and must allow for theological discourse within the civil, public forum.

Murray's adoption of the new ecumenical perspective led him, secondly, to search for another new (theological) perspective that might reintegrate or open another closed wall between the church and its environment, namely, that which separated the church and its generally atheistic civil culture, including Marxism. Here, Murray will attempt to generate the content of new perspectives that will facilitate that conversation. To do so, he will again formulate a notion of civil, but also, more importantly, intrachurch differentiation in terms of belief and morality. The church as well as civil society itself, he will maintain, must be understood as internally differentiated by varying degrees of unbelief and immorality.

Third, within these ecumenical and belief perspectives, with their consequent notions of a (possibly) permanently differentiated church, Murray took up a form of intrachurch and intrasocietal differentiation which must be considered a good for both human society and for religious society, namely, the differentiations of human consciousness as defined by Lonergan. Murray considered cognitional differentiations to be permanent factors of any modern society, but also to be potential sources of social walls, or of intrasocietal war. That diverse individuals and subgroups can have different understandings and (in Lonergan's terminology) different self-appropriations of human consciousness implies a permanent state of social pluralism. Murray will suggest "diction" as a method of conversation that might bridge those permanent social divisions, and another "new perspective" through which they might be reintegrated.

Shortly before his death, with these three new perspectives more or less firmly in place, Murray again turned to the problem of integration within the historical, social church. For this, he tried to generate an image of the church, or a fourth new perspective which would grant a primacy of importance to those forces which could generate social meaning within the church's field of developing social and historical questions. He did manage to shape the main outlines of this perspective, and he suggested some of the ethical requirements that such a perspective places on the authoritative structures of the church, as well as on the church's *studium* and the people in general. But, by way of conclusion to this chapter, I will return to the notions of reason with which he was then operating, and suggest what appears to be a fairly radical limitation placed on the church's magistery. The reasons for this limitation will be found to rest in his notion of the church as a social, historical body that is called to act morally in the modern world.

For all four discussions, the need to breach social walls will be seen to arise for the church from the gospel imperative to preach the good news.[1] But the very historical nature of this public quest for socially held truth generates, according to Murray, some of those walls and also demands the methods of freedom in their breaching. Murray now had a common social, moral perspective for parallel discussions of responsibility toward public meaning in both civil and religious societies.

The following, then, is a presentation of four new perspectives that Murray adopted, in order that he and his church might deal more responsibly with the world in which they lived. The radicalness of his conversions to these perspectives will be highlighted by an initial presentation of his preconciliar attitudes toward ecumenism, atheism, and civil and religious societies. It will appear that only a deepening sense of the historicity of even religious meaning can account for the postconciliar shifts in his thinking. The adoption of these perspectives, in Murray's judgment, is a requirement for his church to respond ethically to its God.

I. THE ECUMENICAL PERSPECTIVE.   At no time during Murray's life did he entertain the notion that the institutional and credal religious divisions of Western society were a good thing, good for either civil society or for the religious fabric of the people. For him they always remained a scandal, a social structure which was against the will of God and, therefore, a source of social disintegration. He did at one point accept religious pluralism as an "eschatological fact," but the force of that judgment was directed only toward the Catholic argument for religious liberty, not toward a theological affirmation of good within the Protestant churches.

Murray's distrust of the possibility and effectiveness of intercredal conversation was deeply rooted. In his first published article, "A Crisis in the History of Trent," he claimed that the ecumenical attempts by Charles Guise merely demonstrated that the chasm which had opened between the churches was in principle unbridgeable and permanent.

> [Guise] did not realize that what had happened was not a split on any specific problem of theology which could readily be patched up by a little sweet reason . . . , but that it was a complete revamping of man's whole relation to God, a subversive questioning of the very foundational principles of religious life (1933, 768).

Within his 1940s intercredal argument, Murray denied even an analogous base for intercredal discussion of theological issues (and even recommended against them), even though he insisted on the need for social-ethical discussion and cooperation. And during the Second Vatican Council, Murray asserted that the Roman Church has its own way of theologically grounding religious freedom, the Protestant churches have their own, and neither should get in the way of completing the intercredal affirmation of juridical religious liberty (1966d, 676, note 3).

Something of a radical shift in Murray's own attitude toward, and definition of, ecumenism occurred during the Council. In 1963 he began a secondary argument for religious liberty on the basis of a "new ecumenical perspective."

> We are living in the age in which a great ecumenical hope has been born. The goal of Christian unity lies, of course, beyond the horizons of our present vision. We do, however, know that the path to this far goal can lie only along the road of freedom—social, civil, political, and religious freedom (1966j, 703).

A year later, Murray referred to this new ecumenical spirit as a fundamental shift in perspective, akin to the political shift from the people as passive to the people as the primary social, moral agents, and akin to the cognitional shift from classicism to historical consciousness.

> Another theological instance of perspectival shift confronts us today, as the polemical question (Who has the one true faith—Catholic, Protestant, Orthodox?) gives place to the ecumenical question (How shall Catholic, Protestant, and Orthodox move together toward unity in the true faith?). A change of perspective has occurred which affects almost every single theological issue and will surely result in an enrichment of the Christian tradition (1964c, 239).

Then Murray suggested that the notion of religious freedom, even in its theological dimensions, might be a beginning point for ecumenical discussions, since the Vatican decree was consistent with the World Council of Churches' definition of juridical religious freedom (1966a, 581).

Murray readily admitted that the new ecumenical spirit had its first birth among the Protestant denominations, as the movement resulted in, and was facilitated by, the National Conference of Christians and Jews and the World Council of Churches (1967g, 91). But, with the 1964 Vatican Decree on Ecumenism, the movement has been given a new birth. Murray described himself as only a new convert to ecumenism, for he was trained theologically to view an interest in ecumenism to be something outside of his own Catholic faith. Now, however, "we have to see to it that theological students are, as it were, born ecumenists ... that ecumenism becomes a quality inherent in theology, as it is an impulse intrinsic to Christian faith itself." This imperative to preach the Gospel, therefore, was considered the first basis for the Catholic initiation into intercredal theological conversation.

Further, the Vatican Council newly recognized a second base for ecumenical discussion through its realization that the definition of the church as used by Leo XIII was no longer sufficient to the reality of the Christian church (1966h, 582–83). For Leo the church was simply the Roman Church, and his discussion of church-state or church-society problems remained institutionally specific. The Vatican Council, however, has affirmed that the contemporary religious problematic must be defined in terms wider than Leo's: "religion in its full ecumenical sense and human society throughout the wide world" (1966h, 583). Further, the Roman Church now recognizes that its very reality as a salvific agent is fractured, and that all divisions of that Christian church have had and do have a role to play in the constitution of Christian society and in the advancement of salvation history (1967g, 91). In a clear reversal of a 1944 statement, Murray judged that the Protestant churches are constituted as agents of salvation by valid preaching, baptism, and other sacraments (1969, 79). In sum, then, the Council has affirmed a valid, essential place for the Protestant churches in the order of grace.

Murray would now grant both an internal and an external basis for the Roman Church's entry into ecumenical discussions. The internal basis is the Gospel imperative to preach to all peoples, including Protestants. The external basis is the "fact" that the church's own salvific reality has been historically fragmented. Although such fragmentation is scandalous, Murray then concluded that no full discussion of theological issues within the Roman Church can take place except in dialogue with the other Christian denominations, in conversations which have as their ultimate goal Christian unity (1967g, 91). The truth of the ecumenical church's fragmentation implies common interaction in the pursuit of new religious truth.

It is in light of Murray's "conversion" to an ecumenical perspective, I believe, that some of his Trinitarian discussions should be understood. In the last chapter, similarities were noted between Murray's discussion of the Nicene problem and the nineteenth and twentieth century religious problematics. Both entailed fundamental shifts in perspective, which were brought on by shifts in governing questions and were affirmed by the magisterial church. In the notes to Murray's own Trinity course, he attempted to adopt and use comprehensively (toward the end of his life) Lonergan's notion of the Nicene perspectival shift (1966j, 3).[2] The Arian problem brought the church from a *quoad nos* to a *quoad se* theological perspective, from a biblical descriptive to a definitional or definitive realm of discourse. The Nicene decrees not only rejected the Arian answers to the new questions, they also sanctioned a differentiation of human intelligence and the use of that differentiated intelligence in religious matters. To return to a solely biblical, descriptive mode of discourse would have been an archaism. Further, the Nicene decrees initiated the scholastic theological tradition, which culminated in the further differentiation of religious language in the systematization efforts of Aquinas and others.

In the midst of another discussion of Trinitarian doctrine and theological development, Murray commented:

> I am not at all sure that this whole complex issue has yet been recognized as decisive in its import for the ecumenical dialogue. I shall, however, register my own conviction in this regard. I do not think that the first ecumenical question is, what think ye of the Church? Or even, what think ye of Christ? The dialogue would rise out of the current confusion if the first question raised were, what think ye of the Nicene homoousion (1962d, 53).

Now, if Murray was being true to his new ecumenical perspective (and I think he was), then it would seem that he understood a primary item standing in the way of reunification to be an acceptance of the various differentiated modes of approaching revelational issues, as the modes and their methods had developed over two Christian millennia. He was, of course, still concerned with structural, institutional differences and doctrinal discrepancies, as well as with the entire notion of religious authority. But, within an ecumenical perspective, Murray appears to have been defending a cognitional *pluralism* as based on historically developed differentiations of consciousness. That which is distinct about the Roman Church is its recognition and preservation within its own self-definition of (some of) those pluralistic modes of theological and ethical discourse. An ecumenical conversation or dialogue which has as its ultimate goal the reunification of the fragmented church must face the cognitional differentiations of the Christian tradition and the resulting social pluralism within the Christian community.[3]

Murray was never very happy with the institutionally specific claim that no salvation was to be had outside of the (Roman) church. In his new ecumenical perspective he further granted that the divided churches are indeed institutional agents for the salvation of non-Catholic Christians—Protestants did not simply have to make it on their own. And, as I will argue, his notion of ecumenism and of the forces of grace as active in institutions spread far beyond the institutional Christian church(es) (1969, 75). The question of Christian reunification, therefore, did not, at this point, immediately nor absolutely involve the problem of salvation. The question, however, did entail a recognition of the breadth of the human response to grace—as that breadth was developed through the various differentiations of human understanding. The ecumenical problem therefore became one of the preservation and development of the human understanding of God. The role of the Roman Church in ecumenical discussion was at the very least the preservation of some modes of the perception of the divine, the defense of a type of pluralism. In this, Murray's concern for the ecumenical discussions was similar to his concern for discussions within civil society.

II. THE SOCIAL DUALISM AND "BELIEF" PERSPECTIVES.   The Protestant-Catholic wall of unintelligibility was considered to be insurmountable throughout most of Murray's life, but that wall which separated the Catholic and the atheist was even more formidable. Prior to the Council, Murray had encountered three distinct types of atheism. The first was the Continental *laïque* political philosophy which would restrict religion entirely to the internal forum, and which initially defined democratic freedoms as extensions of social atheistic principles. A second brand of atheism was American secular humanism, with its near total control over the American educational establishment. And, finally, there was Marxism, the antithesis of Western cultural ideals, driven by a conviction that all reference to God must be eliminated from both the social and the private arenas. Prior to 1960, Murray had achieved something of a standoffish truce with American secularism (a recognition of its permanent place within the American social scene), but he was hesitant to grant it any theoretically valid place within that scene. He called for a united Protestant and Catholic effort to eliminate the secularistic vacuum at the core of the American social spirit. In the early 1960s, Murray's response to Continental laicism and to Marxism, however, was undaunted by any hint that the Christian churches had anything to learn from either of them, much less that the churches must enter into dialogue with them and thereby forge social links with them.

In this section, I will again set up an initial contrast term, this time a fairly recent, 1962, article on the rights of the atheist. Then, under the impact of Murray's extended ecumenical perspective, I will outline his attempts to generate new perspectives which might lead to a new break in the wall between Christianity and atheism—new perspectives that would facilitate conversation. The first such attempt was based on an understanding of secularism as an outgrowth of Christian social dualism, and as in part a reaction to the church's use of coercion. The problem here is understood to revolve around legitimate secular freedom and the church's inadequate response to it. The second perspective for the Christian-atheistic dialogue was an analysis of the call to faith at the core of the revealed order of grace. The first perspective was an attempt to understand the links between the church and nineteenth century political atheisms, the second was a search for links between the church and twentieth century forms of atheism. Now, both of these perspectives, taken together, generate a third perspective that must enter into the Christian-atheism conversation, namely, the perspective of the faithlessness and sinfulness of the church, not only in its parts, but also in its institutional entirety. The church itself is thereby understood to be internally and historically divided in religious and moral terms. This final perspective, Murray maintained, is necessary for the Christian-atheist dialogue—a dialogue itself necessary for the preaching of the Word.

In 1962, Murray was still attempting to ward off any suggestion of a legitimate place for atheism in the social conversation, or of a valid ethical argument for the civil rights of the atheist. In his 1962 article,[4] "Le droit à l'incroyance" (1962e, 91–92), Murray discounted any ethical argument which would support equal legal, social rights for believer and unbeliever. In this article (which was similar to those conscience-based arguments that he had rejected since 1947), he claimed that the rights of the atheistic conscience, as an internal matter, did not lead to a right of social expression. So far, this was consistent with his denial that one can derive a social right from the individual forum. As he had already claimed, the rectitude of conscience is not particularly germane to an argument for a political right. Murray went further, however, to claim that the state could not be indifferent to the social promotion of "a-theistic," "a-social," "a-moral" propaganda within the body politic. As a-social and a-moral, atheism could claim no social rights of expression (1962e, 91). Missing from Murray's argument was any notion of limitations placed on government. While the state is not competent to judge between revelationally based claims, apparently for Murray the judgment between theism and atheism was within the natural law state's competence.

Murray, however, did find a pragmatic reason for not using police methods to suppress atheistic expression.

> Political experience demonstrates, in effect, that in our modern societies, the censure of the state and the measures of police are bad means of assuring the repression of ideas and activities, even those which work to sap the foundations of the common life. The worst evils which follow this type of repression are more grave than the worst evils which one seeks to eliminate. In this conjunction, a government could not prefer to exercise its right to repress atheistic propaganda (1962e, 92).

The atheist can claim no rights against God or government, but may be granted immunity only in the sense of tolerance. Further, "for a number of reasons, today, the defense of religion and of morality ought to return, in large part, not to repressive measures of government, but to the pressure of the common conscience and of public opinion" (1962e, 92).

Since the last of these 1962 French publications defines the form of atheism under consideration to be French Continental, and since the article appeared only in French, albeit in Montreal, one might infer that it was directed only at continental forms of atheism. However, there is little indication that prior to this date Murray considered any other basis for not suppressing atheistic secularism in American society. Even his appeal in 1959 to the permanent, "eschatological fact" of socially held atheism concludes only to the "permanent" judgment that suppression will lead to more social evil than will nonsuppression. No positive grounds for tolerance of atheists was offered.

If the Christian must civilly coexist with Continental and American forms of atheism, even in 1963 Murray resisted the notion that any such pragmatic basis for coexistence (and conversation) with Marxism could be reasonably advanced. Although he had found much to praise in John's *Pacem in Terris,* he did struggle over John's suggestion that the church must distinguish between "historical movements that have economic, social, cultural, or political ends" and "the false philosophical teachings regarding the nature, origin, and destiny of the universe and of man" which originally animated these movements (1963f, 613). Murray continued:

> I am not sure just what "historical movement" the Pope chiefly had in mind. I suspect that it was continental socialism, whose primitive inspiration was largely atheist. Perhaps the Pope's distinction has some relevance to the whole Marxism movement, but here its application would have carefully to be made (1963f, 613).

Murray then argued that John recognized that the nineteenth century Continental problem of God is now passé, but also that John acknowledged Marxism as presently a virulent attack on all that Western society holds dear. Even with this last alleged admission on John's part, Murray was still uneasy. He continued:

> There will be those who will think, as I do, that we have been given only limited guidance. The Pope did not choose to deal with an aspect of the matter that has been carefully covered by his predecessors, notably Pius XI. I mean the profundity of the current crisis of history out of whose depths the Cold War itself has arisen (1963f, 613).

Then he even suggested that "the spirit of confident hope which the Pontiff courageously embraces fails to take realistic account of the fundamental schism in the world today" (1963f, 612).

Murray's movement from a definition of Christian-Communistic relations as a state of all-out war advanced rapidly. He had, of course, praised John for opening a conversation with "all parties within and without the church" (1963a, 855). A rightful (not simply expedient) inclusion of atheism in that conversation seems to have jelled in Murray's thought during the Council. In contrast to his 1962 statement (1962e), Murray claimed in his annotations to *Dignitatis* that the *right* to civil religious liberty was understood by the Council to extend to the atheist, even though some at the Council (perhaps including Murray) were reluctant to put such a claim explicitly in print (1966d, 678, note 5). The need for a social conversation with atheism appears to be based on the church's mission to the secular order and the church's need to be responsive to the legitimate claims of that order. Such a conversation demands for its inception "reciprocity" and "equality" (1969, 6).

Murray proposed two distinct bases for a conversation with contemporary atheism. The first was the legitimate differentiation of the sacred and the secular orders; the second was intrinsic to the act of Christian faith itself, that is, intrinsic to the Christian historical, Trinitarian experience. I will consider these two bases separately.

A. Christian Social Dualism and Its Violations.   Just as the new ecumenical perspective had transformed Protestant-Catholic relations into a form of conversation, so Murray looked for a new perspective within which a Christian-atheistic conversation could be situated and initiated. His first suggested perspective was generated out of his notion of Christian social dualism (1966b, 6–7). For Murray, of course, the social, "ontological" shape of the contemporary world was divided between two distinct, relatively autonomous societies: the civil order and the (ecumenical) church. This notion of social dualism was itself a result of Christian revelation; the historical differentiation of the church and civil societies was consistent with, and indeed a historically induced dictate of, the Christian doctrine itself. The contemporary developmental term of the dualism principle was the self-denial on the part of the state of any competence in religious matters, as expressed in the American Constitution and the United Nations Charter. The principle of social dualism also entails a "self-denying ordinance" on the part of the church, an ordinance which finds its first expression in the refusal of the church to use coercive means for the advancement of Christian faith (1966b, 10). And, further, the church has had to admit that moral and perhaps even religious insights can legitimately arise outside of the church's own visible boundaries, to which the church must be attentive. The church has now affirmed the *secular* value of religious liberty.

This differentiation of the contemporary social arena, while legitimate, cannot, according to Murray, be the final term of Christian thought and action in the world. And, by way of forming a perspective which can lead to a reuniting of those two orders, without eliminating their differentiation, Murray turned to a notion of the causes of contemporary social atheism (1970, 17).[5] Within the proper autonomy corollary of dualism, the church must admit that its own use of coercive force has been, in certain situations, a cause of that atheism. "This itself was first recognized by Jacques Biennassis, in the sixteenth century, but has not become a dominant insight within the Church until contemporary times" (1970, 9). Just as have certain forms of modern atheism, so also the church has at times violated the principle of proper autonomy, thus generating the atheistic reaction.

As a correlative to this judgment of the church's complicity in the generation of atheism, Murray went so far as to suggest that Marxism itself was based on an ethical cry against the injustice of the social order, or, more explicitly, on "an exasperation with a God that forbears evil" (1962d, 104). Marxism is a response to the problem of evil and an attempt to "bring good out of evil," but without the God who would deny to peoples the freedom to transform their social environment.

Finally, this choice against God for the sake of the people's moral freedom and responsibility was at least in part spurred by the church's reaction to those legitimate civil freedoms by which the moral directions of society are, in the contemporary world, to be generated. It is, however, unclear in the present discussion if this causal activity on the part of the church was simply based on ignorance or further on moral or religious, willful fault. So far, Murray has simply argued from a common violation of proper autonomy by both the church and the atheist.

Murray has then attempted to understand contemporary atheism and the present state of social war in terms of the historical interconnections between Christian institutions and militant Marxist action. The task of the contemporary Christian is the generation of a new nonantagonistic atmosphere in conversation with the atheist that can lead to a new social reality. But this new social reality and a new conception of God's relationship to the social order can only reach term in conversation with the atheist, including the Marxist. The process of arriving at a term is an historical process, and as any historical term, novel insights and judgments must be allowed to arise in freedom (1970, 17). The truth that both the Christian and the atheist seek must be cooperatively formulated.

B. *The Perspective of Belief.*   Murray's search for a higher perspective for Christian-atheistic conversation did not stop at a history of institutional interactions or the need of mutual emerging intelligibility. He further attempted to situate different forms of atheism within a polarized conception of (graced) human consciousness, as human consciousness in faith confronts the reality of God. In his 1964 *The Problem of God,* Murray swept through biblical, Nicene, medieval, nineteenth and twentieth century attempts to face the Judeo-Christian God. In these attempts he sought the sources for multiple forms of atheism. Three millennia of the Western theistic problem have been determined by the answers which God gave to the Mosaic question "What is his name?," or in its Christian form "Who do they say that the Son of Man is?" (1962d, 6, 26). In response to Moses, the answer was given "I shall be there with you in power," and to the disciples of Jesus, "You are the Son of the living God" (1962d, 6, 26).[6] The questions and the responses set up four related levels of inquiry: (1) the "existential question" of whether God is with us now, (2) the "functional question" of what he is toward us, (3) the "noetic question" concerning how he is to be known, and (4) the "onomastic question" of how he is to be named (1962d, 16–17). The four questions, according to Murray, have governed the ongoing problem of God.

The biblical approach to the problem found expression in functional terms of interpersonal or intersubjective discourse (1962d, 23). God is with his people and God is with us in Jesus Christ. God will deliver his people. He is to be known in the history of his people and in the history of the community which formed around Jesus. However, in the enigmatic historical utterances of God and of God in Jesus Christ, there remains the fundamental mystery of God's own freedom (1962d, 12). The name of God is ineffable. This ineffability of God, in conjunction with his action in history, has set the basic terms of the Western theistic problem. God is "known" in the biblical sense of intimately involved with people and human history, but he remains transcendent to the realities which people can control through human reasoning. Finally, the person who would deny God's existence or, more precisely in interpersonal terms, his presence among us, is a "fool," a person of culpable ignorance who ignores the divine action and presence in human history (1962d, 78–79).[7]

Again, Murray followed Lonergan's Trinitarian analysis in suggesting that Arius had initiated a transposition of the problem of God to a new level of human discourse, from the biblical interpersonal categories to those of definition. Arius asked not what the relationship of Jesus to us is, but what the relation of Jesus to his Father is, whether Jesus is creature or creator (1962d, 39–40).[8] The Nicene responses were the affirmations that Jesus is on the side of the Godhead, preserving in a different mode of discourse the biblical affirmation that God is with us in Jesus Christ. This response, however, was doctrinal or at the level of judgment, not at the level of adequate understanding (1962d, 45). At this ontological level, Nicaea preserved the ineffability of the name of God by a "gnosticism of affirmation" and an "agnosticism of definition" (*homoousion* is not a "category"). A biblical paradox was transposed to a theological paradox.

Eunomius then tried to resolve the paradox by claiming that he did know the name of God, and that is *agennetos*, the Unoriginate (1962d, 61). This violation of the original historical experience of God and of Christ among his people was countered by the church fathers and eventually led to the Thomistic concept of analogical language. Murray held that Thomas' treatment of the five proofs for the existence of God is, in fact, an attempt at theological understanding, an attempt to scientifically control human language concerning the divine reality, not an attempt to rise from the level of understanding by simple logical operations to the level of doctrine or judgment (1962d, 75). In such analogical language, faith and reason have a point of contact, without reducing the one to the other.

The seventeenth and eighteenth century forms of atheism were called by Murray "academic" and "aristocratic" (1962d, 86). They were primarily attempts to attack the awareness of the existence of God through the forms of the theological understanding of God, and by understanding the human person and the world without God. They argued from the condition of the world to the conclusion that God does not exist. They ignored the fact that the human recognition or ignorance of God is at base a matter of affirmation or choice, not a matter of understanding (1962d, 88, 97). From the negative affirmation that they made (without realizing its nature as choice), they actively promulgated in the general social arena a single mode and method of knowing. Then followed the multiple attempts to reduce religious historical experience to the empirical sciences. There also followed the nineteenth century atheism of the bourgeois marketplace—a conviction that "man can prosper in the world without God" (1962d, 86). Atheism was therefore itself transposed from the level of understanding to that of action. From both the realm of understanding and the realm of action the denial of God's existence was thought to follow. In a sense, both were rejections of the polarity at the core of

Christian faith between *gnosis* and *agnosis,* as well as a rejection of the dualism of a sacred and a profane order of existence.

Twentieth century, "postmodern" forms of atheism have returned to the biblical problematic. Contrary to the modern pretensions about disproving through reason the existence of God, the Marxist and the existentialistic person of the theater admit that God is a beginning point of argument, not a conclusion (1962d, 105–6). The Marxist confronts the evil of human existence; the existentialist, the lack of human freedom. Within those historical problematics, they both conceive that they must choose for good and human freedom, on the one hand, or for God, on the other. And their choice lands on human good and freedom. The action following from that choice then is the active suppression of the notion of God in both public and private life. Neither argues from the experience of the absence of God, as do the death of God theologians.[9] Both argue that God must not be allowed to exist, he must be killed.

The Christian approach to the postmodern forms of atheism must center on the dialectical question of whether or not human existence is indeed more human and more free within the premise of God's nonexistence. Can human life be in any sense human without an awareness of God which includes both *gnosis* and *agnosis,* a knowledge and an ignorance of God which are both necessary aspects of the human turning toward God, or at least toward the Christian God who has manifested himself in history? (1962d, 120–21). Can a temporal political or philosophical system attempt to draw people's openness to the transcendent to itself without creating human tyranny? The choice is between recognition of ourselves as a people of God or a people of the state, in Murray's view. As the experience of God has been situated in history, so the resolution of the contemporary dialectical choice for or against God will have its effects in history (1969, 69).

Murray has attempted to understand the two dominant forms of contemporary atheism as outgrowths of the original biblical experience of God as present but ineffable. (Secularistic academic atheism was more or less written off as a transcended nineteenth century archaism, similar to the death of God theologies.) To opt with the Marxist for the materialistic dialectics of history is to opt for *gnosis.* To choose with the existentialist freedom within a universe which is ultimately absurd is to go with *agnosis.* Christian faith has itself given rise to the choices which threaten to enslave man.

In an article entitled "The Unbelief of the Christian" (1969), Murray reshaped in more familiar terms what he saw as the contemporary dialectics of choice concerning God. "Are there two histories or only one?" he asked (1969, 79). The notion of two histories grants that there is a history that is ultimately formed by man through the use of human intelligence, but also holds there to be another history, salvation history, "whose basic agent is the Spirit of God." These two histories are thought to be "distinct but not separate or separable.... They began at the same moment and they run together, but they are not homogeneous in kind" (1969, 70). The two-history perspective further asserts that "the salvation of man even within the finite horizons of human history is mysteriously dependent upon another mode of salvation of which the theandric history is the bearer" (1969, 70).

The "counterposition" to this Christian view of history is that there is only one history, shaped solely by humans. It is an atheism, but it is new in that it is based on the positive affirmation "of the human person, his dignity and his freedom" (and therefore a common starting point for conversation) (1969, 69). Yet, will not the goal of the enhancement of human dignity, as espoused by the new historical monists, be short-circuited by their very practice of historical, social monism?

Murray's immediate concern here was not, however, with the dialectics of choice. He rather sought to understand contemporary atheism "in the light of faith, and the immediate theological question is whether or not atheism can be integrated into the Christian understanding of the world, that is to say, of the two histories in their relationship" (1969, 71). First of all, the church must view itself as "situated in the interior of history and not above it, ... in the world and not apart from it" (1969, 74). The church therefore shares in all the movements which form the civil and cultural order; it does not exist in some "Platonic" universe. However, the church has not always recognized (one might say, "believed") that "the order of grace is not coterminous with the visible, historical, empirical church." To be true to its own faith, the church must recognize that:

> [t]he frontier between the kingdom of light and the kingdom of darkness does not coincide with the boundary, as it were, between the visible Church and something we call the world. On the contrary, an order of grace is pervasive through all human history, and the action of the Holy Spirit which supports history and is also somehow supportive of all human history, including secular history (1969, 75).

In a word, the claim of "no salvation outside of the (institutional) church" is now judged by Murray to be a sign of unbelief within the church. The church has denied the God who is with us in power.

Within this new perspective of the church's historicity, which also includes the notion of grace as operative outside of the church, the church must face its own unbelief, and in that recognition, realize that "by her own unbelief [and the isolationist slogans it has asserted] the church bears an intrinsic relationship to the unbelief of the world, as well as a responsibility for that unbelief" (1969, 81).

Further, Murray argued that the recognition of grace as operating outside of the church (the "anonymous Christian") must not dissolve the original biblical problematic of the believer and the willful "fool." But the original statement of the problem of God, in both the Old and the New Testaments, was shaped by a primarily *polemical* concern and was addressed primarily to the believer (1969, 74). The new conversation must be with the unbeliever and must be nonpolemical; such is within the new perspective set by Pope John. Willful unbelief must still be understood to be possible in today's world, but even as possible within the church itself. The institutional boundary separating belief and unbelief is dissolved, but not the reality of unbelief.

Murray was arguing, then, that because the church is involved in history, it remains open, as does secular society itself, to the possibility of unbelief. This possibility would seem to be inherent in the (historical) nature of faith itself, as outlined above. "Faith ... contains within itself the seeds of its own imperfection; belief itself contains the seeds of unbelief" (1969, 74). Both the church and the secular order as engraced fall within the same potential of salvation and damnation. But Murray did try to form an image of the (ecumenical?) church which would still preserve its special place within the working out of salvation history. The church must revisualize itself, Murray argued, as a "sacrament" in the more general biblical sense, as "even now" and "not yet" fully a manifestation of the Spirit's action in the world. "Even now the Church is, and is one, and is holy, and yet the Church is not yet one and not yet holy" (1969, 72). The church stands vertically within salvation history, while standing horizontally within human history.

Murray did not, within this discussion of a common perspective with atheism, pay much attention to the "holy" side of this eschatological definition of the church. One possible way of separating the "not yet holy" and the "holy" would be to claim that the institutional church is holy (sinless and believing), while the individuals within the church, including some of its leadership, are yet sinful and unbelieving. But Murray would not settle for this basis of differentiation according to faith. In a discussion of the Council's Dogmatic Constitution on the Church, Murray commented:

It was I who finally devised the formulation in Section 12: "even though there were some people among the people of God who did not act up to the example of Christ in regard of Christian freedom." That is the best that we could get from the Fathers, and you have no idea what a strain it was to get this much into the documents, namely that somehow or other, here and there, now and again, one or another person in the history of the Church may have not lived up to the fullness of Christian revelation (1969, 77).

He continued that, even within the image of the church as a sacrament of God's presence in the world, one has to admit that the institutional church "has been guilty of default, defect and sin against the proclamation of that Christian and human freedom which is inherent in the Gospel" (1969, 77). Of the institution, then, one must predicate Luther's *simul justus et peccator* (1969, 78). And, again, the ultimate ground for this sin toward the Gospel has been the unbelief of the institutional church itself.

By transposing the sacred-secular distinction from the institutional level to the level of history (without entirely dissolving the former), and by situating the institutional church within two coterminous sets of historical movements, Murray attempted to form a "higher viewpoint" within which the sacred-secular distinction (which had been previously taken to the point of dichotomy) might be reintegrated. He thereby removed the sharp biblical dichotomy between believer and "fool" from its role in defining the borders between the church and the world. Murray recognized that the church as a people is differentiated by its more or less holy members, and that the church as an institution is likewise differentiated from one age to another in religious-ethical terms of sinfulness and in soteriological categories of belief and unbelief, as these two indices are related to the church's witness in the historical world. Even the church within history can be more or less moral, more or less believing, more or less a clear witness to the reality of God in its midst. For Murray, history has entered into the heart of the church, thereby allowing room for the recognition of cultural, ethical and theological pluralism within the church and among the realizations of the institutional church at various times—a long move from his 1940s conception of the church. The church remains related vertically to the order of the Spirit's activity and horizontally to the secular history which is primarily the work of humans. At the level of interaction with human history, the church shares in all the moral and intellectual deficiencies, differentiations, and resulting pluralism that compose any human, historical society.

Such was the result of Murray's attempt to find a common perspective in which the Christian and the atheist could understand one another.

III. ONE MORE COGNITIONAL PERSPECTIVE.   In his attempts to initiate conversations with Protestants and with atheists, Murray fortunately had a fair amount of time to develop some perspectives for the conversations and to work out some of their consequent ecclesiological implications. In the ecumenism discussion, he started from the premise of an institutionally differentiated church, and formulated some notion of the manner and means by which those resulting divisions might be transcended. In the atheism discussion, he started from the premise of rightful differentiations between the sacred and the secular, and again tried to develop perspectives by which the Christian and atheist might work toward mutual intelligibility.

In this section, I will consider "differentiation"[10] in the specialized sense of differing perspectives on the attainment of truth. Much of this discussion depends on Lonergan's conception of those differentiations as spelled out in *Insight* and developed in *Method in Theology*. And the "cognitional differentiation" that most concerns us here is that of "historical consciousness," a notion that, as I have previously noted, Lonergan was himself developing in the mid-1960s. Here Murray adopts the notion, but only partially follows through on the ecclesiological consequences of it. More will be said in the next section and in the last chapter on the implications of such a recognized differentiation, and resulting pluralism, within civil society and within the church.

Again, it was only about 1966 that Murray began to catch on to Lonergan's notion of "historical consciousness" as a distinct differentiation on human understanding, a new perspective on the contingent and social nature of all human truth claims. Before that date Murray had used the term "historical consciousness" only as it applied to his own understanding of the prudential nature of ethical judgments. But by 1964 Murray was familiar with other Lonergan differentiations as spelled out in *Insight*, a familiarity that surfaced in an article on American education—the viewpoints and recommendations of which will be used in this section to guide my reflections on Murray's own response to what he considered the church's affirmation of historical consciousness. He regarded this affirmation of historical consciousness to be on a par with Nicaea's affirmation of dogmatic consciousness, and as therefore placing imperatives on church thought and discipline. But first, his discussion of cognitionally differentiated America.

A. Commonsensical, Humanistic, and Scientific Differentiations. Murray dealt with an epistemologically pluralistic American society in his 1964 "On the Future of Humanistic Education" (1964c). For many years the American educational system had, of course, been his battleground. As he now defined the problem, the battle at the core of the American spirit divided between three distinct manners of knowing: the "commonsensical" manner of most people; the humanistic understanding of the arts, philosophy and theology; and the scientific mode of the technological community. Relying heavily on Ellul, Murray claimed that the scientific mode had assumed, out of the battle between the ancients and the moderns, the top of the intellectual hill, from which it was gradually taking control of American social meaning (1964c, 232–33). There is a growing sense that "the People are to be managed," to be transformed into a "Freudian Proletariat," to be molded by a starkly limited scientific elite.

At stake here is Murray's notion of the moral direction of society by democratic means—the relation between the wise and the people in democratic interactions and conversations. Since society is becoming more complex, it does require increasing depths of expertise for the understanding of social forces and in the formulation of social policy. Despite his use of Ellul, Murray never could outrightly reject science as some type of compromise with the devil. Scientific and technical differentiations of consciousness are legitimate cognitive differentiations, resulting in legitimate forms of social pluralism. But the problem for a democratic society is the reintegration of that differentiated society, the generation of understanding between these legitimate sources of social pluralism. Otherwise, the direction, and therefore the moral direction, of civil society will be stripped from the people, and those of solely technical sensibilities will gain control of society's moral future. "Will civilization, which is an affair of the sciences, have overwhelmed *culture, which is the moral state of man?*" (1964c, 233).

Where scientific understanding does touch social policy and moral directions, there must be developed a form of "diction" through which scientific understanding is somehow conveyed to the people (1964c, 235–36, 242–43). This task, according to Murray, falls to the humanist, the person who can effectively convey meaning and the force of logic through common language. But, further, a new perspective must be formed within which the multiple forms of social meaning are reintegrated (1964c, 236, 245–46). All social sectors must come to "understand what understanding is" and how it "moves from the moment of wonder to the moment of the attainment of truth" (1964c, 242). They must come to recognize the differences in "the criteria whereby to test the validity of insight and the certainty of affirmation" in all that the mind can search out. If the American social conversation is to access the root American problem of meaning, then:

> One would understand the meaning of the verb "to know" and of the correlative verb "to be," when there is question of Aquinas, Aristotle, Locke, Spinoza, Newton, Einstein, Bohr, Goedel, Spengler, Shakespeare, Picasso, Mother Hubbard, and the man in the street, to cite random symbols of the modes of knowing: theological, philosophical, scientific, mathematical, historical, artistic, commonsensical. Here, I suggest, is the broad area in which the true lines of the philosophical battle of the books are to be drawn (1964c, 242).

Much of this presentation is, of course, consistent with *Insight* and the notion of the multiple forms of human knowing suggested there. But Murray's further concern is that complex and multiple forms of knowing must be socially recognized as valid and socially communicable, at least in what concerns public policy. As the moral core of democratic society, "we the people should know what [the scientists] are saying and what they are up to" (1964c, 243). Their conversation concerning social goods "ought, therefore, to be somehow open to the public." The integrating viewpoint which would make this conversation possible would concern the different methodologies and different orders of truth which must circulate within a truly human society.

Murray's divergence from Lonergan's interpretation of common sense will be treated later. It is obvious here, however, that Murray considered common sense to be the proper and valid mode by which the moral directions of society are publicly discussed, shaped, and appropriated. (This notion of common sense is nearly identical with his notions of consensus and prudential determination, as will be discussed in the next chapter.) He focused rather on the establishment of communication between those in the scientific mode of thought and those within the commonsensical, and seems to recognize that a potential tyranny can arise among both those of the commonsensical and those of the scientific differentiations of human cognition. He looks for a viewpoint on knowing that recognizes the legitimacy and limitation of both camps, i.e., a viewpoint that affirms a legitimate cognitional pluralism.

B. Historical Consciousness within the Church.   Murray had already judged that the church, either through a lack of insight or even perhaps through sinfulness and unbelief, had missed "the truth which is at the core of every error," in that case the truth of human dignity and human freedom as those truths were asserted by nineteenth century laicism (1966e, 7). By 1966, Murray added another truth to the list of those which the church had at least temporarily missed seeing in the midst of error. The modernist crisis had at its core the truth of the historical nature of human knowledge and of the church. Modernism was a false systematization of those truths, but the church initially reacted by throwing out the baby with the bath, taking or maintaining a "Platonic view" of itself and the truths which it holds (1966e, 11-12).

Happily, however, the affirmation of *Dignitatis Humanae* and the attitude of the entire Council indicate that the church is now pervaded by "historical consciousness." The church has recognized and affirmed the truth at the core of the modernist heresy, just as it has affirmed the truth of human freedom and dignity at the core of laicism. Murray therefore judged that at last the church's magistery has recognized and adopted a further differentiation of human consciousness, much in the line of the Nicene definitional mode and the Thomistic systematic mode.

For Murray, this optimistic evaluation of the magisterium's appropriation was partially reinforced by the church's 1967 majority report on artificial birth control. In that report, a majority of the Pontifical Commission endorsed the use of some forms of artificial birth control. Murray responded to the majority report by claiming that the majority recognized the historical nature of church teaching.[11] That report, he held, was permeated by historical consciousness and the insight that truth must be "intelligently conceived and rationally affirmed." Within the modern world, the church's theology of marriage is now inadequate to the new social forces which in part define marriage. The majority recognizes that one must examine the "total situation of the problems of reproduction, including the novel demographic dimensions of the human community" (1967j).

The minority, classicist view has not recognized the new historical perspective of the church. They consequently ignore the shift in the total cultural and demographic factors which must lead to a redefinition of the birth control problem. But at core, the minority viewpoint remains locked within the classicist view of authority.[12] They do not recognize that the "church reached for too much certainty too soon and went too far" in preconciliar attempts to address the problem, and that the issue of certainty is distinct from the issue of authority. The majority opinion recognizes that a caution in arriving at moral truth might itself be a proper function of church authority, as church authority is understood from the perspective of historical consciousness (1967i).

The birth control issue, like the religious liberty question, was an ethical problem, only indirectly touching theological issues of a

Nicaean caliber. Recalling, however, Murray's judgment that a major point of the new ecumenical discussion must concern the doctrinal, definitional, and systematic modes and methods of understanding theological truths, then surely this development of historical con-sciousness, another mode of knowing both religious and ethical realities, was, in his own understanding, joining the languages by which faith legitimately expressed itself in a historical church. Thus, Murray's conviction that the Second Vatican Council had endorsed a differentiation of consciousness on a par with Nicaea would have perhaps made *Humanae Vitae* particularly difficult for Murray to endorse.[13]

Be that as it may, it seems clear that, among the other differentia-tions within the church which Murray had recognized in the ecumeni-cal and atheism discussions, a further set of differentiations in the Lonergan perspective of human consciousness could be added to the list. The church that he was now encountering was permanently and legitimately pluralistic, with a constant need for reintegrating view-points and discourse. Murray needed a new perspective on the church by which these multiple differentiations might find unity in the one church, and structures within which unity could be repeatedly generated. I will now turn to Murray's attempt to bridge the gaps between these multiple differentiations.

IV. A NEW ECCLESIOLOGICAL PERSPECTIVE FOR UNITING A NECESSARILY DIFFERENTIATED CHURCH.   It is not surprising that Murray's 1960s conception of the internal life of the church circled around the notions of freedom and conversation. There were, however, two distinct movements in the formation of this new perspective. Murray first attempted in 1963 and 1964 to parallel his civil political theory (as developed in *We Hold These Truths*) with his longstanding, fairly unexamined, ecclesiology. The basis for this paralleling was the notion that both the body politic and the church are societies, although distinct in origins and ends. It should be recalled that at this time Murray was arguing for civil religious freedom on the grounds that it was a legitimate moral insight that has arisen independently in the secular order, to which the church ought to be attentive. However, this grounding for democratic social theory and its application to the church ran immediately against his conception of magisterial author-ity, leaving Murray with a dialectic contradiction that required a higher perspective within which to relate church authority and the forces needed for the church's own internal growth.

Murray's second attempt at a new perspective, which surfaced in 1965, reached beyond his democratic social theory (based in a rightful autonomous development in the secular order) to his notion of moral agency developed after the Council. Within this new perspective, the languages of freedom and conversation remained constant, but some rather distinct changes in Murray's understanding of the church as a society (now called a "community") and his understanding of Christian freedom within the institutional church, led him to a stronger emphasis on the forces by which the church ought to be integrated and reformed. Murray had to expand his notion of the church, and thereby to transform and balance his notion of church authority.

A. A Contradiction Calling for Dialectic Resolution.   Soon after he was admitted to the conciliar discussions, in an address to Catholic journalists, Murray attempted to define the functions and freedoms of the public press within the church by an appeal to his American sociopolitical theory. Although the church is a society *sui generis*, it is still possible to find an "analogy" for understanding Catholic journalism's function in the church in the secular press' freedoms and functioning within civil society (1964d, 8). Within contemporary social organization, the freedom of the press is judged to be a "social necessity" based on the need for the moral direction of society.[14] Modern political theory is based on two principles: "the consent of the governed to executive legislation," and "the participation of the people in the processes of government" (1964d, 8). These principles of consent and participation require a dialogue between the people and the government, the vehicle for this conversation being the press. The dialogue between the people and government as facilitated by the press is the structural basis through which the further dialogues of society take place. "The multitude is civilized, made civil precisely by the fact that throughout the whole social body there is continually taking place this conversation among the people" (1964d, 9). These ongoing conversations concerning politics and culture are the means by which society is integrated. In principle, the need of a free people for information, for conversation, is "unlimited," although in some cases the people may judge that certain information concerning "such things as military security" should be held from public discussion (1964d, 9). But it is the people who are the judge of such limitations.

The application of this political theory to the "analogous" church society begins to show its differences immediately in the fact that "there exists among the people no *right* to judge, correct and direct the actions or the teaching of authority" (1964d, 9). Murray's longstanding but mostly unexamined principle of final magisterial authority still apparently holds. However, the church as a *social,* human reality "creates a public *right* to information about all that concerns the

Church" (1964d, 9). The cultural, social, integrative requirement for information exchange still holds for ecclesiastical society. Murray therefore concludes that "within the Church, as within civil society, the need of the people to know is in principle unlimited," and therefore "there ought to be no arbitrary limitations imposed upon the dissemination of public information within the church" (1964d, 9). (Presumably, the church has no "military security" concerns.)

Murray has, then, claimed that there exists "no right to judge, correct and direct," but also that there exists "a social right" to information. The crunch point in Murray's argument is a definition of "arbitrary limitation" and the location where such judgments are to be made. In another context, he stated that church conversations should be governed by the principle "as much freedom as possible, as much coercion as necessary," without offering a basis for this principle (1966a, 581–82). But here he offers two possible grounds for the application of this "jurisprudential" principle to the church's internal life. The first is the new personal and political consciousness of the people, their recognition of their own dignity and their right to direct political reality. One cannot demand a schism within the Christian people in their political and ecclesiastical living. "The self-conscious citizen within the civil community cannot be expected to be simply a passive subject within the community of the church" (1964d, 10). Second, Murray suggested that the press has a responsibility (and therefore a right?) publicly to note abuses of authority and thus to "serve the true interests of authority." It is to the interest of authority that its method of exercise should be "pure, free of all taint of the arbitrary" (1964d, 10). If such mutual openness and information exchange between the people and authority is not maintained, then a spirit of confidence between them will disintegrate, taking with it the general pastoral effectiveness of the church.

To my reading, there is here a dialectical contradiction between Murray's absolute authority principle and his theory of socially constructive moral agency, a contradiction which in chapter 1 concerned the secular action of the laity,[15] but now applied to action within the church itself. In his discussion of the internal life of the church, there is no stated responsibility, and therefore no right, of the people to judge, correct, and direct the collective existence of the church. That is, the people are not conceived as having an actively shaping, ethical role toward their common religious meaning. And yet, in his civil social studies, Murray has been increasingly basing his case for natural law theory and for the necessity of freedom on the authorization principle—the active, ethical agency of the people—which principle he would in 1965 generalize beyond its mere Anglo-

American incarnation. In civil society the people are under obligation to shape the institutions under which they live; in the church that active obligation of forming ecclesial institutions and beliefs has not yet been recognized or formulated.

The ultimate culprit behind this activism in the one arena and passivism in the other appears to have been Murray's earlier notion of civil-social knowledge as temporal and church-revealed knowledge as permanent/timeless. The temporal/permanent distinction had initially allowed Murray to claim the impermanence of church-state institu-tionalizations, while yet maintaining his own "Platonic" notion of revealed truth. The residual of that distinction still affected his arguments in 1964. However, as described in the next section, Murray's postconciliar move toward active moral agency allowed him to develop beyond this contradiction.

But there was also another basis for letting the contradiction ride in 1964 that rested in Murray's quite practical evaluations of the state of the church. In a 1963 interview, Murray reiterated his mid-1950s negative judgment concerning American Catholics. In a discussion of a possible revitalization of the laity and lay assumption of religious responsibilities, Murray wrote that, in regard to "the run of the mill American, I am very skeptical" (1964e, 351). Again, concerning the bishops and collegiality,

> I believe that the bishops themselves do not really believe in [collegiality]. ...Practice has shown that the individual bishop considers his own vertical line to the Holy Father rather than anything like a horizontal line of unity with his fellow bishops in governing the Church (1964e, 347).

Any transformation of the people, or the bishops, or even liturgical practice will be extremely difficult and a long time in coming. With such estimates of the ability for responsible action among the bishops as well as among the people, it is little wonder that Murray was slow in facing the social and cultural forces of his church.[16]

B. A Dialectic Shakedown.   It appears, however, that the conciliar discussions, particularly during the third session, significantly boosted Murray's hope for conversation within the church, and consequently gave him a practical ground for changing his own perspectives on the church. Within the religious liberty discussions, Murray had briefly sought a new conception of the church in the image of a "family of God," but quickly shifted from this interpersonal image to the sociopolitical image of the "People of God" (1963i, 451–52). He had encountered the conciliar difficulties in arriving at an affirmation of religious liberty, and then at a common understanding of the grounding for such an affirmation. But the conversation did indeed result in a consensus. After the third session, with its delayed vote but with the affirmation clearly in sight, Murray wrote: "in the end, a doctrinal decision on religious freedom was postponed for a year because it had already been postponed for some two hundred years" (1965c, 43). And the reason for both postponements "was that free discussion of the real issue had been inhibited within the Church by the power of the Holy Office." No consensus could develop in the church without free discussion, but now that consensus was developing in that great "event of freedom."

Soon after the adoption of *Dignitatis Humanae*, Murray noted that some of the opposition to the declaration was based on a fear that the political concept of religious freedom would be recklessly applied to the internal life of the church (1965c, 42; 1966d, 694, note 58). With little hesitation, however, he himself began to work toward an "analogous" notion of Christian freedom and its role within Christian society. For him, this again meant the formation of a higher perspective within which apparent contradictory principles could be integrated, in this case the principles of authority and freedom. Murray's first call was for an elimination of the bureaucratic blocks between the pope and his bishops, between priests and laymen, thereby decentralizing the church, initiating more freedom and more direct contact between the various functionally differentiated orders within the church (1964e, 10).

However, as he had done for the ecumenical, atheism, and cognitional discussions, Murray tried to move beyond mere structural suggestions to a new image of the church which would facilitate conversation within the church across the moral, religious, and cognitional differentiations that he had discovered. He abandoned the term "People of God" (but not the notion of consensual society), preferring rather the term "Christian community." The Christian community is composed of two distinct sets of relationships. One is the relationship which defines authority, the critical relationship of command and obedience. Another, horizontal relationship is that of dialogue, by which the evangelical freedom of the Christian engages in the building of the church (1966i, 741).[17]

According to Murray, the modern problem for the church is not that of authority, nor even of freedom, but rather a "crisis of community" (1966i, 734).[18] The ongoing problem of community has been raised to the level of crisis by the historical problematic in which the church has found itself. Seventeenth and eighteenth century social forces directly challenged the authority of the church in moral and social-religious matters. The nineteenth century cast the problem in terms of the authority of God himself. The church accepted the terms of the challenge, and responded by "a certain hypertrophy of the principle of authority, and a corresponding atrophy of the principle of freedom" (1966i, 735). This problem was compounded by the type of authority models which were available to the church for its understanding of its own authority. The then socially dominant political models were clearly paternalistic and authoritarian, with the correlative imaging of the people as purely passive. Murray, therefore, now understood the church to have adopted a (faulty) political model understanding its own authority structures and role.

Any historical society "always has some kind of authority," entailing some form of obedience. But the insight which was lost to political and ecclesiastical societies was the dialogic, free nature of a community's historical relationships (1966i, 736). Vatican II has recognized, in the modern affirmation of human dignity, the parallel truth of the Christian equality in dignity and freedom within the church. It has recognized that the church is primarily a community, a communion in meaning, with the common functions of service and witness. The church is also, but only secondarily, a structure of authority and a juridical order.

In a sense, then, the church has relearned the truth of its basic constitutional dynamisms from a suggestion offered by secular society. Christian freedom has been recognized as a type of achievement which is never complete. "Man is never more than an apprentice in the uses of freedom. Their mastery eludes him. The possession of freedom, like the possession of truth, is the term, always only proximate, of an arduous education" (1967l, 320). The eclipse of the importance of freedom was in part "a failure on the part of the Church, her magistery and her people, chiefly the intellectuals" (1967l, 321). The "forgotten truth" is that of

> . . . the positive value of freedom within the People of God. It is the principle of doctrinal progress, of the growth of the Church toward more perfect inner unity, and of the widening and strengthening of relations between the church and the world, both religious and secular (1967l, 323).

Christian freedom is, in the final analysis, the love which forms the heart and reality of the Church as community. It is the will toward Christian community.

This newly regained insight into the requirement for, and primacy of, freedom/love within the Christian community should lead to a redefinition of the role of authority. Authority principally stands in the service of the freedom/love which constitutes the community. Its first function is to facilitate the "dialogue of salvation" (1966i, 737). It further performs this primary "unitative function" "through [its own] dialogue with the charismatic body of the faithful," recognizing "all manners of legitimate diversity and pluralisms—in rites, theologies, spiritualities, apostolate, etc.—which, so far from damaging the unity of the community, constitute an enrichment of it" (1966i, 737). The authority's second function is decisive or directive, a function which again is a requirement of most social bodies. The church lives by truth, by judgment, and therefore by decision and direction. However,

> ... [t]he performance of this *secondary* function supposes that the primary function has already been afoot between the community and its teachers and pastors; that therefore the decisions and directives, without ceasing to derive their force from apostolic authority, are also the decisions and directives of the community, whose common good they serve (1966i, 740).

The third function of authority is corrective or punitive, an accidental function which derives from the sinfulness of the church. The exercise of this function, however, is also in service of the primary unitative function, requiring therefore the exercise of due process.

> The demand for due process of law is an exigence of Christian dignity and freedom. It is to be satisfied as exactly in the Church as in civil society (one might indeed say more exactly) (1966i, 740).[19]

Murray, then, was attempting to break the Roman Church's preoccupation with a "hypertrophied" authority principle by suggesting that a fuller image of the church would include a social reality which was not simply, or primarily, the result of submission of the will. The authoritative instruments of the church are functionally defined as protective and instrumental toward the development of unity. Any diehard ultramontanist would, of course, agree that church authority had as its principal function the facilitation of Christian unity, without perhaps much concern for due process in corrective situations and for ongoing dialogue as a constitutional aspect of the directive function. What Murray seems to have been arguing for, however, is the recognition that the basic forces which unite the church must arise at the most basic level of Christian social reality: in the free interactions of the Christian individuals and in the free interaction of subsidiary or differentiated groups within the church.

And this interaction in freedom, which is an action of love, must be clothed in languages[20] that generate common understanding. The will to community responds to and furthers expressions of humanly formulated meaning. And the blind imposition of authority, outside of any communication of meaning, cannot generate the core reality of the Christian community. Save for the magisterium's decisive function (which will be taken up in the conclusion), the role assigned to church authority here is similar to Murray's notions of the role of governmental and educational-establishment authorities. It is a servant to the forces of public reasoning which generate public understanding.

Why should the church authority proceed within the maxim of "as much freedom as possible, as much authority as necessary"? Because the forces which constitute the church as a social reality are beyond the effective range of coercion or of blind direction. In one final article Murray again took up his three functions of church authority (as cited above), but here he specifically focuses on the church's *studium*. Concerning the relationship of the theological community and magisterial authority, Murray suggested that "the spirit of theological inquiry is immanent in the very dynamism of Christian faith itself," driven by a love of truth concerning God (1967c, 111). As new questions are asked throughout history, the theological community finds itself at the "growing edge" of the tradition. And

> ... the dynamism of this progress in theological understanding is, I take it, freedom and not authority. Hence I assume that the first function of authority is to foster the freedom of theological inquiry (1967c, 112).[21]

The theological community is somehow a "fraternity" in its own right, that is, it is in some sense differentiated and relatively autonomous. It is the role of the bishops to encourage a spirit of theological inquiry in those who are clearly in the theological "fraternity," and even among those Christians who are not.

Paralleling his discussion of the directive function, Murray discussed the directive role in relation to social, moral questions (not theological questions). And, of course, he had already suggested that the Church was a dialogic *partner* in the resolution of such issues. Further, the church must in its social statements practice a "self-denying ordinance." It must speak in terms of "what the whole Church can say for the whole Church, speaking to the whole Church, and speaking also to all men in the name of the Church, out of her own treasury of truth and wisdom" (1967c, 115). He continued that "this canon would surely make for responsible utterance." He has implied, then, that some form of consensual basis plays a role in the fulfillment of magisterial responsibility, if not for the "truth" of its utterances (although perhaps that), then for its social and moral effectiveness.

Finally, in the matter of heresy, paralleling the church's coercive function, Murray called for a distinction between adventurous answers which may well be mistaken, and hardened positions which deserve to be called errors. "The former are an affair of deficient intelligence; the latter, of deficiency in what can only be called good will. Errors in faith are a matter of will" (1967c, 116).

The church has claimed to be a community of faith, but a publicly scandalous discontinuity has opened between this claim (which is a religious reality) and the forms of Christian interaction. Until the church encourages the practices and reality of community (i.e., Christian freedom in conversation), its religious witness will remain clouded.

In the final reel, Murray has suggested a type of relative autonomy for the theological community, restraint in the exercise of the magisterium's moral directive functioning, and responsible use of coercive force, a responsibility based on ongoing discrimination between naive enthusiasm of immature understanding and hardened wills of unbelief and immorality. There has been, then, a gradual application of Murray's political terminology of rights, responsibilities, and autonomies to the interior life of the church. However, it might be good to thematize the shifting basis of those terms as Murray applied them.

In his civil religious freedom argument, the right of the people to judge, correct, and direct civil authority, with its correlative limitations placed on government, followed from the authorization principle—the ethical warrant for government action resting ultimately with the people. Religious liberty and all other freedoms as immunities were both a dictate following from and a means of facilitating the moral agency of the people. In Murray's 1964 journalism address, the authorization principle, as the heart of his ethical argument for civil religious freedom, was cut out of his intrachurch freedom argument by his notion of magistery. As yet, he appeared to find no basis for such freedom except in the rather expedient problem of a dissonance between civil moral agency and a lack of positive activity within the church. In that 1964 address, the right to information and the obligation to point out arbitrary uses of authority seem to hang, once again, in midair, as would perhaps the terms from any democratically formed language against an "adopted monarchical" image for church authority. Murray's suggested "right" to information did not seem to connote an active agency by the People of God. The conversation which follows from that right appears geared primarily to the formation of unity within the church through the passive reception of correct knowledge. The obligation to point out abuses in the use of authority does connote an active ethical function for the press, but the tone of Murray's argument seems to rest simply on the moral, professional integrity of the journalist (not being tied to any subdivision within the church); the press should simply present the facts. The basis for judgments of arbitrary usage is left suspended, the magistery having apparent warrant to final word on what is arbitrary and what should be disseminated through the press. Such was not Murray's intent, but he had not given sufficient bases nor criteria for those rights, obligations, and practices. His use of political language remains something of a foreign injection in his discussion of intrachurch actions.

That which created an integral place for such languages was the notion of the church acting through time. Murray's mid-1960s deepening awareness of the historicity of church thought and meaning led him to a preoccupation with the "growing end" of that meaning, and therefore with the ethical prerequisites for the advancement of that growing end. With these new concerns, his image of the church has in a sense been "turned on its head," and, in that new stance, the language of rights, responsibilities, and most particularly relative autonomies found a logical place within his discussion of freedom within the church. His conciliar civil religious argument was anchored in the ethical notion of human dignity (individual and social) and its protection; therefore, the rights there discussed were primarily thought of as immunities. Rights as empowerments were not central to a conception of civil religious liberty. Here in his intrachurch freedom argument, however, a right to freedom arises principally from a notion of freedom as an empowerment—an opportunity and an obligation to participate in the "growing end" of the church's necessarily new understanding of its past and present moral and theological universe. His notion of historicity, then, has been the key which unlocked his own long held conception of absolute papal authority. Limitations on that authority are found to be ethical requirements for the advancement of the church's understanding. Historicity did for Murray's intrachurch freedom argument what authorization did for his civil freedom argument: it constituted the main body of church membership as dependent on dynamisms which could not be violated by authority without risk of collapsing moral and religious meaning. The People of God and its various subgroups are relatively autonomous for ethical reasons; from them new meaning must arise.

Or rather, Murray had two distinct social-ethical bases for his limitations on the church's authority structures. One was the just mentioned requirement for new insights as the church spanned time—its Gospel-inspired response to its own historicity and that of the societies in which it found itself. Members must be empowered to respond creatively over time. The second social basis rested in the multiple legitimate differentiations within the church, differentiations in piety, morality, and cognition—the problem of church unity generated over space. As the church faces its own temporality and its own extension, conversations must be encouraged if the church is to forge its deepest reality, i.e., the bonds of love freely given. The people must be empowered, based on their ethical obligations and responsibilities toward their church itself and toward their civil societies, so that they might recreate those realities when they face the socially new and the socially diverse. Murray's church was now fully historical and fully social, requiring active moral agency on the part of its members.

The boundaries between the magistery and the church at large are, however, still somewhat unclear. Murray had one further index for the identification of those boundaries and the violations of those boundaries in arbitrary uses of authority. In the conclusion to this chapter, I will take up his distinction between understanding and judgment as a means by which responsible moral action within the church could be understood and the rights and relative autonomies situated.

V. CONCLUSION.   In Bernard Lonergan's 1972 *Method in Theology,* four essential imperatives are understood as rising from the four dynamic operations of human reason: "Be attentive, be intelligent, be rational, be responsible," corresponding to experiencing, understanding, judging, and decision or choice (Lonergan 1972, 6–13). Murray never did appeal to this explicit formulation, although all four imperatives and operations were active in his own thinking about civil society and the church.[22]

Now, there has been a movement in Murray's last ecclesiological considerations to limit the hierarchical structures of the church primarily to the intellectual operation of judgment. As Murray argued, any historical society demands a forum in which decisions and judgments are formed, where the truth of that society is addressed and consciously constituted. And within the church this responsibility is principally located in the magisterium, as exemplified in the Vatican Council, even as this process of coming to judgment is to be facilitated by free conversation.

But questions perennially emerge concerning the meaning of church affirmations. Murray pointed out that the original Nicene affirmations were not really acts of understanding, but rather judgments placed on the false responses of Arius and others. The word *homoousion* was not basically a category of understanding; it was a sign for an affirmation that the Son and the Father are the same in all things, except in name. It was then left to theologians to try to understand insofar as possible the truth which was being affirmed by such a magisterial judgment. Further, it was for the theologians to understand the differentiation of human consciousness that was being simultaneously affirmed by the Nicene Council, a differentiation of which the conciliar fathers were mostly unaware. Similarly, in the religious liberty decree, that which was affirmed by magisterial authority was the civil right of religious liberty. It is now the task of the theologian to understand what the affirmation means, and the grounding for that affirmation. Further, again, it is the task of the theologian to understand the inchoate affirmation of the historical differentiation of human consciousness that is implied in the declaration and the development of that affirmation from the time of Pius IX. Murray, then, has been separating the teaching or content communications function away from the primary definition of magisterial authority. How are these operations of understanding (localized in distinct theological discourse) and judgment (localized in the hierarchy) related?

The theological discourse of the church is an attempt to understand the truths which the church proclaims, as opposed to the act of judgment by which those truths are constituted as the church's. Now, since the church is a historical reality, its affirmations of truth are framed within specific historically complex factors that shape and form those questions which call for response. The constant task of the theologian is to understand the factors which entered into the church's doctrinal affirmations, perhaps with a clarity that escaped those who first pronounced those judgments, such as the political versus theological components of Pius IX's and Leo XIII's judgments concerning religious liberty. It was Murray's conviction that such judgments are always true, but that their truth must be understood afresh by a penetration of the complex factors which framed governing questions and perspectives. That which was rejected in nineteenth century political movements and in the modernism movement was rightly and truly rejected. But the perspectives out of which the rejections arose did not and do not exhaust the values which were at stake in those movements. The theologian must define the specific questions which were doctrinally addressed, and isolate those questions and responses from other valid questions concerning them.

Nor is the task of the theologian simply to come to a clearer understanding of the truths which the church has affirmed in the past. After the Council, Murray wrote that, with the time of doctrinal definition past,[23] theologians are not simply to quote and paste together such affirmations in the discredited nineteenth-century manualist style. It is the further task of the theologian to penetrate and understand the social and theological universe within which the church is presently situated (as a requirement for the pastoral mission of the church), and to know better the relationship between past problematics and doctrinal responses and present problematics and possible new doctrinal responses. New questions and new perspectives always present archaism as a possibility. If the church is to exercise its missionary function within the moral universe, and its soteriological function within the realm of grace, then it must gain insight into the frameworks which form the contemporary questions. And all of this searching for past and present understanding is not especially a function of the hierarchy.

Murray's suggested relative autonomy for the theological community was based on this notion of the magistery differentiated from the theological community in terms of judgment and understanding, respectively. He wrote: "the magistery is not a scientist—an exegete or a theologian or a professor of history. Its function is magisterial, not scientific. It is a function of judgment, not discovery; of affirmation, not explanation." A bishop, he said, can be a theologian, but only accidentally to his office (1967c, 112–13). His office is primarily one of judgment.

But, who then are the theologians of the church? In his discussion of the exchange of information in the church, Murray preferred to speak of the *studium* (1967c, 111). It is the function of the *studium* to be the forum for intrachurch dialogue. But Murray again, just as in his American discussions, had some problems defining the boundaries of that *studium*. The church's *studium*, he wrote,

> ...no longer exists in its medieval form, of course. It is more scattered in an age of general learning. To it now belong seminary faculties of theology, faculties in church-related colleges, Christian intellectuals (in universities, as writers, etc.), religious journalists (the latest accession). All are somehow engaged in "inquiry" in the wide sense that the word "theological" has today (1967c, 111).

It is this diffuse body of inquirers that the magistery is to encourage and grant "as much freedom as possible." Further, the magistery is to encourage theological inquiry among the general body of the faithful. One might explicitly suggest (as Murray did not) that in purely theological questions, the *sensus fidelium* can be, and must be, a source of theological understanding within the church, as that *sensus* was suggested as a basis for the dogmas of the Assumption and the

Immaculate Conception. Certainly, within Murray's thought, there is a strong base for suggesting that the forum for the church's understanding of ethical issues is the general body of the faithful, as the church must be reasonably responsible for the moral values that develop in civil society. Further, we can extend the notion of collective responsibility for theological understanding to all sectors of the church, as a requirement for active social participation in the shaping and appropriation of the theological truths that bind us together. And, if the people are to be so empowered, it would seem reasonable and moral likewise to extend the application of jurisprudential limitation on the church's authority structures vis-à-vis the full church community concerning all the realms of intelligibility that the church can and ought to intend.

If we take "understanding" in the broad sense as implied by both the church's historicity and pluralism (as discussed in the last section), then the restriction on the magistery would appear to be considerable. Coercive restraint can only be used against free conversation when there is involved a matter of hardened will, a matter of heretical judgment, rather than of immature understanding. And under the jurisprudential principle the burden of proof would seem to rest on the magistery. But, even in this case, a judgment that would issue in coercive restraint must, according to Murray, be made in conjunction with the relevant theological and moral "fraternity," since dialogue is to proceed and accompany authoritative judgments. Further, even the magistery's directive function (in both morals and religion) is constantly open to inquiry and examination, as theologians and the people seek out the intelligibility of such directives. Such scrutiny and the possibility of finding hidden factors which have entered into a directive could exercise considerable restraint on the hierarchy. Be attentive, be intelligent, be rational, be responsible! Murray finally suggested the court of public reasoning as the forum for the church's ongoing search for religious and moral truth.

Such were the results of Murray's last application of political, civil, and social analogues to the church, and their transformations within that consideration of the church. Murray had consistently maintained throughout these discussions his conviction that the church, even as a social body within a historical field, has its own particular ends and its own particular methods, that it is both a society and a society *sui generis*. But as a society situated in time, the church, he found, is governed by some factors which are common to all societies. Differentiation, coercion, and the requirements for the generation of insight and consensus remain inescapable factual and ethical elements which constitute a viable social-ethical conception of the church. Human reasoning in a collective sense permeates his analysis of the bases for the church's new understandings and judgments, as well as the bases for the fulfillment of the responsibilities that arise out of its God-given missions.

Despite the complexity of his argument as he weaved it together through the 1960s, Murray was not yet finished with it. Attentiveness, understanding, judgment, and responsibility have so far been considered in relation to the moral truths which develop within society at large, and to the religious truths which develop within the (ecumenical) church—as foundational operations for civil and religious societies. The operations and dynamics involved in the generation of common understanding and judgment have recast both civil and religious societies as social and historical. With responsibility for such operations and dynamics an element common both to religious and to civil society, Murray then attempted to generate another "higher perspective" within which to integrate further the relatively autonomous realms of civil and religious meaning. In the next chapter, the further point of integration will be found to be in a responsibility to the God who is the ongoing creator and redeemer of both societies. The agents of social development and decline, Murray will finally admit, cannot and should not cloister their conscious theistic responsibility within the narrow confines of their personal beliefs, away from public discourse, any more than they should ignore the distinctive realms of social realities and the obligations arising from those realities by confining their perspectives to the interpersonal. But, the starting point for such a public discussion of responsibility toward God will be a critique of the church's (and society's) witness to that God.

Chapter Six

HUMAN RESPONSES TO THE GOD OF HISTORY:

From an Ethics of Institutions to an Ethics of God's Presence

Throughout this study I have attempted to present Murray, not simply as an abstract arguer within the calm and dispassionate waters of academia, but rather as a social actor initiating dialogue with, and responding to, other social actors and the institutional and cultural forces of his historical environment—and this for at least two reasons. The first was to demonstrate that Murray himself was caught in the historicity that he was discovering, that only in interaction with the actual social realities surrounding him could he come to descriptive and normative definitions of forces—such as law, principles, consensus, social moral agency, state and church—that would be adequate to the social problems he faced. The second reason is correlative to the first, and foundational to it. Only as a social actor could Murray face the ideological elements of his own thought and attitudes, and thereby dialectically remove those elements. Murray's implicit practice of ideological criticism and the ethical requirements following from that criticism are the topics of this last chapter.

Now, the term "ideology" admits of at least two general definitions. In the first, ideology is used much as was the term "perspective" throughout this study—the recognition that governing viewpoints are formed in a social matrix and that the most fundamental viewpoints are more a matter of choice than of empirical or logical derivation. Those who hold this definition of ideology might differ considerably among themselves concerning the way a person or society shifts fundamental viewpoints, but the core of their sometimes strident stances is the recognition of the historicity of all human knowing. This definition of ideology is primarily descriptive.

A second and much more common definition of ideology regards as ideological any symbolic or rational belief system which masks those realities that are relevant to understanding and judgment, and particularly to a fuller understanding of the moral factors involved in human action. In common usage, ideology in this second sense conveys a judgment that someone's perspectives (the screens through which reality is interpreted) are personally or socially destructive.

That is, the term is used in a pejorative sense, and even in a morally pejorative sense. Again in common usage, the cry of "ideological" is most often applied to the arguments of those with whom we disagree. But, where more honestly employed, the recognition of the potential ideological warping of almost any human language demands the ongoing task of self-, as well as other-, criticism. The criticism suggested by this second definition of ideology is considered to be not simply descriptive, but rather normative, in the task of social ethics.

In this chapter I use the term primarily in its second, pejorative sense. Having been born into a specific historical age, with its own perspectives on the human person and social reality (ideology in the first sense), Murray found that some of those perspectives were ideological (in the pejorative sense), that they stood in the way of responding ethically to his world and to his God. He therefore had to shed those perspectives, generate and take up other perspectives, if he were to be a responsible member of his civil and ecclesial societies. The last chapter outlined that process of taking up new perspectives for the sake of increasing social dialogue, particularly as those perspectives concerned the church's own self-definition. In this chapter I review some of the earlier conceptual and perspectival shifts that Murray did manage to effect, but I also suggest directions in which his ideological criticism could, and ought, to proceed. Doing so requires studying somewhat more closely the root of that impulse, the drive to act ethically as a social ethician within his two societies.

The first, ethically inspired shifts to be examined here reach back to the epistemological theory that was encountered in chapter 1, primarily the tradition's definitions of conscience and principles, and, as an aspect of the latter, the differentiation of philosophical and theological knowledge. The ideological aspects of these definitions and their overcoming will be dealt with briefly in the first two sections, principally in terms of specific ethical judgment, the historicity of theoretical modes of thought, and moral agency.

In the third section I attempt to push Murray beyond his own work. I question the rationalism of Murray's own understanding of social meaning, and suggest that that theory blocked Murray's recognition of other legitimate and necessary forms of social communication and meaning, a blockage that renders his theory insufficient for (but not irrelevant to) an adequate understanding of the forces that direct social life. But, in the process of criticizing Murray, I also question the dichotomous dualism implicit in most challenges that are presently directed at his theory of the meanings and the processes by which societies are constituted.

Then, after having accepted Murray's own criticism of his earlier cognitional theories, but also having attempted to broaden them, I follow, in section IV, Murray's redefinition of God's power, not according to the institutional categories that had dominated much of his public life, but rather in terms of God's present historical action in the church and also in general society. I attempt to show that the perspectival shifts described in sections I and II prepared the way for this more explicitly theological perspective on social communication and meaning (and that the critique in section III would enhance such a shift). As will become apparent, it seems to me that, toward the end of his life, Murray became a consciously *theological* ethician, arguing in both civil and religious societies in explicitly theological categories. This new consciousness was the result of a final break with elements in his earlier epistemological and ecclesiological theories that blocked what might be called a social spirituality—a conscious recognition of, and interaction with, an historical God.

In section V, I interpret the just described major shift in Murray's spirituality in terms of Lonergan's notions of cognitional biases, and in the process question Lonergan's notion of common sense bias, siding with Murray in what appears to be an unacknowledged disagreement between them. At stake will be, once again, Murray's notion of the type of morality that is demanded of the people, of all those who have a say, or ought to have a say, in the development of any society.

The final section of this chapter is an attempt to define the tasks of social ethics in the light of Murray's own practice of social argument.

To claim, as I do here, that a social ethician can correct theory in the face of social action is to affirm that theory and action stand in a circulating relationship, i.e., that theory and action can be mutually self-correcting. To claim further that some theories or aspects of theories are ideological in the pejorative sense is to posit normative ethical requirements incumbent on the theological, social ethician.

I. THEORIES OF SPECIFIC CHOICE WHICH RENDER SOCIAL ARGUMENTS INADEQUATE OR UNETHICAL.   James Gustafson has recently lauded the convergence between Catholic and Protestant conceptions of what has here been termed specific prudential determination (Gustafson 1978, 114–24). Arising among the Roman Catholic "contextualists" and among mitigated forms of Protestant "situationalism" is the perception that acts of judgment must enter into the application of principles to concrete cases, that the link between principles and specific judgments is historical, not deductionistic. With this reaffirmed notion of prudential determination, both traditions are escaping, respectively, magisterial legalism and biblical legalism. To my reading, Gustafson is affirming the prudential nature of individual ethical choices—how one is to come to a choice concerning a specific act, in a specific situation, with perhaps other specific actors involved.

Although the theory attempts to take account of the historical situation in which individual decisions are made, the resulting notion of judgment is still fairly individualistic, without, however, denying the possibility of socially formed specific judgments. And, Gustafson is also reaffirming the dignity, responsibilities, and rational operations of the moral agent in arriving at specific ethical judgments.

Now, true to his Thomistic background, Murray began his professional career with a notion of the prudential nature of specific ethical choices, and this in regard to both individual and social choices. Based in his notion of individual conscience, he insisted that the applications of principles/laws to specific situations involved human judgment, and that that judgment was to be respected as long as serious common good dangers were not involved. Yet his first discussion of conscience tended toward an ethical legalism, because (1) it confused laws as principles, on the one hand, with laws as specific ethical determinations and civil proscriptions, on the other; (2) it presumed a timelessness to the principles which were to govern conscience; and (3) that argument was permeated by a notion of absolute magisterial authority, as Murray inherited such a notion from his tradition. All three of these limiting factors took the dynamic force out of his notion of specific prudential judgment and, along with it, the notion of the individual's responsibility for knowing what was going on in his or her world and for making hard choices in dialogue with others. He did not yet have the notion of human person (living under the stark responsibilities to act constructively and maturely as a publicly thinking creature) that would become the cornerstone and goal of his later reflections on specific, individual human choice.

As I mentioned in chapter 1, the prudential nature of specific determinations was more clearly present in his discussion of "political judgment," the third of his initial religious liberty arguments. Here, the legal institutionalization of church/state relations was always, and in every case, tied to the concrete historical situation, primarily to the actual social consensus. The choice of the form of those relations required continuous discernment of what existed in the real world, and acts of understanding and judgment prior to the imposition of law. Here, however, it was unclear who was doing the discernment, understanding, and judgment. While his notion of individual determination was not yet fully prudential, his notion of social determination as yet had no clear social subject. Political judgment was primarily distinguished by the object of those specific prudential acts, that is, by the laws that are formed, not by the thinking peoples that form those laws, much less by the social rational processes that must supply the foundation for legal formulations.

The residual legalism of Murray's initial theory of individual prudential determination and the individualism, the social disembodiment, of his theory of social prudential determination led to the collapse of his first religious liberty argument and also kept him from recognizing the socially active forms of reasoning required for both types of determination, and particularly for the social. As I suggested, Murray's notion of the permanence of theoretical and, especially, theological knowledge, impelled him to keep that knowledge outside of the historical flow, and therefore outside of the range of acting, discursive human subjects. The danger he feared was historical relativism. So, rather than extending an analogical analysis of human reasoning from the social realm (where his notion of prudential judgment was more clearly developed) to that of individual choice, he argued from individual cognitional acts to the social, and found that he could not develop a sufficient notion of human, civil rights.

Murray's historical studies first of all tore one realm of theoretical knowledge, the philosophical, from its timeless universe. In the process, he had to notice the social dynamics of coming to collective understanding and judgment. It was only then that he could return to the world of individual human choice and recognize the fully prudential nature of all human choice. But by then he did not need, and insisted that others not use, individualistic theories of human cognition to ground social obligations and rights. Murray ended up affirming the dignity, responsibilities, and rights of individual and social subjects in arriving at specific prudential determinations. His path for getting there was not a direct examination of his initial cognitional theories. Rather, he confronted both past and contemporary social arguers (including himself) and learned from them what human dignity entailed.

Murray's laborious path toward notions of individual and social prudential determination and the notion of human dignity based on the responsibilities for the use of reason in both arenas of judgment, stands as a warning for the social ethician. If one wishes to affirm human dignity, one must develop sufficient theories of social cognition to ground that dignity. Individualistic cognitional theories can yield no more than individual inviolability, in a fairly private sense. And if one encounters theories that apparently do not want to affirm human social dignity, it would be a good bet that buried in those theories is an individualistic understanding of human cognition. I at least would argue that any ethical theory which does not account for the social forces involved in argument is ideological, and ought to be challenged as unethical through inattention, if not through bad will.

II. THEORIES OF THEORETICAL KNOWLEDGE THAT BLOCK THE MORAL AGENCY OF THE HEARERS OF SOCIAL ARGUMENTS.   Situationalism and contextualism, as theories of particular prudential determination, have at times been advanced or branded as theories of sheer ethical relativism. Some have claimed that situationalism offers no guidance in moral discernment, and therefore no ethical truth claims can be formulated. Murray's initial, sharp divisions between practical and theoretical reasoning (and as an aspect of the latter, between philosophical and theological reasoning) was, I have argued, his first attempt to deal with the historicism problem. Yet one after another of his theoretical principles and arguments was cast into the historical drift, first his political philosophy, then the principles of justice. Murray's notion of the contingency of general philosophical principles grew out of his appreciation of civil society's historicity and its pluralism. For a long time, however, he still clung to the notion of noncontingency of theological affirmations and of the church's self-understanding, until Lonergan gave him a way out of the historicism problem. By the end of his life he did admit the contingency of the theological propositions that guided church thought and action. But then he could so face them, without, as will be discussed further, having to settle for moral and religious relativism.

Before turning to the historicism problem and the cognitional theories that handled that problem, however, I first want to examine the root impulse behind Murray's situating of even theoretical knowledge within a field of historical development. In contrast with some anguished European responses to the recognition of the historical contingency of human social meaning, for Murray the notion was quite freeing. For:

1.   In the realm of specific choice:

   if   the moral worth of all human law is tied to historically specific social realities,

   then   judgments concerning the legal forms of church-state relations can alter from one historically specific society to the next.

2.   In the civil realm:

   if   a society's philosophical understanding of the state is contingent on the emergence of insights and perspectives concerning, among other realities, the moral agency of the people, *then* the political philosophy by which one society defines itself and its state need not tie another age to forms of power and ethical analysis that are clearly archaic and inadequate to new social configurations of power and moral strength.

3.   In the ecclesial realm:

if the church's own understanding of its mission in the world is at times informed by adequate political philosophies, and at times infected by faulty political philosophies,

then the church need not be tied to its own past policy definitions of its mission, such as the preservation of its own integrity through isolation, or to the preservation of its own freedom through suppression of all opposition.

4. In the realm of faith:

if the very religious truths by which the church understands itself and God are dependent on the emergence of insights and perspectives as these arise in the course of historical development,

then the church's understanding of itself as a timeless embodiment of Christian truth, preserved through corrective restraints, must give way to a recognition of itself as principally and primarily a community of ongoing historical inquiry and of transforming love.

Now, Murray's adoption of the above four consequential clauses was, in his manner of arguing social issues, a liberation. He recognized in them a call and occasion to act maturely, to reason responsibly. Given his desire to remain within the developing thought of a religious community that had been reflecting on religious and political issues for two thousand years, and given, at the same time, his own perceived obligation to address the ethical dimensions of his present church and civil society, Murray in fact needed such an enveloping concept of historicity. It allowed him at once to analyze the impact of political facts and philosophies on earlier church thought, to affirm that within the available perspectives of, say, Leo XIII, the church's responses were intelligent and ethically correct (or limited and incorrect), without having to affirm that such responses are timelessly intelligent and ethical.[1] Political philosophies and public recognition of moral goods such as rights have emerged in the process of historical development, and their emergence and affirmation can be reasonably defended as rational or challenged as irrational. Social reality is composed, i.e., constituted, by such types of meanings. For Murray, one cannot (and should not) aprioristically claim the eternal validity of any political philosophy or rights theory, or, for that matter, of any ethical theory regarding social reality, familial structuring, common moral affirmations, or even the principles of justice themselves. To do so would be to deny the need to adjust to the new configurations of values that might arise, but also to deny the need for each age to appropriate in a mature human manner the values which ought to survive from one age to the next. This notion of historicity and contingency, he found, was necessary for his own and his church's moral response to the world in which they found themselves.

However, it is precisely his gradually enveloping conception of human historicity that has drawn criticism from both Catholic and Protestant commentators. For example, Edward Goerner has faulted Murray for having abandoned any classical discussion of ideal political form (Goerner 1965, 172–91). And Faith Burgess has likewise criticized him for never giving a theoretically timeless grounding for religious liberty (Burgess 1971, 238– 42).[2] These criticism are at core concerned with the claimed contingency of Murray's theoretical and his policy affirmations, respectively. In asserting a timelessness in either realm, Goerner and Burgess miss both the social nature of the knowledge Murray was recognizing and the mature moral response that he was trying to evoke. First, the social nature of that knowledge.

If Murray did indeed relativize all human social judgments of moral value, judgments of justice and rights, perspectives on political and ecclesiastical social realities, by linking them to the emergence of insight, he did not, in his own understanding, abandon any rational discussion of social and ethical values or the possibility of invariance in general or specific moral judgments from one age to the next. Answers which are posed to the moral questions of any age can achieve, through the self-correction involved in public discussion, a closure of judgment or, in Lonergan's term, the "virtually unconditioned" (Lonergan 1958, 280–81).[3] But Murray did eventually recognize that changing questions concerning seemingly identical ethical problems could, in fact, betray either actually new, or simply newly recognized, factors that must be rationally addressed in new deliberations. If a person (or a society) is to be true to the new problem or the restatement of the problem, he must rationally achieve closure of the relevant value questions that emerge in the consideration of the issue; one must achieve a "virtually unconditioned" judgment. And for Murray, this process of reaching judgment is of necessity a social activity, capable of reaching the virtually unconditioned only in the broadest possible conversational field. Murray at once therefore claimed the historical flux of emerging insights and ethical theories, but also claimed that true judgments of value are possible in a social body, precisely because of the self-corrective action of shared social meaning. A rational case can and must be made for the affirmation of emerging social insights, definitions, and theories. One can and must understand the reasons for their emergence and the criteria for their continued affirmation.

But, beyond even the possibility of achieving public affirmation of true value claims, Murray rested more and more of his argument for public rationality on the individual and social agents of those arguments, and therefore on the moral responsibilities of those agents. In the early 1950s, Murray had configured the meaning which is the core of society to be a series of value-laden propositions ("We hold these truths"). In the early 1960s, and certainly by 1967, he had to admit that the affirmation of those principles (and their alteration) could only at core be generated by processes of social self-correction in the face of changing perspectives and changing relevant social realities. In the process of responding to changing questions, there stands the possibility of human attentiveness, human intelligence, human discussion and application of criteria of judgment. But, further, it is in the public commitment to human attentiveness, intelligence and judgment that, finally for Murray, the core and timeless moral reality of human society resides. Without personal and collective commitments to the processes of human social reasoning, the discussion of any moral, justice, or religious issue quickly resolves into a factionalistic play of blind force. This is not to claim that the scope of one's social viewpoint in itself somehow automatically grounds the moral content of a judgment. But it is to claim that true judgments of fact and value have a better chance of emerging in the broadest conversational field possible.[4] To arrive at moral truth, one must converse. To converse, one must be committed to conversation. Murray eventually found the ultimate point of ethical reference in personal and social commitments to reason in public, that is, in the underlying realities of human moral drives as they reach out to all that is of value and shape and direct all discussion of human value. From the imperative to be responsible in public discussions, as well as from his notion of society as a field of emerging insight, conversation, and judgment, he could then situate the principle of "as much freedom as possible" both in civil society and within the church as the first imperative for the moral and intellectual development of both societies.

Murray, then, began to view social ethics as having two sides or directions that mutually revolved around the free practice of social conversation. The first side is that of emerging insights and the public discussion of particular policy issues, and also of general value commitments and the public understanding and adoption of those commitments. This side of social ethics is the application of constructive social reasoning to specific actions, such as laws, and to the general value orientations which guide social action. Both specific social acts and general commitments require the ongoing, creative exercise of reasoning.

On the other side of social freedom, however, stands first of all the abstract capacity to enter into the processes of social inquiry and judgment. Behind this capacity, there resides a responsibility for the full and effective use of public reasoning, an obligation addressed to actual human beings who are born into specific historical societies. And behind even that still rather general responsibility for reasoning, stands the moral agent, as Murray eventually defined that reality in his religious liberty and church freedom arguments. The moral agent who is pertinent to both of those arguments is anything but abstract. That agent breathes and acts, hears and chooses. Arguments thrown into the public forum attempt to engage that listening, acting being. They seek to facilitate a choice against the tribal methods for definition of social reality. They seek to engage the agent as a lover of the truth and value of social living and of the search for the truths and values in and by which large-scale social realities are constituted. The moral agent is a destroyer of walls, while remaining attentive, intelligent, reasonable, and responsible for actual human beings wherever he or she may find them. The moral agents addressed by Murray's later arguments are in part constituted by the hope that Murray had for them.

It has been pointed out that Murray was not very insightful or a very good social ethician on issues ranging from racial relations to the war in Asia (Coleman 1976, 705). And what he had to say about nuclear war seems to a later time overly naive and, strange to say, overly optimistic. All these issues, however, are on the first side of the perspective offered here. One might suggest that those who effectively argue against his specific views on such issues do so by the very methods of prudential, historical discussion that he claimed were essential for the public formation of consensus and policy commitments. Murray himself expertly and insightfully argued the issue of juridical religious freedom, and then of general social freedom, in much the same manner.

But toward the end of his life, his understanding of what ultimately concerns the social ethician did change. As perhaps old and seasoned people are wont to do, he began to view all public, prudential discussions in terms of what effect the style and content of those discussions would have on collective moral will, whether in civil society or in the church. The social prudential processes of particular determination, the theoretical modes of understanding social realities and their processes, and the institutions which organize political and social action, are all made servants of the ethical drives which must be invoked for long-term development, not just for short-term resolution, of social questions. Murray increasingly concerned himself, not with the Communistic or secularistic enemy without, but with the possibility of rational and moral contraction within, with the latter's resulting social jingoism. He looked into social morality and found at its core a moral will and, as will become evident in section IV, an enabling love.

It is this moral agency, common to both practical and theoretical reasoning, and common likewise to civil and theological thought, that dissolved those aspects of his practical/theoretical and philosophical/theological distinctions which had masked the ethician's task of recognizing and evoking that moral agency. Murray came to recognize that any and all social arguments either encourage or deaden that moral will, sometimes unknown to the person who is arguing in public. No argument for a social policy or a commitment, advanced in public, can be neutral in its effect on social moral will. The fact that we and what we know are historical places demands on us to live creatively and maturely.

III. PROPOSITIONAL VERSUS SYMBOLIC MODES OF PRUDENTIAL KNOWLEDGE AND DETERMINATION.   To claim with Murray that civil society is abstractly capable of ethical discrimination through public, rational discourse is often to provoke the response: So what? Even if there might be a distinct form of human reasoning proper to large-scale social bodies, that type of reasoning, it may be claimed, is seldom engaged in public fights over moral issues. And since the forum is left solely to juridical instruments and techniques, a public discussion of viewpoints, of insights into the historical social situation, and of the values involved, is de facto impossible. Murray himself noted the limitations of what is possible in juridical discussions. The only way now to gain public endorsement of a value is by juridical imposition, as many in the present American abortion debate contend. Murray's claimed "great act of faith in the reasonableness/moral sense of the people" is dead, if it ever did exist.

My own reactions to the cynicism expressed in statements such as this are often shaped by the recognition that those who have renounced the attempt to convince others of the values they hold are usually those who, through lack of knowledge or through the irrationalism of positions they choose to adopt, are not able to win a public argument. So they have to settle for simple imposition of their value commitments by coercive means. Here, however, I wish to address another response to the decrepit state of American or church public discourse, a suggestion of an alleged way to bypass our lack of collective commitment to public discussion. What is needed, it might be claimed, are nonrational forms of discourse, such as the symbolic, the artistic, the interpersonal, which carry with them modes and models of evaluation that can bypass the dominant juridical, technical, or even linguistic rationalism of the American public forum. We currently need the generation, adoption, and application of common civil religious symbols that can function as umbrellas under which we may then find common meaning and come to common commitments to programs of action.

I do not want to discount the notion that new, common symbols are necessary for the reunification of a pluralistic America or even a pluralistic church. But I do suggest that there is something in the ethical orientation of the rationalistic Murray that might help evaluate the generation and use of symbolic languages in the public forum. Here, I will suggest that what Murray had discovered about conceptual social knowledge might be, and ought to be, applied even to our understanding of symbolic forms of social meaning. In what follows, I will use the term "figurative" language to include symbolic, artistic, and interpersonal forms of communication,[5] and the term "conceptual" language to designate the common sense modes of public discourse (primarily formulable in terms of propositions) that were Murray's favorite. I argue that both forms of knowledge are prudential, both in specific and general determinations.

It seems to me that figurative and conceptual languages operate in a similar fashion both in human consciousness and in the public forum, in terms of their generation and in terms of their applications. Both the figurative and conceptual languages through which we share common social meaning and commitments are the product of experience. Neither arises full blown from the head of Zeus. The "truth" that they convey rises out of the experience of actual human living, and the expressions of both forms of public language are shaped by the concrete reality of commonly lived experience, rather than by abstract, so-called timeless patterns of disembodied myths or theoretical reasoning. Further, figurative or conceptual contents are born into a world of meaning that already exists, and therefore the "truth" of those new meanings will at least in part be judged according to how they fit into that prior world, either in terms of reorganizing that world or in terms of their compatibility with the more important value expressions of that world. The accumulation and interrelations of the contents of figurative and common sense knowledge are nonsystematic and can only be systematized at risk of losing the richness and depth of their content. In both cases, it is people that generate meaning and integrate that meaning into the general orientations of their lives, and they do so by similar human means—nonsystematic integration that is nonetheless open to communication and public comprehension.

Likewise, figurative and conceptual languages are applied in a similar manner to evaluations of particular worth. All languages of public ethical discourse require mediating insights into particular situations by which the accumulated but concrete experiential patterns are related to particular historical instances. Just as there is the possibility of a legalistic imposition of propositional meaning on particular acts or situations, likewise figurative meanings can be similarly imposed, as in the case of someone marrying the image of one's parent, or rejecting a person with black skin because of appropriated collective myths about blacks. But we generally do not hold the immediate imposition of either legalistic conceptual meaning or of figurative meaning to be responsible. To be ethically applied, both types of meanings require mediating insights.

And, finally, judgments of artistic worth, symbolic significance, or moral value are all open to the same type of public exchange and public criticism which, in Murray's opinion, correct and advance public prudential determination. One can and must criticize symbolic, artistic, and intersubjective realms of meaning much as one can criticize the propositional assertions of a person who purports to be wise, by pointing out values and contents which seem to be lacking in the symbolic or rational evaluations of any particular issue, and by further pointing out the lack of insight into the particular situation under discussion. And this "pointing out" may be done in conceptual or figurative languages, or more often, in the public forum, in a combination of both languages. Wisdom and insight can be applied analogously to all normal modes by which a social body arrives at common meaning and evaluation.

Now, if the generation, organization, and applications of figurative meaning are similar, within the public forum, to those of common sense meaning, then the dangers involved in not noticing their identical human source are also similar. Without a recognition of their common structures and procedures in the multiple forms of common meaning, one's analysis of social figurative meaning tends to get away from the subjects (individual and collective) who are supposedly engendering, in a way that can be self-correcting, those meanings and evaluation. In the processes of human development from infancy to maturity, emotional or symbolic meaning may indeed at first be a given, introjected reality, much in line with some interpretations of Durkheim's collective consciousness, to which the individual blindly submits or succumbs. But emotional and symbolic meanings, if they are to be active in the lives of individuals and communities, must be constantly acted on by those individuals and communities, both in terms of their use in shaping the actions by which we express ourselves and the institutions under which we live, and in terms of the reaffirmation and adjustment of the general meanings themselves. In the realm of application, for example, even a smile is ambiguous and potentially destructive without individual and social interpretations of what is before us (mediating insights) and self-correction. Sadists and dirty old men can smile too. If our theory of the dynamics of symbolic languages disregards the subjects of those meanings and the actions required by the subjects, then the directive role of figurative meaning becomes irrelevant or impossible, but in any case damaging. Just as Murray insisted that the moral agency of the individual, social subgroups, and society at large must be recognized and engaged in shaping the concrete realities of our society, likewise the role of subjects in expressing those figurative meanings in concrete ways must be recognized and consciously engaged—if those subjects are to be morally responsive to their actual world. We ignore the subjects of figurative, particular value determinations at risk of reducing those subjects to the status of moral automatons.

Nor can we escape penalties for ignoring the subject in the collective generation and appropriation of the figurative meanings that shape our identity and fundamental orientations. Just as general, propositionally expressed value commitments must be reappropriated, and perhaps adjusted, by each new age, likewise the self-appropriation, self-correction, and responsibility of the individual and society toward general figurative and symbolic meaning must be recognized and engaged even in the realm of nonpropositional common meaning. Otherwise, it can be argued, the social reality defined by those meanings becomes alien and reified. The meanings by which a society is constructed stand in danger of becoming clichés and therefore socially irrelevant. Or they become ideologies and therefore dangerous: they exist as answers that keep people from asking further relevant questions. In Murray's terms, the moral agent must be recognized in one's theory of social meaning. With no recognition of social self-appropriation and self-correction, there is no notion of agency, and therefore no notion of moral responsibility. Murray's final defense of freedom in civil and ecclesial societies revolved around such a notion of moral responsibility for the common, general meanings which we share. Basing those freedoms in moral agency was the only way in which he could reasonably defend those freedoms and yet adequately position them within legitimate concerns for the long-term development of both civil and ecclesiastical societies. But, beyond simply a defense of freedom, he judged that self-appropriation and self-correction are as necessary for society as is the meaningful application of a society's value orientations. Free moral agency is a requirement for all those meanings that we share in common. And, not so surprisingly, a notion of human ethical agency can lead us to better theories of those common meanings, figurative and conceptual, by which we are constituted.

Murray's theory of social decision-making and consensus formation should indeed be criticized. But I think the problem with his epistemological theory, at least as it applies to these issues of particular and general ethical determination within society, is that he did not extend it far enough. He himself never noticed the similarities between public figurative and propositional languages of value, as both come to determination out of accumulated experience and mediating insights. Further clarifications of the similarities between these public languages of moral evaluation, which I have chosen generally to call "prudential," must be developed if his case for the full possibilities of public social ethical discourse is to be adequately recognized and exploited.

Murray was himself a rationalist, whose rationalism kept him unaware of the role of symbolic modes of knowledge in shaping public value perspectives and policy determinations. But to criticize him while accepting his own polarized division of reason and the symbolic, and opting for the isolated primacy (and reification) of the latter, is to miss the essentially social nature of symbols and the ethical agency involved in their generation, appropriation, and self-correction. And to miss that social nature of symbols is to miss the ethician's task of engaging the human, moral will of the actual people he is facing.

IV. GOD'S HISTORICAL PRESENCE AND THE EMERGENCE OF ENABLING LOVE. In the 1940s, Murray had insisted on the necessity of a natural law consensus for the common pursuit of international justice. The consensus was thought to be a motivational content that would unlock the forces of civil love or friendship, although not the forces of religious charity. As Murray developed his notion of civil consensus as involving emerging tertiary principles that would guide prudential ethical discussions, the evocation of love or charity receded to the background of his thought, perhaps because of his concentration on rights as immunities, not as empowerments. Only once during the American discussions did he explicitly question the temporal viability of the preconciliar American experiment, if there was no public awareness of Christ. That outburst came only after years of rather disillusioning attempts at consensus formation.

What is the relationship of God's grace to social development and decline, and therefore to those who argue social ethical issues? Murray never did publish any clear or systematic responses to this question. But a movement in his later perspectival changes suggests an understanding of that relationship at a far deeper level than the simple motivational relationship of religious propositions or symbols to human drives. The ideas which mediated Murray's transition toward a new understanding of God's action and social action were (1) his new awareness of the problem of God as primarily a problem of and in history, (2) Lonergan's recognition of the historical emergence of "theoretical" religious meaning within the People of God, and (3) the notions of *gnosis* and *agnosis* as forming the necessary but unstable grounding of Western social consciousness. All three elements, in combination with his ethical grounding of rights as positive em-powerments, moved Murray to reconceptualize the source of social healing power, not simply as emergent propositions (or symbols), but also as outbreaks of God's action in the general, historical human community. Here I will briefly follow this development and suggest an underlying problem that Murray was apparently trying to solve.

In his 1964 *Problem of God,* Murray established as foundational the affirmation of God's action in human history—the distinction be-tween, but relatedness of, sacred and secular history. As he spelled out that foundation, the problem was initially and constantly "existential," only secondarily "functional," "noetic," or "onomastic." The contem-porary problem of God has once again invested primacy to the question of whether God can and should be affirmed as intimately involved in human history, or whether God should rather be eliminated from history by human choice.

Second, the return to the "existential" historical arena, however, did not entail a neoreligious primitivism, a rejection of theoretical modes of thought. Lonergan had taught Murray that the human understanding of God is dependent on the emergence of human intelligence, both in terms of questions, propositions, and judgments, and in terms of distinct modes and methods of thought. Just as the foundational religious problem concerns God's presence in history, so the terms and perspectives for its resolution arise in a graced, historical church at multiple levels of discourse. That is, our knowledge of God and the power by which the church rightly addresses the changing forms of the problem are both eventually understood by Murray to be of the nature of emerging possibilities. Our awareness of God in history is conditioned by God's power and by our ability to be insightful, decisive, and authentic—this power and this ability related in some fashion as cause and effect. If human insightfulness, decisiveness, and authenticity are made possible by the enabling presence and power of God, Murray could then discuss the possibility of God's presence wherever there is found insightfulness, decisiveness, and authenticity—even outside of the church. The church's own responsibility to witness to God and its responsiveness to God's action in history would demand such recognition and affirmation.

Finally, Murray's theme of *gnosis-agnosis* suggested that the ongoing problem of God is at its base a problem shaped by God's gracious presence at the heart (and mind) of human civilization. Because persons stand before the divine reality, they and their civilizations are caught in a constant dialectic between a gnosticism of existential affirmation and a fundamental inability to capture the divine reality conceptually. Murray further suggested that the health of human society depends on the ability to maintain both its gnosticism and agnosticism. Any resolution of the tension by eliminating one of the poles leads, he argued, to totalitarianism (one society, one history) or to the destruction of social reality in mutual incomprehension (no society). The manner in which we live in this grace-induced consciousness of God will have its historical, social effects.

Behind all these formulations is a conception of the emergence of God's power and presence as beyond human control and human limitation. The church has been unfaithful to God by its claim of no salvation outside its borders, by its denial of God's action within human society. Part of contemporary atheism's strength is its denial of the God who sanctions injustice and of the church that claims God as its sole possession. There is here a presupposition that all human reality can be a source of divine action and love. A "natural" universe was now, in Murray's thinking, turning into an abstraction untrue to the constituent consciousness of historical society.

How can one locate the saving presence of God in historical society? The problem here is similar to the locating of the intelligent and the wise in the ethical arguments. Murray suggested, but only suggested, that wherever there exists a will to community which is

212 J. Leon Hooper, S.J.

expressed in and through public conversation, there is a possible indication of God's power. The church is to be a witness to God's actions in history, even to God's action arising outside its own institutional circle. The Protestant churches must be recognized as involved in that history which is salvific. Modern personal and political (or communal) consciousness is a rightful exigence of the human spirit, demanding from the church protection and encouragement both within and outside the church. That will toward community is the grounding for his new conception of the church primarily as a social reality based on love, only secondarily as an authority structure. And that will is the ground for breaking down the walls between the churches and between Christianity and Marxist atheism. Wherever one finds a will to community that seeks expression in conversation, one finds a truly redemptive drive within both the church and the larger social arena.

Further, a conversation toward unity begins in the mutual recognition of sinfulness and leads to mutually agreed determinations that come as surprises to both parties, since they are truly new. Murray here went beyond the simple recognition of multiple modes and methods of knowing as a solution to social divisiveness. He suggested a type of historical process akin to religious conversion, but the process arises within the social body as a whole, not just within individual human consciousness: a collective drive toward unity, a recognition of the actual bases of differences, an admission of sinfulness, a quest for, and eventual attainment of, new perspectives. Only after the attainment of such perspectives do the questions of a proper institutionalization of church-society relations come to the fore.

In Murray's later "conversion" to ecumenism (in the broad sense), there is a long delayed deinstitutionalization of the locus of God's gracious activity in the world. The recognition of prudential determination, and the further recognition of the role of his adopted cognitional transcendentals (be attentive, etc.) in all forms of human meaning, prepared the way for this deinstitutionalization. Then the notion of the historical emergence of insight and perspective and its parallel in the notion of the historical emergence of God's gracious presence in a will to community could lead nowhere but to that deinstitutionalization. Once Murray had allowed (in fact, demanded) in light of the Gospel, the public discussion of theological truth, he was forced to discuss the religious grounding of social existence and to bring the languages of grace to bear on such public discussions. The God foundationally known in history becomes the focus of Murray's own confession of Christian faith and also the focus of his own practice of social ethical discussion. While still including the church and the propositions which the church determines in his conception of the proper objects of religious discourse, there is here a turn to the God who founded that church through a historical action of dynamic love—a love that levels those barriers which separate humans from God and humans from other humans. Evangelical freedom has been engaged by God and has found its expression in the core historical reality of the Christian community as a will toward an even larger community. That such a drive can authentically arise outside the church, even among atheists, is a manifestation of God's universal salvific will. God is not just the authenticator of one or two institutions; God is a person who presently acts in the social world.

Finally, this turn toward a God who acts in human history was not an attempt on Murray's part to ground ethical principles that had been cast into an historical, relativistic drift. Murray thought he had, in Lonergan's notion of "virtually unconditioned" judgment, a sufficient grounding for the truth of particular ethical determinations and of general value claims. The ethical responsibilities that fall on the moral agent to be attentive, intelligent, and rational, however, placed the notion of active ethical agency in the center of his social theory. And for a person of God—a God whose salvific presence and will is active throughout human history—the confession of that presence is as imperative as the confession or affirmation of the moral values which direct behavior within historical society. Any theory that denied or ignored that presence would be ideological, demonstrating a faulty participation in that enabling love that reaches across the distance which separates us from other historical actors and that attempts to level those walls which separate us.

V. PUBLIC THEOLOGICAL DISCOURSE AS THE OVERCOMING OF ECCLE-SIASTICAL GROUP BIAS.   How might this move toward the unpredictable God in general human history be interpreted? One such interpretation might be John Murray Cuddihy's judgment that Murray was in the process of capitulating to American civil religion—a rejection of the social solidarity claim of ecclesiological uniqueness with its concomitant methodology of cultural isolation (Cuddihy 1978, 77). But there is another possible interpretative framework that is truer to what was going on with Murray, a framework which at the same time could serve as grounds for criticizing Cuddihy's own religious and social presuppositions. It is Bernard Lonergan's notions of common sense, as presented in *Insight*.

In his section on "Common Sense as Understanding," Lonergan distinguishes three types of common sense biases (Lonergan 1958,

218-44, esp. 218-28). The first is "individual," the blocking of emerging insights by the individual because of unauthentic or psychologically determined perspectives. The second bias is that of the "group." Group bias expresses itself in the dominance of minority or impotent groups by those who presently and temporarily hold the coercive and cultural power to impose their own will. Group domination is limitedly self-corrective: suppressed groups will unite and take over the control of the social body. And, all things being equal, the new dominant group will simply impose its own will on the out-groups by purely coercive means.

Third, Lonergan also speaks of the "general bias" of common sense. Here common sense appears much like the prudential methods of social knowing as outlined through my own study. Its general field of governing insights is particularistic, accumulated through collective experience, and self-corrective through further questioning. It forms judgments by mediating insights into the particular situation and by reflectively grasping the adequacy of questions and of the answers to those questions. For Lonergan, however, this general common sense manner of knowing and judging is intrinsically biased by its concentration on the short term, on the practical. Since it deals in insights and judgments concerning the particular, it cannot of itself achieve adequately critical self-understanding. Since it is mostly interested in efficiency, it misses the dynamics of the longer cycles of social ethical and religious development and decline. General common sense is biased against the emergence of those insights and perspectives which concern social, cultural reality over time.[6]

Now, given Murray's heavy reliance on so many concepts from *Insight*, it is notable that he made neither explicit nor implicit appeal to this tripartite distinction of the biases of common sense. The individual bias as described by Lonergan was not of immediate concern to Murray, as the latter argued questions of meaning at the cultural level of social organization. But Murray's apparent disregard of the notion of general bias can, I think, be explained by what we have seen before of his understanding of the contemporary forms of public consciousness. Murray had argued for the possibility of reasonable, prudential ethical discourse within large-scale social bodies. Much of his life was a defense of such a possibility. He did criticize the American tendency to reduce social problems to technical questions, but for him this tendency was initiated by the interaction of the academic community's scientistic viewpoints with the general culture and the adoption of those viewpoints by the latter. Murray's society was "post-scientific."[7] He also argued against a growing, pervasive ethical relativism, but again the source of that general social attitude was thought to be the interaction of (unauthentic) historical modes of understanding with the general populace. His age was also "post-historical." The closest Murray came to a notion of general bias was in his discussion of the capitulation of the American Catholic community to a purely sociological sense of Catholic solidarity, but this sociological solidarity can be more adequately understood in terms of the second bias of common sense, that of the group. All his other Catholic criticisms focused on an indiscriminate adoption of the American scientistic or historicist viewpoints.

However, even beyond his understanding of contemporary society, much of Murray's own manners of dealing with social questions, and some shifts in those manners, become intelligible in terms of the breaking of group biases. Murray the social ethician never subscribed to the notion that the church could or ought to go it alone in the definition of civil social reality. Even in his early cooperation debate, he argued that the frankly pluralistic nature of the international social arena impelled the church toward cooperation at the level of social action (law), contrary to some of his Roman Catholic opponents. But under the impact of his expanding notion of specific and general prudential determination, he had to admit the validity of some general value commitments that arose outside his church, and to insist that his church be attentive to them. Then, as he uncovered social moral will at the heart of civil and religious societies, he could recognize the institutional, collective sinfulness of his church, paralleling the similar sinfulness of other social groups. One more strand in what might be considered an ecclesiastical group bias was broken. But only with the notion of faith as foundationally an affirmation of God's action in history was the final strand broken. The growth of purely theological knowledge must be an ecumenical affair, and the results will emerge out of a common social discourse. This was not to deny the truth of the great theological propositions that the church had previously affirmed. It was merely to shed a group bias about theological truth in order to respond to an age that is pluralistic, but open to God's salvific power. Murray did briefly try to spell out a special role for the Roman church in the historical development of secular and sacred history. Yet, this role was described primarily in terms of witnessing to the presence of God in general society, and it did more to highlight the stringent ethical requirements for the purity of the church's own witness than it did to enforce a general Roman Catholic bias toward its own uniqueness.

All this suggests that the bias with which Murray was concerned (and which he recognized) was that of the group. Murray recognized, as perhaps the Lonergan of *Insight* did not, that any mode of human cognition can be totalitarian in its designs, because it is actual, living people who practice those modes of knowing, and that actual human choice (the heart), not isolated conceptual intelligence, leads to the intending of whatever good there is to be found in historical societies, or to an ignoring of that good. Again, he agreed with Lonergan that a shift from the perspective of the group to that of the general (international) society could not and would not automatically yield true judgments of theological and ethical value. But he did recognize that an intending in love of real persons, of peoples, and of all people with whom we share this earth, is the only moral force that can break those jingoistic biases that restrict our accepted definition of humanity to those who look or think like ourselves. He did count on the God who is active in history and who can give rise to a drive toward "community" within many (and any) social groupings, and who, in the engagement of evangelical freedom, is the source of salvific action and thought in both civil and religious societies. Murray's final challenge to those social conceptions that enhance group bias are theologically grounded in God's emerging presence in general history. One can then interpret Murray's later ecumenical perspective as a gradual stripping of his own group bias, first, under the guidance of his study of social and theological reasoning, and, then, in a confrontation with the Christian God of history. To allow one's own group biases to be challenged, and to facilitate the shedding of the similar biases of one's opponents, is a task of the theological ethician, by which that ethician participates in the redemptive activity of the Spirit.

VI. THE SHAPE, THE LANGUAGES, AND THE ROLE OF ACTION FOR A THEOLOGICAL SOCIAL ETHICS.   Finally, what can be learned from Murray concerning the content and practice of social ethics? Murray was more, rather than less, intelligent and decisive. As time went on, he became more, rather than less, attentive to the physical and cultural forces that permeated his social environment—forces such as law, other institutions, Protestantism, atheism, various orders of meaning, and variations of group bias. And he loved American society and the church, loves which directed him throughout his life toward a responsible use of his own intelligence in his attempts to understand and help direct the forces which constitute those societies. Four propositions concerning theological social ethics are suggested by Murray's attempts to act responsibly in the public forum:

(A)   Social ethics is a distinct field of ethics which is not reducible to personal, psychological, or even juridical considerations. For social arguments to be true to the reality addressed (and to be effective), they must be based, not only on the juridical methods particular to the social arena, but more especially on the manners and methods by which we maintain and develop common meaning.

(B) Because of the reality with which the social ethician deals, the languages that he or she must employ are particularly dependent on the emergence of new insight and judgments, i.e., are dependent on social, historical generation.

(C) Since the ethician's object is a historical, social reality, the principal methods of social transformation which must occupy the social ethician are the self-corrective processes of developing social meaning.

(D) Three coequal aspects of social ethics place increasing demands on the social agent for consistency between theory or teaching and social action.

A. Social Ethics Is a Distinct Field of Ethics Which is Not Reducible to Personal, Psychological, or Even Juridical Considerations.   From the beginning of his publishing career, Murray had insisted that the life of a social group does not reduce to the aggregate of individual drives and individualistic goods of the person. There exists a common good that spells out an arena of distinct social concern. However, his initial manner of distinguishing that social arena was primarily in terms of the juridical—the limited range of law's effectiveness and the contingency of legal institutionalizations. He also asserted the necessity of a commonly held field of meaning, the natural law consensus that was to ground social action. But the cognitional categories that he used to configure that common meaning were inadequate, as was in a backhanded manner confirmed with the collapse of his first religious liberty argument. Thus, in his postconciliar attempts to found religious liberty, he went to great and sometimes tortuous lengths to ground that right in a concept of human dignity which is internally social (which includes a notion of institutions as expressions of moral discernment, and a theory of human cognition that recognizes the initial and ongoing social nature of even individual acts of understanding and judgment). Murray's arguments for freedom in both civil and religious societies were based on an insistence that the *social* good of both societies is dependent on such freedoms, distinct from the needs of the individual or small intersubjective groups. Just as Murray had in the cooperation debate argued that the historically novel, recently developed forms of international interaction required the structuring of that international arena by law, so later he argued that the scope of the newly emerging social reality required a distinct consideration of manners by which common meaning and commitments are developed, those social forces which could cast that arena as a state of war or as a field for the attainment of the international economic, political, and moral good.

Murray's understanding of the common good shifted from the institutions or tangible products of collective action to the meanings and commitments which bind peoples together. Society itself became those common understandings. Society is a field of meaning. Social ethics deals primarily with that field of meaning, only secondarily yet importantly with the tangible products of social reasoning.

We need not advance far beyond Murray's own work to confirm that an attempt to found civil, economic, and political freedoms in more personal realms of human action cannot but fail to be convincing, when the potential scope of modern social self-destruction is brought as a claim against such individually based freedoms. To attempt to so found social freedoms is to leave the social field to those who conceive society as distinct merely or exclusively in that here the forces of coercive restraint and constraint have some legitimate place. Any argument for rights and freedoms, whatever else their bases, must include a foundational appeal to our collective methods of knowing and our collective commitments—social realities which can be destroyed without the protection of those freedoms. Only an argument grounded in collective cognitional requirements stands a chance of being reasonably defensible and publicly perceived as such. If the ethician claims social reality as his field, his or her claims and calls for freedom, public virtue, and the goods of that social reality must be based on an intelligible recognition of the distinct dynamisms and relatively autonomous processes of common meaning. The social ethician's arguments and objects of study are distinct.

B. Because of the Reality with Which the Social Ethician Deals, the Languages that He or She Must Employ Are Particularly Dependent on the Emergence of New Insight and Judgments, i.e., Are Dependent on Social, Historical Generation.
Murray gradually moved away from a classical manner of conceiving social reality (almost exclusively in terms of permanent institutions) to a conception of that reality as constituted by the types and manners of human knowing that it affirms. That the languages the social ethician uses are contingent, that they emerge in a process of social development, became apparent to him in the very process of dialectic challenge and reformulation. And this notion of emerging languages can legitimately be extended even into the meanings by which the people of God are constituted. The church thinks within history, interacting with the social realities that it encounters, acting within the range of the conceivably possible. The early, interpersonal church did not confront the Roman Empire with quite the same range of the

imaginably possible as did the later church. Nor did the early church have to face questions of long-term social development. Again, the biblical church did not initially have to adjust to the large-scale historical reality that it itself later became. The languages appropriate to large-scale social realities, those realities to which the church in its ethical and religious concerns must attend, require the emergence of new forms of analysis. Murray never objected to, say, rights languages as not directly situated in biblical affirmations or in biblical symbolism; he merely objected to the expressed or implied individualism of earlier forms of seventeenth century rights theories. For him, rights as well as virtue languages, if properly understood in terms of the governmental, cultural, and institutional forces against which they were developed, are legitimate and helpful languages for the protection of the moral forces that are to drive historical, social living. But those languages must be so understood if they are to have a legitimate position within a public ethical argument and also have a publicly recognized (and effective) force in such arguments.

The continual problem facing the social ethician is the adequacy of those languages with which he or she attempts to understand and shape that social reality—a reality that has at the very least undergone radical changes in scope. Before a social problem can be resolved, social ethicians must critically approach the languages by which they attempt to comprehend that reality. Particularly crucial is the recognition that the level of potential group bias in large-scale social realities far exceeds the effective scope of intersubjective feelings and attachments, and therefore must be consciously addressed and ferreted out. A continual task for social ethics, then, is the exposure of ideological dimensions within those very languages which social ethicians use. Languages that were adequate in one social context can become ideological in another. This brings us to the third proposition.

C. Since the Ethician's Object Is an Historical, Social Reality, the Principal Methods of Social Transformation Which Must Occupy the Social Ethician Are the Self-Corrective Processes of Developing Social Meaning.   It is now a long-standing, often lamented truism that our contemporary patterns of interdependence have shifted the problem of social pluralism to a central position that it had never occupied in past ages. Not only must the social ethician admit, as Pius XII frankly admitted, that the emerging international society is religiously pluralistic. That society is also culturally, ethically, economically, and politically pluralistic. Some of this pluralism is indeed based on bad will, on willful limitation of insight and supported judgment. But much more of it is morally legitimate, based on differentiations of human meaning that are enhancements of human culture while at the same time serving as potential rallying totems for social division.

Murray never did pay much constructive attention to racially, ethnically, and nationally based pluralism. But a case can be made that, at least in part, differentiations that are so based have a legitimate place in international society, that the pluralistic groups based on those differentiations have a right to relative ethical autonomy, while also having an obligation to contribute to the moral direction of their larger societies. Murray did recognize religiously, theologically based pluralism. At first, he sought to keep theologically based perspectives effectively out of the public discussion, but then came to admit that those perspectives must reach public expression (for the sake even of theological truth). And even early on, he recognized the legitimacy of cognitional differentiations, a notion that was expanded by his later contact with Lonergan.

Now, if these perspectives and the groups that embody them are legitimate, and if they are under an obligation to contribute toward collective cultural, moral, and religious understanding, then the manner by which they interact cannot be by an assimilation of all the various perspectives by every member of society, nor by an elimination of some by the others, nor by the domination of some over others. To respect the human dignity of those who hold these perspectives, the manner of their integration must be directed by the difficult processes involved in the generation of new insights and inclusive perspectives. It involves a process of give and take, a process of concrete attentiveness, intelligence, reasonableness and responsibility, as Murray adopted this notion of "reason" in the last few years of his life. Just as social ethicians must critically approach their own languages, so must they do so in conversation even with those who are initially cast as the morally ambiguous or as the enemy. The ethician searches after new meanings by which disparate peoples who have been thrown together can be constituted as a people.

D. Three Distinct Aspects of Social Ethics Place Increasing Demands on the Social Agent for Consistency between Theory or Teaching and Social Action.   In his breaking away from individualistic starting points for social ethics, Murray uncovered the dynamic structures of public policy determination. According to Murray, the resolution of particular policy issues, such as those of abortion or nuclear disarmament, will always and in every situation be constrained by the instruments that are available in the public forum. While it might be true within smaller groups that the resolution of specific ethical issues has at its command forces of interpersonal fellowship and intimate group self-definition, at larger levels of social existence the primary tools of public determination are much closer to those of reason—reason defined as concrete attentiveness, etc. Contemporary society is a nonnatural reality in the limited sense of the novelty both of its scope and of the dangers posed by group biases—biases that have no automatic, natural predators to keep them in check save those of public discussion (whether that discussion be conducted primarily in figurative or in conceptual languages). As a novel construct, society must be capable of self-criticism and self-correction which can only be supplied by public reasoning, by disciplined public conversation, by the generating and appropriation of inclusive viewpoints.

Simply within the context of particular policy determination, then, the image of society that Murray presented was intrinsically conflict ridden. If large-scale social institutions are principally constructions of concrete reasoning, with a primary and necessary ordering force in particular problem-solving being civil law, then the resolution of any specific moral or justice issue will be in terms of public peace. A conception of society as shaped by these forces suggests further that a change in the public consciousness of immorality or injustice can and will only initially reach the public forum through the disturbance of public peace, whether through attempts to change the law or through disobedience of the law. Conflict is the key by which a society advances first of all to a public discussion of particular issues. But ultimately, a lack of polarizing conflict spells out the resolution of those issues. A law can become enforceable only after there has been a public weighing of that issue, a discussion of the values involved and of the proper relative weighting of those values. For Murray, then, one arena of social ethical discourse is intrinsically conflict ridden, although it can be brought to practical resolution only through the action of public prudential reasoning. To ignore these forces, either by denying the place of conflict or the place of reasoning, is to condemn a society to anarchy or to a totalitarianism which is itself an anarchy of meaning.

At the first level of social ethical discussion, the languages of law, of conflict, and of particular prudential determination in the public forum have their legitimate place. But Murray, even in the cooperation debate, insisted further on the need for public discussion of general evaluative claims within that public forum. At first, these general value claims were simply givens, definitions which allowed or required little discussion. But, with his eventual recognition that general moral claims, including the principles of justice, develop over time, he adopted a more dynamic notion of those general value claims, more importantly as directive rather than as simply, timelessly

222 J. Leon Hooper, S.J.

descriptive of human concern. The general languages of rights, the novel forms of the authorization principles as well as the general authorization principle itself, and the tertiary principles of justice must be publicly argued and, through conversation, publicly affirmed and given directive roles in social policy discussions. Thus, Murray extended his notion of prudential determination to include theoretical discussions and to place those discussions in the public forum.

These discussions of the general values which a society maintains, then, constitute a distinct, second realm of social ethics, one that is not amenable to the languages of law, but is more properly discussed in terms of commitments which are to be actively preserved, even as they are being advocated. Here, the values endorsed by the social ethician must be carried in the manner by which that ethician addresses the public forum. One might coherently argue the ethics of a specific issue, say, a protocol for animal experimentation, without moving to act, without taking up a scalpel or an electrode. But in arguments concerning general value commitments, the actions advancing the argument will be readily perceived to be coherent or not coherent with the proposed values. Action is intrinsic to the attempt to shape the general principles that come to govern public policy discussions.

But, in itself, this move to include theoretical evaluative discussions in the public forum did not, Murray came to realize, reach to the foundational task of social ethics. To get at the forces of social commitment, Murray had to appeal to the active ethical agency of the actual people he was addressing, in a manner that, again, did not contradict that agency. Murray's insistence on active ethical agency constituted a shift from a primary focus on the social good to, in a sense, the individual and collective agents who were to affirm and develop that good. At this point, he recognized a further specificity to any ethical argument—that it is conducted with concrete human beings in particular situations. Murray's shift to moral agency, and his love of that agency in concrete peoples, broke him away from his own institutional biases. But the deeper implication of this turn is an imperative placed on the social ethician: a requirement of a love for ethically mature peoples, and a subsequent commitment to work with them in a manner that is consistent with, and evocative of, that ethical maturity. At this level of social ethics, the public languages or actions one employs are even more intimately tied to the values to be pursued than is true even in general commitment discussions. Love of peoples who ought to be morally mature defines, it does not simply motivate, one's social action.

It is at this point that Murray became an unapologetic and uncompromising *theological* social ethician. For Murray, the power of

God was indeed considered necessary for long-term social development. But, in the end, he did not present the discussion of that necessity in an apologetic fashion, as a divine answer to a troublesome question posed in the secular order. The church's mission is to witness to and to advance the action of a God who is already operative in that order. Consistent with his notion of love for the social good (i.e., maturely reflecting peoples) as the grounding of social development, he claimed in a parallel fashion that a love of God must lead to a witness to his power, a witness that reaches as far as God reaches, which was certainly, even empirically, beyond the church's institutional boundaries. The notion which mediated this viewpoint was his claimed *gnosis-agnosis* structuring of human consciousness. The denial of that consciousness spells the denial of God's gracious presence (constituting a break with that God), and therefore facilitates the possibility of social, totalitarian monism. Just as an ethician must be aware of the agency of the particular peoples with whom he or she deals, so must that ethician be aware of the agency of a historical, incarnate God. The God one faces is himself a mature social agent, and must be responded to accordingly—in free, responsible acknowledgment of his historical action. A mature God evokes mature human responses.

Be attentive. Be intelligent. Be reasonable. Be responsible. For a person of faith (faith in the social good, in the moral agency of the social person, in the power of a historical God), the commitment to such imperatives rests ultimately in love for actual persons and for God, as that love breaks beyond the bonds of limited insight, attention, and response. For Murray, a theological social ethician is one who speaks out of love, over and above all the conceptual formulations that he or she critically uses.

What then, according to Murray, ought a theological social ethician do? The task, it would seem, is threefold. First is the nitty-gritty involvement within the church and civil society in the prudential processes of particular determination, the formation of mediating insights by which both societies can come to common judgments of fact and judgments of value. This task in itself involves an understanding of the nature of the powers available at those levels of organization for enforcement and development. It also involves an accumulation of experience in those particular issue areas that are the ground out of which wisdom can arise. It is an arena in which argument is always difficult, but an arena that is the first and most public line of defense against social disintegration. If an institution, a social subgroup, or a society becomes blinded to the necessity of, and forgoes public discussion, then it will be buried under its own lack of insight.

However, this first task always carries with it a second, that of forwarding in the public forum the discussion of our general value commitments, of those things for which we as persons and as peoples are willing to suffer and die. This is the realm of the ideal, without which any society loses its sense of purpose and its hope. But it is also a realm that develops over time, and therefore must continually reenter the public discussion; our general values also involve a form of ongoing prudential determination. At the same time, this realm of general value discussion must be kept distinct from the first, lest our loves die amid conflict and our ability to respond to the particular historical world in which we live be blinded by our theories.

The third task of the theological ethician is a confrontation with the people's ethical will, and, ultimately, a confrontation with the God who acts in history. As Murray became increasingly preoccupied with this level of social-ethical public discourse, he gradually renounced his own much enjoyed polemical style; he recognized the role of the church in evoking the historically, if not theologically, justified atheistic cry against God; and he called on the church to observe the ethical procedural rules as well in its own internal dealings as in civil society, "and one might even say better"—all in order to evoke that mutual recognition of ethical agency which can only be born in love. Further, the church is to be a witness to God's action in history, that action toward unity through the difficult act of public discussion. Its own faith in the God of history, in his existential presence in our time, becomes manifest in its witness to God in word and act, a witness that continually challenges the church's own group bias. Beyond group bias and its instruments of war and limited insight, are the forces of conversation and freely emerging insight into the social reality that has been universally offered redemption.

Murray's later work on the notion of God in history transformed his own thinking from that of a natural law theorist, for whom reason stands publicly isolated from grace, to the framework of a theological ethician for whom the reasoning persons of faith confront their historical social world with the insights and languages of faith. More than a little historical analysis pushed home the point that the location of the intelligent, the morally wise, and even the holy within historical society could not once and for all be determined along institutional or group perimeters. If the church is to follow the God who redeems, thereby being true to its own mission and also true to the core consciousness of human society, it has to surrender its own group biases (hidden as those might be behind institutional and theological theories and symbols), while at the same time maintaining its own self-consciousness as a people who witness to God's historical presence. Whether or not that is sufficient to hold the solidarity of a siege church, after that siege has ended, remains an open question. For Murray, the role of witnessing to God's presence was not only sufficient. It was liberating in his sense of evangelical freedom, a freedom that allows both criticism and love toward civil and religious social realities to grow hand in hand. Reason and love are locked together in faith in, and in the power of, God's redeeming presence.

Notes

1. This issue of cooperation was intimately involved in the maturation of the American Catholic intellectual community—the first issue around which the Catholic Theological Society of America was formed, as described by Eugene Burke, C.S.P. (Burke 1980, 339-40).

2. Throughout this study, any text citations with just a date and page reference will be Murray's; all other author citations will include author, date, and page. Full publication information is given in the bibliography.

3. Indifferentism as described here is consistent with 1945a, 201-209, Murray's consideration of *Notre Charge* and the Sillonist movement. Indifferentism can also be described as a belief that Catholic doctrine is irrelevant to eternal salvation, but Murray did not concern himself with such a form.

4. According to Murray, the discussion of spiritual integrity as an organic and "different" group awareness is within the context of Harnackian liberalism which "reduces religious pluralism to unity on the religious plane," while the Catholic position "reduces religious pluralism to unity on the social plane." The former operates through a "sentimental tolerance," the latter through a "hard intellectualism" (1943b, 273-74).

5. From Murray's review of Connell's work, 1942b, 414-15.

6. The term "lexical" is used in the following sense: if condition *a* is fulfilled (unity or integrity), then condition *b* can *possibly* be acted upon (temporal common good). If condition *a* is not fulfilled, then no action *may* be taken toward condition *b*.

7. Murray did endorse the Sword of the Spirit movement with its parallel federation, but the movement included local mixed study groups, much along the mutual organizational structure. Such decentralization and grass-roots mixing "prevented an overcentralized organization, with consequent loss of spontaneity and freedom" (1943b, 283-84).

8. I have found it necessary to distinguish between two different types of generalized principles (as used in natural law or in theological arguments), and have chosen to call them "directional" and "definitional." In the ethical sphere, directional principles guide the attention of the moral inquirer to aspects of a moral problem which might lack clear definition, but which are generally considered important in moral considerations. For example, here the mission of the church is thought to be guided by the two principles of Christian integrity and the temporal common good. Directional principles, therefore, call up human intentionality, serving as premises for criticizing arguments that ignore aspects of these intentionalities, without necessarily and immediately offering clear formulations of the terms of these intentionalities. On the other hand, definitional principles, as particularly used in Murray's first

religious liberty argument, are thought to be essential definitions of the terms of human intentionality. Murray appears to have initially held that definitions of certain general social and cognitional realities (such as "church," "state," and "conscience") admit of clear, precise, and permanent definitions, which then serve as premises for moral and theological arguments.

9. Murray relied heavily in his definition of systematic theology on Mortimer Adler, "The Order of Learning" (Adler 1941, 334-36).

10. For some people theoretical distinctions work better than meta-phorical distinctions. Murray attempted the following metaphorical distinc-tion—only once: "By divine constitution, the sheep are not the shepherds. And it is hardly fitting that we should either invite the sheep to draw up a chair to the shepherd's table, or ask the shepherds to crawl about cropping grass with the sheep" (1944c, 376). One might wonder about latent paternalistic ideologies.

11. The argument described in this section was "theoretical" in the sense that it prescinded from the question of laymen working within a religiously pluralistic society. However, the notion of relatively autonomous realms (of action, theology, and spirituality) was not far from Murray's thought when he dealt with objections to pluralistic cooperation. Two sets of objections highlight a similar epistemological conception of theology and spirituality.

The first was Benedict XV's choice not to allow even Catholic laymen to participate in the World Council of Churches 1919 Stockholm accord on international peace (1943a, 102-4). In response to claims that this disapproval witnessed to a long-standing Vatican condemnation of mutual cooperation, Murray countered that Benedict approved of such cooperative social goals and even of the charity behind the accord. What Benedict disapproved of was the founding charter of the World Council of Churches, which Murray under-stood to be the principle that the doctrines of all members stand equally before the Lord. Benedict therefore condemned an organization which had as one of its founding principles a religious, ecclesiological doctrine contrary to Catholic teaching. And although this was an interference of the spiritual power in a concrete temporal organization, the interference was based on and directed toward a purely religious, but institutionalized, truth.

The second papal condemnation that Murray had to address was Pius X's condemnation of the Sillon movement in 1912 (1945a, 201-9). Murray contended that Pius' condemnation was not directed against the lay autonomy premise of Sillon. Pius objected to, in Murray's view, the strongly anti-Catholic vision of founding father, Marc Sangnier. Sangnier was driven by an image of a future society which he hoped would replace Catholic notions of a just and religious society. The problem, then, was one of a spirituality which was to replace Catholic spirituality. Murray used as evidence the fact that Sillon accepted into equal membership even men who were atheistic. This accep-tance of atheists indicated a vision which was at odds with the Catholic vision of the importance of religion for society. It constituted Marc Sangnier's spirituality as contrary to even the natural foundations of Western civiliza-tion. This question of atheism will be discussed further, but suffice it now to say that Murray considered Pius' condemnation a justified intrusion by a spiritual power in the temporal realm, concerning a natural, not revealed, religious premise of that organization. Murray again claimed the judgment of Rome was directed at a spiritual reality.

At this point, Murray's argument was that Rome in matter of fact intruded into temporal organizations only when a founding theological principle or spiritual vision was involved. This argument will become stronger in time.

12. In "Christian Co-operation" (1942b) Murray considered the views of Francis J. Connell, W. Butterfield, Maurice Bèvenot, Canon Mahony, and Jacques Maritain. In "Further Views (1943a)," he followed through, with strong approval, the position of Max Pribilla.

13. To the objection that non-Catholics contest or doubt the existence of natural law, Murray quickly responded with the usual natural law contention that they could only deny it theoretically, not in practice: their behavior betrays such a belief.

14. Murray wrote in "Pattern for Peace" 1944a, p. 12: "We may not doubt their [i.e., truths of the natural order] power to found a just social order; no such doubts appear in the papal documents. Moreover, we must remember that the Gospel and the natural law are not, as it were, two alternative foundations for social reconstruction. The natural law exists within the Gospel; and a social order which would conform to the demands of the natural law would already be fundamentally Christian. Therefore a Catholic program of co-operation on the basis of the natural law would be in perfect harmony with the program of Catholic operation on the basis of the integral Gospel."

15. Faith, in Murray's use of the term, involved both cognitional and volitional elements. In "The Role of Faith in the Renovation of the World" (1948c, 15–17), he wrote of faith primarily as an energy, an energy that was lacking in modern social reconstruction, despite all the application of intelligence. But he more consistently (and not inconsistently with the *Messenger* article) discussed faith, and therefore spirituality, in terms of both "cognitive" and "affective" elements, as his praise of Scheeben's doctrine indicates (1948e, 21).

16. Murray had suggested that Catholics should initiate such organizations, thereby guaranteeing that the governing principles of such organizations would be consistent with Catholic thought and that scandal would not be given (1943a, 109).

17. Compare to "...it is generally recognized today that even a general 'will to peace' on the part of individual nations will not insure a stable international order unless it is institutionalized in an international organization, that will function as a sort of collective conscience and be able to enforce its imperatives. The principle is clear: action for social organization must be social and organized in its principle. There is hardly need to belabor the point" (1943b, 262).

18. Murray's first religious liberty article, "Current Theology: Freedom of Religion" (1945b) was primarily a review of Protestant M. Searles Bates' *Religious Liberty: An Inquiry* (Bates 1947) and F. Ernest Johnson's *Religion and the World Order* (Johnson 1944). Bates' book was a result of the 1943 meetings of

the Joint Committee on Religious Liberty of the Federal Council of Churches and the Foreign Missions Conference of North America. Johnson was editor of his book, and it is his contributions to the book that drew Murray's strong, if cautious, praise.

In this section, I will not take up the interactions between Murray and American Protestants. Such will be considered in the next. But it is interesting to note that it was initially an attempt at Catholic-Protestant dialogue that led Murray to the topic, and that he started out in a balanced, yet critical, and even mildly sympathetic tone. Murray's religious liberty debate quickly confronted less "civil" responses from his American and European Catholic colleagues, and thus his primary "dialogic" partners, as well as the general tone of argument, quickly shifted. In the next chapter we will see that both the tone and content of Murray's Catholic-Protestant dialogues also shifted, but for somewhat different reasons.

One point in this first article should be noted, since it suggests the agenda that Murray appears to have set for himself in subsequent articles. Concerning some Protestant attacks on "the Catholic position," he wrote:

I suggest that this attack will not be successfully met simply by the strenuous defense of the position that the Catholic church is the one true church. The position, of course, must be guarded at every point. However, all the Protestant literature that I have seen and all the Catholics whom I know manifest a full awareness that such is our position. So far as freedom of religion is concerned, what is properly at issue and what troubles a good many Catholic as well as Protestant minds is rather the *political* implications of our position in the present world situation. In that field the confusion lies, and from that quarter the attack is made. (p. 90).

The term "political" that I have highlighted here should be compared with the term "political" in its usage as one of the three distinct arguments that must be formulated, as will be outlined further on. The political in Murray's present usage is the prudential determination that is responsive to societal religious consensus. It is this theory of prudential determination that Murray appears to have thought would remove Protestant fears concerning the Catholic position. We will note later that not very many of his Protestant colleagues appear to have understood what he was talking about, and those who did were not particularly relieved.

19. Commenting on M. Searle Bates' book (Bates 1945), Murray writes: "Hence, in the first two sections [on history and contemporary forms] it is constantly, both explicitly and implicitly, passing judgments of value on contemporary or historical situations without having first made clear the premises that justify these judgments" (1945d, 2-3). This disdain for historical argumentation should be remembered at the beginning of chapter 2.

20. Also "In the hypothesis of a supernatural order, perfecting the order of natural reason and human conscience, the rights mentioned would be subject, not to extinction or to revision, but to further completion. I believe that they remain intact in the supernatural order; but they are no longer an

adequate statement of the case. This is one of the cases in which human reason is 'humiliated' in the supernatural order, in order that it may be perfected and exalted" (1945d, 12).

21. For Murray's most unequivocal rejection of any political rights for the atheist, see 1945a, 103.

22. Reason "certifies" and "validates" theories about the natural order, although Murray does not spell out how this is done, that is, he does not discuss the epistemological presuppositions of his "perceptions" of essential realities. At issue seems to be the assertion that this moral order is "perceived, not created," by reason, despite his use of the term "architect" in the above. See 1945e, 249.

23. For example, "laws are mediated to the person by conscience" (1945e, 244). Murray is again vague on the intuitions or methods by which these laws are perceived. And it would be quite possible to interpret the relationship of these internalized laws and specific acts as immediate applications, which of course is a legalism.

24. Preliminary forms: 1945d, 4, 15. Final form: 1945e, 243. Whatever the arrow directions meant to Murray is not apparent in either the preliminary or final forms of the argument.

25. This inclusion of beliefs as a term of the operation of conscience is another extension beyond a narrow definition of conscience.

26. Note that religious life is situated in the personal half of the moral universe in the preliminary schema. This of course is out of line with much of even Murray's present thought. But it does suggest that his restriction of religious liberty to the internal forum rested in part in an unexamined if incomplete privatization of religion, at least within the natural order. (This apparent privatization will be discussed in the conclusion of this chapter.) The supernatural order included the quite public reality of the institutionalized church.

27. Here is the epistemological grounding for his rejection of the sufficiency of common will and/or charity as the sole basis for intercredal cooperation, discussed in the last section. We also need a spurring and directing content.

28. The missing third source for the will of God was "(b) through paternal authority in domestic society" (1945d, 4), which Murray claimed was not germane to a discussion of religious liberty.

29. "The prime point to be recalled is that the same man, the same community, is at once religious and political, subject to the authority of the moral law and to the authority of the State. Hence the prime obligation of the State to its citizens is to be itself subject to the moral law in all its actions. . . . The reason is that only thus can the conscience of the citizen, and the public conscience, be at peace, in the harmony of the obligations it has to God and to the State." Here is one of the few references Murray makes to "public conscience," but he does not define its meaning or utilize it in his argument.

Murray has so strongly emphasized the divinely required moral role of the state for the common good, and has so strongly connoted a purely private content to the "moral law" on the left side of his schema, that it is difficult to understand how the dictates of the state and the private morality of the citizens could fall into disharmony, unless the state encroached beyond the elements of the common good, into that realm of private or family life. At least in the first schema there is no commensurable content between the moral law and the civil authorities, a fact which I will show to be linked to Murray's private notion of conscience.

30. See also 262, note 9a. Such entails also the need of education and the development of virtues.

31. There is no thought here of having an obligation to shape ethical principles, at least for the common person who is to make moral decisions. (Such a notion might have sounded too much like the *conscientia exlex*.) The only obligation apparent in the present discussion is that of passive adoption of those principles. Had Murray been able, at this point, to visualize such an obligation incumbent on all people, he might have maintained a consistency between his notion of "law" in "natural law" (as perhaps backed up by a divinely sanctioned constraint) and those notions as used in the correlation of conscience and civil law, preserving thereby his implicit ethical legalism, at least as far as the common man goes. Fortunately he will have broken free of this thinly veiled legalism about the same time that he discovered the general dictates of natural law to be principles within the contingent, historical flow of human cognition.

32. For the purpose of establishing religious liberty, Murray claimed that he could prescind from consideration of the family (1945d, 4). Murray posed as one of the positive empowerments of conscience "the right to marry according to one's choice, to raise a family and to educate one's children to faith in God and obedience to His law" (1945d, 11; 1945e, 274). Why or how this right should be based on conscience is not obvious. If it is merely an extension of individual rights to an intermediate institution, then its effective scope is privatized, as will be discussed further. Murray seems to be granting more reality to, and an independent basis for, the family than to and for voluntary organizations, but the irrelevance of intermediate institutions to his present argument did not push him further.

33. Murray handwrote such a claim into the preliminary manuscript (p. 4) and incorporated it into the final form (p. 242). His only other treatment of intermediate institutions was to put them on a par with the state as potential violators of individual rights (1945e, 274–75).

34. Thus the entire structure of his presentation, first obligations (1945e, 263–73), then rights (pp. 273–78).

35. There is some ambiguity on this. As we shall see, the right of the individual to immunity from coercion in the realm of belief or opinion is not based on an obligation to the state, but rather on the obligation to act reasonably, as commanded by God. There is in Murray's thinking at this point no major emphasis on the individual's obligations toward the common well-being of society. And, while the state has an obligation to conform its laws to general natural law (the "private" law of the individual), this does not carry with it the state's right to morally act in the public forum. The right to so act arises from, again, divine command or obligation placed on the state by God.

36. It should be remembered, though, that in the natural universe there existed only one socially relevant moral authority, the state, and one authority with a scope only within familial matters. One might wonder where the dubious conscience was to turn, especially in conflicts with the state. Murray lacked carriers of general moral meaning.

37. Murray even speaks of there being two wills of God. "Initially, there is His supreme will that the reason of man and its practical judgments should be in harmony with the eternal order of reason which exists in His divine mind; in other words, God wills that man's conscience should be always right and true. There is also His will that the voluntary acts of man should be in harmony with his own reason and its practical judgments; in other words, God wills that man should act according to his conscience." He calls a lack of correspondence between these two orders "an eccentricity in the moral order, which illustrates at once the dignity and the misery of conscience" (1945e, 260).

38. Murray's definition of the (Roman) "Church" does admit to some limitation on the church. All salvation comes through the church; it is a necessary society. But it will pass out of existence with the passing of the temporal order. "The magisterial authority of the Church, her hierarchy of jurisdiction, and her sacramental system are divine in their origin and institution, but temporal in their finality." From which he concludes that the church "does not exist to save itself, as it were, but men" (1945e, 237).

39. One might ask, whatever happened to conscience as an autonomous source of moral discernment in the revealed order?

40. Murray's sense of religion as taking up space in the temporal order and as being capable of acting and being acted upon in that order established for him only three possibilities for the relationship of church and state, all of which entail some form of legal institutionalization, as we will see in the next subsection.

41. Murray does not discuss why this is so, and he waffles a bit on its force. He writes "There has never been in history a perfect solution of the problem of the relations between the spiritual and the temporal; never will there be one." We will continually fluctuate between clericalism and caesaro-papism. But, then again, "the theological solution is not sheer transposition ... by sheer imposition, either by the force of the State or the *fiat* of the Church .... The solution must be an organic growth, and must be in harmony with the religious and political realities of a particular community." And, "the union of Church and State is not always the correct political solution, for the simple reason that the order of essences is not always realized in the order of existence. (That is not a very good formula.)" (1945d, 16). He calls union an ideal and seems to hold that it can organically grow to a proper juridical expression. How this differs from a perfect solution which is never realizable is unclear.

42. Murray argues that the rights of association and propaganda are civil rights, not religious rights (1945e, 276–77). That is, they are related to the common good, and therefore related ultimately to the public consensus. Religious liberty in a private sense is absolute. Civil rights are never absolute.

43. He had suggested that the individual was under obligation to contribute to attainment of the common good, as directed by the custodians of that common good, i.e. the state. But this obligation was, cognitionally speaking, purely passive—a technical response to evaluations and conceptions of others. The individual is not yet an active moral agent in the sense Murray will develop, particularly during the Second Vatican Council

Chapter Two

1. 1948f, 1948g, and 1949e are used in the discussion of indirect powers (section I); 1949g, 1951c, and 1952a for the Society-State Distinction (section II); and 1952b, 1953a, 1953c, 1953e, 1954b, 1954c, 1954d, and 1955a for the implications of the Society-State Distinction (section III).

2. "From the actuality [of a thing], one can infer [its] possibility." I came across the phrase in one of Murray's commentators, but have not been able to track down its source.

3. Even in 1954, Murray was claiming that "the efforts of the Church toward its [church-state] problem have always been guided by the same set of general principles" (1954b, 11). But, as we will see, he had in mind a different set of principles than had preoccupied Pius IX.

4. Murray followed Bellarmine's five reasons for papal direct power (1948g, 513–18), which he concluded "lead to the conclusion that the primacy of the spiritual means a power on the part of the Church to judge, direct, and correct the political life of man, wherever the political touches the spiritual" (p. 518), with no implications concerning the problem of means.

The slightly effective part of Bellarmine's proof is based on papal examples of use of temporal power, concerning the most effective of which Murray writes: "The second group of seven are all examples of papal action in the founding and rule of Western Christendom: the deposition of Childeric by Zacharias, the transfer of the Empire to the Germans by Gregory V, and four of the string of depositions in the Middle Ages: that of Henry IV by Gregory VII, of Otho IV by Innocent III, of Frederick II by Innocent IV, and of Louis of Bavaria by Clement VI. These are the real foundations of Bellarmine's case; and among them the actions of Gregory VII, Innocent III, and Innocent IV are leading. He appeals to them again and again. . . . In substance, then, Bellarmine derives his theory, in what is special to it, from the most resounding acts of the Medieval papacy in its most imperial-minded representatives" (p. 519).

5. Murray argues that the early Fathers did not assert such a right to use coercive power, because before the Middle Ages, there was a genuine "defect of right" (1948g, 525).

6. Murray does not discuss the fifth and sixth powers. The sixth, of course, raises the question of the state forcing such support, but, as it stands, it concerns church members, not civil or political society directly.

7. Murray had earlier used a society/state/government distinction to attack the logic of opponents, but at that time that was about as much use as he gave to it (1948f, 29).

8. However, his writings are laced with comments such as: "Likewise denied in the *ancien regime* was the principle of the freedom of the Church; Francis I half-cynically conceded that he would probably be damned because of the bonds in which the Concordat of 1516 confined the Church of France and the Holy See." Murray continued: "Yet it is to the *ancien regime* and its imitators, the Restoration monarchies, that the books *de jure publico* point when they are developing the 'thesis' about 'Catholic societies'" (1951c, 349).

9. For example, in "Separation" (1953c) Murray had promised further work on "the cooperation of the two powers and societies, the substance of society, and public religion" (p. 214). The first and third items became part of the last Leonine article; the second was never dealt with by way of "essential" definitions, but became immersed in a study of the state's concern for aspects of culture.

10. One problem with presenting a summation of such a long, inter-woven, and at times backtracking argument is that direct quotation contri-butes neither to brevity nor to clarity. I have therefore used for the most part only indirect citations to the appropriate articles. For the one article that never did reach publication, I have included direct quotations in the notes.

11. Murray relied heavily on J. T. Talmon's *The Rise of Totalitarian Democracy* (1952) for four principles which guided French democracy, also on Christo-pher Dawson's *Beyond Politics* (1938). Murray particularly liked the suggestion that Jacobin democracy *required* an enemy for its very existence, so the church was its target.

12. The *res sacra* or *res sacrae* includes:

> ... the husband-wife relationship, the parent-child relationship (includ-ing education), the political obligation, the human dignity of the worker, the equality of men as all equally in the image of God, the moral values inherent in economic life, the works of charity and justice which are the native expression of the human and Christian spirit, the patrimony of ideas which are the foundation of human society—the ideas of law, freedom, justice, property, moral obligation, civic obedience, legitimate rule, etc., etc. There is also the thing, sacred in its destination, whereby the Church occupies ground in this world, namely, her legitimate property" (1953c, 209).

One might ask, what else is left?

The use of the term "address" in my text is purposely ambiguous. Murray has not yet faced the limitations which might possibly concern the church's ultimate word on moral matters.

13. Murray went to some length to suggest that our "separated breth-ren" were not considered by Leo to be involved in the conspiracy.

14. Therefore Leo's political and social philosophy was at fault (realms of temporal reason), not his (timeless) theology. The term "power" here is simple coercion, not as it is used in the powers argument.

15. Leonine encyclical of 1891, often entitled "On the Condition of the Working Class."

16. It has been suggested that Leo had some contact with the Anglo-American distinction of society and state through the interventions of Manning and Gibbons, concerning the American Knights of Labor issue (Hales 1958, 207). On Gibbons' possible influence on *Rerum Novarum*: Moody 1961, 75–77).

17. Put in terms of a necessary social polarity, "True order rests on freedom *and* authority." Both principles must be held and balanced simultaneously, although Leo missed the first because of the type of debate in which he was involved (1954c, 5). This notion of polarity principles will play an important role in Murray's later religious freedom argument.

18. This consistent use of the society/state was, rather, "nearly" firm. Murray wrote in corrections on the galley proof pages of this fifth, Leonine article. At several key points, particularly in those sections dealing with the relationship of Christian faith to the temporal order, he scratched out the term "state" and substituted "society."

The following references to this article are made up of two parts: the first is a number given at the end of a string of printing data at the top of the pages and these numbers are sequential; the second is a large print galley page number (e.g., S-35) which is not sequential to the article. References for the material of this note are, therefore, in the form "1955a, gal. 24, S-35; gal. 3, Q-33; gal. 10, R-88."

19. "It might also be noted that an act of legislation is not formally an act of the virtue of religion, it is not an act of faith, worship, thanksgiving, or petition. Its formal effect is not an increase of grace in citizens or public officials, but the creation of a juridical situation within the state. It is therefore clear that the question of the care of the public religion by government through the coercive agency of law is to be distinguished from the question of the public profession of religion by society in free acts of faith, worship, and service" (1955a gal. 8, R-31).

20. Murray dealt with the relation of the *state* to revelation in terms of the public care of religion. "It is suggested [in *Immortale Dei*] that the care of religion is indirect rather than direct. What government directly serves is the public advantage, not the Church as such. Governmental care of religion does not terminate directly at religion itself—at the substance of religious faith or religious unity. These are sacrednesses which are to be preserved inviolate—even, and indeed especially, from government. Political action terminates at a political end, which is exactly described in the text; this end is the creation of *opportunitates* and *facilitates*—favorable environment within the body politic—which may indirectly assist men in pursuit of their eternal purposes. Since these purposes transcend the whole order of temporal life, the assistance rendered by government to men in their pursuit can only be indirect" (1955a gal. 13, Q-85).

21. "In presenting the first view I wish to make it clear that I am not attributing it to any particular author. The fact is that I shall deliberately sharpen its propositions, somewhat after the fashion in which Leo XIII sharpened the propositions of sectarian Liberalism" (1955a, gal. 23, S-5). The title of this section is "Anatomy of an Anonymous View."

22. "The quality of the Catholic population does not enter into the argument. That is, little if any attention is paid to the prevailing level of religious knowledge and practice, to the general educational and cultural level, to the level of political self-awareness—in a word, to the question whether laws are being framed for Catholic masses or genuine Catholic people, for an ignorant and apathetic Catholic multitude or for a Catholic body politic that is reasonably literate—religiously, politically, culturally."

Murray then turned to the use of this theory in support of Ecuadorian and Spanish establishment. "You may even find a degree of religious dissension that erupts into assassination, as in the case of Moreno, or into a bloody civil war, as in the case of Spain. You will certainly fail to find the fulfillment of the Western Christian ideal of political life and government, which is certainly not dictatorship. No matter. You find establishment and intolerance, and therefore you find the ideal Catholic state." Again, this article did not make it to publication.

23. This section is entitled: "The Traditional View: Pius XII," which is also the "unitary" view, i.e., Murray's view. Murray's use of the term "unitary" is slightly confusing. When he uses the term "unitary" theory in contrast to the "disjunctive" theory, he is contrasting a prudential judgment theory of ethical determination with the thesis-hypothesis, ideal vs. expedient theory. However, when he refers to the "unitary" social theory, he is referring to the one society, Christendom theory which stands in contrast to social dualism theory.

24. See also 1954d, 1.

After references to the international reactions to Ottaviani, the notes continue:

"Pope sought occasion; offered by invitation to address convention of jurists; carefully prepared.

"First point: 'only he to whom Christ has entrusted guidance of whole Church is competent to speak in the last instance on such vital qq. touching international life, that is, Roman Pontiff.'

"Significance caught in Rome: 'exit auctoritas Em-issimi.'"

25. Both of these aspects are, of course, related to one's juridical theory. Matters of public law concern moral and juridical elements, but Leo and Pius differ on the element which they emphasize. "Leo's emphasis fell upon the moral origins of human law; Pius' emphasis falls upon the political purposes of human law...a choice of emphasis is possible; and Pius XII's is the more traditional choice, the choice dictated by the intrinsic necessities of doctrine rather than by the extrinsic necessities of polemic" (1955a, gal. 26, S-31).

26. The political office holder, when functioning within the role of statesman, gives priority to the principle of peace in the framing of legislation. "The demands of social unity and peace, as they become concrete in determinate circumstances, are the highest and most general norm for the legislative action of government in what concerns the order of religion. By firmly asserting the primacy of this juristic norm Pius XII sets things right side up, so to speak. It is the traditional doctrine" (1955a, gal. 28, S-11).

27. "In affirming the autonomy of the lay authority of the state in matters of legal decision Pius XII is again fully in the tradition of Leo XIII, whose clarification of the traditional doctrine of the 'two societies' had made this principle newly clear" (1955a, gal. 29, S-31).

"What the Church wants—all that the Church wants—is that these norms [peace, international scope of common good] should be honestly applied by the jurist. The Pope does not reserve to himself the right to make the final legal decision for the jurist, or to substitute his own judgment for the jurist's judgment. The legal decision is squarely in the hands of the jurist.

"But the Pope does reserve exclusively to himself the judgment as to what set of principles and norms the jurist is to use in coming to legal decision . . . Pius XII clearly tells the jurist three things, in effect: (1) that in matters of legal decision affecting the relation of religion to the order of law he, the jurist, is the competent lay authority; (2) that in reaching his decision he is to follow the traditional norms of the Church; (3) that he himself, the Roman Pontiff, has just stated these norms—all the norms there are; there are no others" (gal. 30, S-60).

This is, of course, right back in the problem of theological and "temporal" knowledge, the closest Murray came to leaving the evaluation of specific forms to laymen, and the most strained portion of his interpretation of Pius.

28. "The dualism is not natural; indeed its establishment involved a certain dislocation of the natural order, a diminution of the stature and scope which the political power would have possessed in another, purely natural dispensation . . . As the political expression of human reason, the State seems to share that tendency [toward monism], inherent in reason, which has been the origin of all heresy . . . and political monism."

Whereas Murray had earlier consistently insisted on the compatibility of nature and grace, reason and faith, the temporal and the church, there is here an assertion of an ongoing disharmony between the pairs, a lack of synchronization or "natural" compatibility between the two orders. But, if the state is "by nature" as limited as he has been saying, then the problem that he is describing is actually between two societies; the state remains restricted to its limited goals and within that "intention of nature" which the institutionalized society/state distinction is. Previously Murray has seriously objected to the classical view of the *state* as the most perfect society, whether the order be natural or redeemed.

29. "The tendency [to juridical and social monism] was likewise visible in another form in the medieval Christian commonwealth. It appeared not so much in social fact (the Christian dualism maintained itself in terms of fact), as in social theory—in those theories of hierocratic stamp which exhibited a will to reduce the state to the Church, largely under the influence of a principle which derived from reason rather than from revelation, *Duo principia ponere nefas est*" (1954b, 13). Murray's notion of "natural" reason, here, is curious. It will be discussed in the next chapter.

30. "The suggestion here seems to be that the writ of the international community should also run within the territories of all member-states. This

tolerant writ, necessary and rightful within the determinate circumstances of the international community, would establish the 'norm that the free exercise of a religious or moral belief and practice which has value in one of the member-states should not be inhibited by means of laws and coercive measures of state within the whole territory of the community.' This norm of the international community would likewise be a norm within the individual states, in consequence of the obligatory concern that individual states must have for the higher good of the broader community."

This judgment, of course, stands in sharp contrast to Murray's reaction to Furfey in the cooperation debate (chapter 1, section 4).

31. These two principles—theologically based social dualism and the moral priority of civil society—are not, of course, the same. I will discuss Murray's attempt to link them in chapter 4.

32. Refer to note 29 for the "cause" of Catholic Jacobinism. "Repression of religious error a pendant of establishment: because one official state-religion, therefore no public existence for others. Because government represents transcendent truth of Catholicism, therefore does not recognize, publicly, those who do not share it. In concrete and pushed to extreme, a sort of 'Catholic Jacobinism.': those who are not of the faith are not of the nation" (1954d, 8). See also 1953c, 203.

33. My use here of the terms "social ontology" and "ontological dualism" is an anticipation of Murray's own later usage, as will surface in chapter 4. Both here and in Murray's later work, the term "ontology" in reference to society is merely used to suggest the strong realism involved in the assertion that "two there are," even though the assertion might arise from the world of faith. For Murray, the temporal universe has been "recreated" with two distinct sources of social meaning, and it can deny that recreation only on pain of self-destruction.

34. This use of "consensus" differs from that of his first argument. In the essential argument, "consensus" was significant for the practical or political argument, and concerned the type of common religious adherence which was maintained by a society. "Consensus" in the historical argument becomes primarily an ethical reality which is prior to temporal, political and philosophical arguments, and therefore, in a sense yet unexamined, prior to any age's ecclesiastical argument.

35. The poverty of Murray's notion of the church during this period is at the least curious, perhaps reflecting the tendency to deal with religion from a privatized or individualistic slant. There is no notion of the church as primarily concerned with God, or with witnessing to the presence of God in the church or in temporal reality. The church merely facilitates the individual's approach to God. As will be seen in chapter 6, a more theistic orientation to his definition of the church will enter his thinking after the Council.

Chapter Three

1. For a general discussion of the religious liberty constitutional question: Smith, *Religious Liberty in the United States* (1972). Chapter 13 is a good presentation of Murray's thought. Particularly chapters 17, 18 and 19 take up the recent church/state Supreme Court rulings.

Smith's book is the finest presentation that I have found on the religious and constitutional debate concerning the First and Fourteenth Amendments. The first section deals with separationist (Protestant and secularistic) theories, the second with Catholic, and the third with the actual juridical discourse of the Supreme Court. In the third section Smith works with an epistemology of ethical determination that is not unlike Murray's own—the process of prudentially drawing a line between two contrary tendencies within the First Amendment. Murray, of course, would object that one must go behind and beyond the actual constitutional formulation for a proper balancing of those tendencies.

2. As will become obvious throughout this chapter, Murray's notion of Protestantism was about as monolithic as was his initial notion of Catholicism. (Regarding the latter at least, he had to confront pluralism within the Roman Church, and would later incorporate a notion of diversity into his ecclesiology as an essential, not accidental, facet of the church.) Murray never did develop a differentiated notion of Protestantism, nor confront alternative Protestant theories of American society, such as the three-part distinction between Protestant approaches to religion and society, as utilized by Thomas G. Sanders in his *Protestant Concepts of Church and State* (1965), nor H. Richard Niebuhr's five-part classification in *Christ and Culture* (1951).

Murray's own operative categories were "Protestantism" and "secularism." Until the 1960s, he caught his Protestant colleagues in a "catch-22" situation. First, if they spoke of the churches as voluntary associations with equal sanction by God, he would reject their arguments as proclaiming a Protestant ecclesiology, and therefore a theology. Second, if they ignored any discussion of God and the churches, then he claimed that they were dupes of secularism or themselves "unadulterated secularists" who happened to be blessed by liberal Protestantism. Any Protestant who, in Murray's view, made a nonreligiously (natural law) substantiated claim was caught in the general secularistic web that sought to ignore the importance of theistic discourse for modern society. But, third, if they simply claimed ecclesiological rights based on personal rights, Murray would jump on what he considered to be social naivety. After his first failed religious liberty argument, he could not accept individualistically based claims of social rights, devoid of an appeal to a social grounding for those rights—but thus emerges one's understanding of the church.

3. Throughout these notes, the first references for all previously published *WHTT* (1960a) articles will cite both the first publication, and then its location in *WHTT*. All subsequent references to each text will be to the *WHTT* versions, unless original materials from the first publication that did

not make it to *WHTT* are cited. All original *WHTT* materials will be noted. In the bibliography, an asterisk (*) indicates the text version(s) cited in these chapter notes.

4. "Sociological" is used similarly to "social" in H. Richard Niebuhr's *The Social Sources of Denominationalism* (1957), as Murray's discussion of the relation of reason and faith is similar to a parallel discussion in Niebuhr's *Radical Monotheism and Western Culture* ([1943] 1970, 11–16). (The reason-faith topic will surface in section II of this chapter.) There is no indication that I have seen of much mutual recognition, much less discussion, between these two authors, a fact which must be listed as a major loss in American ecumenical possibilities.

5. For a brief history of the Project: MacIver 1955, v–vii. This was the second, theoretical work following on Hofstadter and Metzger 1955, both results of the collaborative project.

The following is a listing of all the correspondence, which are randomly spread through Murray Archive, files 13 and 15.

1. October 19,1951: MacIver to Murray: introduction (MacIver 1954, #1).

2. March 31, 1952: MacIver to Murray: comments on Murray's critique of a first statement on religious liberty, neither of which is on file (MacIver 1954, #2).

3. April 17, 1952: Murray to MacIver: two-page letter and six-page comment on the Project's Communism critique (Murray 1954a, #3).

4. April 22, 1952: MacIver to Murray: brief comment on April 17 letter (MacIver 1954, #4).

5. April 23, 1952: Murray to MacIver (Murray 1954a, #5).

6. August 26, 1952: MacIver to Murray: MacIver's case for scientific starting point (MacIver 1954, #6).

7. Updated: Murray to MacIver: from internal data, a response to the August 26 letter and to further Project publications (Murray 1954a, #7).

8. February 4, 1954: Murray to MacIver: sixteen pages of comments on the Project's "The Greater Mission of the University" and "The Denominational University," which became chapter 14 and appendix A of MacIver's book (Murray 1954a, #8).

9. February 11, 1954: MacIver to Murray: MacIver states that Murray was the only one who substantially objected to the Project's finished product (MacIver 1954, #9).

10. February 18, 1954: Murray to MacIver (Murray 1954a, #10).

11. May 5, 1954: MacIver to Murray (MacIver 1954, #11).

12. May 30, 1954: Murray to MacIver (Murray 1954a, #12).

6. This shift from the natural law as a set of truths to the natural law as a theory of public reasoning was, early in this period, facilitated by Murray's appeal to Heinrich Rommen's notion of the "tradition of reason." But both Ernest Barker's conception of the "tradition of civility" and Walter Lippman's "consensus" discussions expanded Murray's notion of reason beyond the dynamisms of individual rational psychology to the exigencies of social

cohesion and collectively affirmed meaning. As will be argued in the next two chapters, this prepared the way for an adoption of Bernard Lonergan's notions of society as constituted by meaning. Even in this chapter we will find some notions of reason that appear similar to Lonergan's, but a discussion of these similarities will be delayed for later consideration.

During this period Murray himself makes reference to the following works: Rommen, *The State in Catholic Thought* (1945) and *The Natural Law: A Study in Legal and Social History and Philosophy* (1947); Barker, *Traditions of Civility: Eight Essays* (1948); Lippman, *Public Opinion* (1922) and *Essays in Public Philosophy* (1955).

7. This notion of "prudence" is identical, from what minimal definition Murray gives it here, to the notion of political judgment that he developed in the 1940s (chapter 1), but much broader in its application.

The "fundamental option" of the American people for the method of freedom as discussed above, sets up the public situation that "freedom of expression is the rule, and censorship the exception" (p. 164), meaning that one has to have a very clear argument for censorship to contravene the normal rule of freedom.

8. He adds "The chief danger is lest the Church itself be identified in the public mind as a power-association. The identification is injurious; it turns into a hatred of faith."

9. Note here the nonindividualistic interpretation of the presupposition for freedom. Against some views of the Anglo-American tradition as steeped in egoism and isolation, Murray asserts freedom for the sake of a socially moral society.

10. Reflecting Murray's current involvement with "the forthcoming conciliar Declaration" on religious freedom, he did try to argue that the Catholic refusal to impose their minority moral view was based on religious freedom. But for a man who held such a sharp distinction between natural law morality and revealed religion, it is difficult to see what religious freedom (except in a highly institutional sense) has to do with his argument.

11. John Coleman understates that "nor is [Murray's] defense of America's cold-war stance particularly critical or enlightening" (Hollenbach 1979, 705), although Coleman himself has made good use of the principles of "limitation" and "proportionality" in his pastoral letter for Bishop Roger Mahony, "The Call of Christ, Prince of Peace: Becoming a Church of Peace Advocacy," December, 1981.

Murray judged that the Russians pursue a policy of minimum risk and maximum security—they avoid at all cost raising their own survival as the governing index on their use of force. America, on the other hand, considers the use of force only under the question of national survival. In this mental frame, no rational discussion of the use of force by Americans is possible. America should pursue a policy of maximum risk and minimum security.

12. Murray's comments on Smith's position are accurate to Smith's text. For Murray's objection to the reduction of all religious questions to biologisms, see p. 22. Murray does admit the validity and usefulness of a limited empiricism, as long as it is itself limited by other branches of knowledge. Smith prefers the societal adoption of modern science, in part for its limited range of

the knowable. If we realize how close we are to the primitive cruelty of our beginnings (Smith 1949, 18), we will collectively set out to "maximize satisfactions (with deference to the rights of others)," without the brutality which has arisen from absolutist philosophies and religions (pp. 18, 28).

13. Murray will soften his conception of the "constancy" of human nature, while even more strongly insisting that understanding can reach the human person and social reality.

14. This 1958 reference to a realism which is "naive" was not part of Murray's 1950 conceptualism, perhaps reflecting some late 1950s influence of Bernard Lonergan, as I will have many opportunities to note. Throughout the early 1950s, Murray will strongly support what he eventually came to call "naive realism," as opposed to "critical realism." When he did come to reject "naive realism" for "critical realism," he did not miss a beat in his counter-positioning of his new epistemological theory against the opponents mentioned here.

15. It is noteworthy that these three terms were used to describe the rights of the church vis-à-vis government.

16. He continues: "It is indeed one of the ironies of history that the tradition should have so largely languished in the so-called Catholic nations of Europe at the same time that its enduring vigor was launching a new Republic across the broad ocean. There is also some paradox in the fact that a nation which has (rightly or wrongly) thought of its own genius in Protestant terms should have owed its origins and the stability of its political structure to a tradition whose genius is alien to current intellectualized versions of the Protestant religion and even to certain individualistic exigencies of Protestant religiosity. These are special questions, not to be pursued here."

In the second part of this article, which became a separate chapter in *WHTT* (chapter 2), Murray did take up the question of founding theologies. The study concentrates on Edmund Burke, Roger Williams, with some mention of the Cottons and the Mathers, and academic appeal is made to Perry Miller and Daniel Boorstin. His main case is the one that we have seen, that the philosophical conception of law and the practical situation of religious pluralism determined the American conception of liberty. The theologies of equal denominational value were, he maintained, not determinative.

17. Note the terms "understanding," "judgment," and "experience" in this text. For many years Murray held for a two-part general division of rationality: theoretical reason and practical reason, theory and action, etc. As mentioned in note 14, this use of the Lonergan notion of three rational operators has entered Murray's thought in the late 1950s, along with perhaps a notion of the "longer cycle of decline." But a discussion of this influence is postponed for later chapters. Lonergan's *Insight* appeared in 1957.

18. With a clearer notion of judgment (as distinct from understanding) Murray was in a better position to deal with general and specific value determinations than he had been when working with his earlier conception of human thought according to the theoretical/practical division. He was, within a notion of judgment as a rational operation, better able to incorporate a Thomistic notion of tertiary principles (and therefore historical development) within his own democratic social, ethical theory.

19. Highlighting is my own. As we have seen from the beginning of this American discussion, the problem of relativism was never very far from Murray's thought. Early on, he granted three areas of ethical concern at the national level of social organization: the public order, the general ethical beliefs, and justice. We saw in the censorship debate that, under a notion of the limitation of the state to public order, he made the entry of general ethical beliefs into public law contingent on public order—a consensus must exist before a nonpublic order good could be enforced by civil law, and the attempt to enforce such goods without consensus was destructive of public order.

As we will see in the next few paragraphs and in the conclusion, Murray's newly appropriated notion of judgment as operative in both general and specific value determination will similarly cast the notion of "justice" into the historical stream. Whereas he had earlier appealed to justice (spelled out primarily as a set of definitional principles) as the noncontingent basis for judgments concerning public order, he now appealed to the very act of judging, to the rational operations of human intelligence, for such a basis. Murray has now reached beyond norms of justice to the social action of reasonable discussion for the noncontingent grounding of his social ethics. Again, I will discuss the basis and implication of this move in the following chapters.

20. The terms "common sense" and "common sense judgments" are Lonergan's (1958, 207–11, 280–99), and will be defined and discussed more fully in chapter 6. In the next few chapters I will suggest that Murray's adoption of many Lonergan concepts helped his religious liberty argument and his understanding of historical knowledge within the church. Likewise, I will argue that a clearer notion of common sense procedures could have helped Murray clarify the interrelationship between the elite and the people, particularly since he expected wisdom of the people.

21. He continued: "The proper task of the Church is the custody and the development of the deposit of faith, which is a body of revealed truth, a structure of mystery, that sustains and directs the action of the People Spiritual."

22. The Manifesto was published as: "Separation of Church and State: A Manifesto by 'Protestants and Other Americans United,'" *The Christian Century* 65 (January 21, 1948):79–82.

23. Within his directly Catholic-Protestant exchanges, this is the earliest that I have found a concern on Murray's part for due process (perhaps in response to others and his own inflammatory language). This lack of an earlier affirmation of due process is understandable within the context of his fear of a "religion of democratic process." During this period he was, however, also involved in talks for Catholic lawyers' "Red Masses" and was doing some writing on civil rights and the role of due process within democratic political forms. See "Free Speech in Its Relationship to Self-Government" (1949c), and "The Problem of Free Speech" (1953d).

Murray's later conversion to the ethical primacy of due process was in part born out of these confused Catholic-Protestant exchanges.

24. In response to Murray's "Reply," Bowie did cite the Roman Catholic

"totalitarian claim to be the only church of Christ" as the ultimate ground of their mutual hostility (Bowie 1949b, 637).

25. According to Thomas G. Sanders (Sanders 1965, 68–69), during this period Blanshard was criticized even by some of those who shared his separationist presuppositions for undervaluing the dangers of secularism to American culture. Murray had little if any understanding of positive Calvinistic theological background for Blanshard's agenda of limiting church power (see H. R. Niebuhr 1959, 75–87). Sanders himself criticizes the separationist movement for its excessive anti-Catholic bias and its lack of critical reflection on its own highly political activity in the public forum.

26. Murray's four procedural rules were: (1) "each minority group has the right to censor for its own members . . . "; (2) "no minority group has the right to demand that government should impose general censorship . . . " where "judgments of harmfulness" are not shared generally; (3) "any minority group has the right to work toward the elevation of standards of public morality . . . by the methods of persuasion and pacific argument"; (4) "no minority group has the right to impose its own religious or moral views on other groups, through the use of the methods of force, coercion, or violence" (1956f, 168).

27. Once again, it is difficult to figure out which group of Protestants Murray was talking about. I have had occasion earlier to note his monolithic view of Protestantism in the education debate (see note 2). After Murray's serving on a Fund for the Republic committee with Reinhold Niebuhr, he seems aware that Niebuhr and Bowie differed, but as we shall see there is no serious theological engagement with Niebuhr. I suspect that Murray's use of the term "fundamentalism" covered both contemporary forms of uncritical biblical positivism and also the entire evangelical tradition.

28. It has been suggested that Murray was playing off Niebuhr's technical term "ambiguity," without really understanding it. Murray did not know much about Niebuhr's theology, nor even his political ethics; he had only met with him in the forum of ethical discussions, with mixed results. What bothered Murray most was the ethical individualism implicit in the formula "moral man and immoral society," the title of Niebuhr's 1932 book which Murray quotes in the present article (p. 285). Such individualism (and even theological individualism) has been criticized by others (Stone 1972, 84) and by Niebuhr himself (1965, 15). See also Novak 1966, 92–112.

29. At work, of course, is Murray's notion of ethical determination as prudential judgment, in both the private and the public spheres. For this reason he views the dichotomy between "moral man and immoral society" as a "pseudo-problem," and the complexities of foreign policy as open to moral action, more difficult perhaps to isolate, but nonetheless open to enquiry.

30. Several elements of Berle's own argument, which Murray considered important, have not been presented here. One such element is a distinction between "consensus" and "opinion." Consensus concerns the general principles out of which specific ethical judgments are made; opinion is a commonly held, specific judgment, or a commonly accepted policy decision (1960a, 102–3). In the terminology used in my conclusion, specific prudential

determination or policy decisions would be "opinion," while general principles would be "consensus." Berle did help Murray establish his terminology and keep these two cognitive ethical realities distinct.

Further, Murray argues throughout the article that the "consensus" elements serve as the directing factors in the businessman's drive to be, or to at least appear to be, reasonable. This would imply that the businessman himself is the agent of particular moral determination within economic society (remembering Murray's argument for relative economic autonomy in the Leonine series). The businessman must make moral choices; he cannot simply follow specific laws since law can never cover the complexity of all valued situations. The businessman is himself, then, a moral agent, and therefore society itself is an arena of particular ethical determination.

My discussion through the next few pages primarily concerns consensus elements, one of which is the generalized commitment to practice public, prudential reasoning.

Chapter Four

1. Throughout this article and elsewhere, Murray repeatedly appeals to the "emergence" of new states of the question and of the principles by which judgments are formed. This concept of emergence is dear to Lonergan's *Insight*, particularly as developed in a subsection entitled "Emergent Probabilities," pp. 121-24.

2. The information here was taken from Donald Pelotte's *John Courtney Murray: Theologian in Conflict* (1976, 74-114) and Richard Regan's *Conflict and Consensus* (1976). For an historical study of the Council and *Dignitatis Humanae*, I would especially recommend Regan's book.

3. In a May 10, 1959 letter to Fredrick Crowe, S. J., Murray included a one-page outline for the Jesuit meeting. The discussion was to be based on Lonergan's *"Divinarum processionum conceptionem analogicam evolvit Bernardus Lonergan, S.J.* (Rome, 1957)" and *"De constitutione Christi ontologica et psychologica* (Rome, 1956)." Of primary concern was the development of Trinitarian doctrine. In the Crowe letter, Murray wrote: "The theme I have in mind is Bernie Lonergan's treatment of the divine missions and the inhabitation of grace. I went over to his theory this last year in class."

4. *De Constitutione Christi ontologica et psychologica*, 1956, (the doctrine on Christ as subject—useful for 'interiority').

Divinarum Personarum Conceptio analogica, 1957 for *intelligentia fidei*).

De Deo Trino, 1961 (for genesis of dogmatic and theological categories).

De Verbo Incarnato, 1961 (for development of Christological dogma, satisfaction, redemption as dialectic law).

A series of articles on *Gratia operans* in *Theological Studies*, 1941 and 1942, illustrate the genesis of the category of the supernatural...

'The Assumption and Theology' in: *Vers le dogme de l'Assomption* (Fides, Montreal, 1948), pp. 411-24.

'Theology and Understanding,' *Gregorianum* 35 (1954):630-48."

The bibliography and statement of "Themes" are in Murray Archives, file 486 (1962a).

5. An address delivered at a meeting of the Canon Law Society of America in October, 1966. Published in Biechler (ed.) 1967, 126–33, and in Lonergan 1974, 1–9.

6. Murray to Lonergan, June 28, 1967: Murray asked for editorial comment on an Anselm Atkins article on "dialectic de-development," an article which was under consideration for TS publication.

Lonergan to Murray, July 2, 1967: Lonergan criticized the article for remaining locked in logic, "not escaping from classicism into the realm of method and an understanding of dialectic, not as within logic but as an analysis of historical process."

Murray to Atkins, July 12, 1967: Murray wrote that "the movement from a static logic to a dialectical logic still leaves you in the world of logic. In other words, you are still in the classicist world, and perhaps captive to the classicist fallacy, namely, that logic is the all embracing science."

The Atkins article was, of course, rejected, this after Murray had suggested that the article went considerably beyond Lonergan's own position (July 28 letter, above). Lonergan obviously felt that it did not go sufficiently far, much less beyond, his own position.

7. "Church and State: The Structure of the Argument" (1958a). On the top of the 1958a manuscript, written in two different hands are "Received from Father Murray, 3/6/58" and "Not published: Rome Censors."

"Unica Status Religio" (1959a). For a discussion of the censorship of this article, see Pelotte, 1976, 57–59.

8. Note the highly developed and highly limited notion of human law, in contrast to that used in his first, essentialistic argument. Not even this, however, could save his argument without an appeal to modern consciousness.

9. Murray was still trying to maintain a certain type of "timelessness" to the theological realm. The sheer fact of international religious pluralism is not of immediate relevance to the theological argument, since such a sheer fact is situated in the temporal order and is therefore contingent. A "theological fact," however, is spoken from outside that temporal, contingent order, and is therefore relevant to a theological argument. In Pius XII's term, it is for Murray a theological *questione facti* which destroys the ideal bias of the conservative argument, without immediate reference to the temporal political order. (This means of preserving religious truth will disappear by the time of the Council.) The sheer fact of religious pluralism is, however, significant to the layman in the formation of law, since "the emergence of this wider (international) human community is the object of a divine intention" (p. 18).

10. My claim of his "proof text methodology" mostly concerns his uncritical use of Scriptures. Murray demonstrated little notion of a fundamental pluralism of theological viewpoints within the Gospels, much less within the entire New Testament. In the present text he merely based his case on Luke 12:51,

"Do you suppose that I came here to bring peace on earth? No, I tell you, but rather division (*diamerismon*, sc., dissension, disunity, separation)." A mysterious necessity attaches to the fact of religious division and moral incoherence .... Religious divisions among men occur, not simply as a matter of naked and inevitable fact, but in accord with the same "messianic necessity" [as Christ's death]. Of them it is also true to say: "Sic scriptum est." (p. 8).

11. Before 1960, Murray never did define in the writings that I have seen what he meant by "doctrine." After that date, as we shall see throughout this chapter, the term tends to cover all judgments of truth and value as affirmed by the magisterial authority of the church. These include his "junctures," but also political philosophies as well as affirmed perspectival shifts such as between "classicism and historical consciousness." The common element behind all of this is Murray's work in Lonergan's Trinitarian theology, as will be discussed further in this chapter, and in the next.

12. The literary source for Murray's image is Santayana, as also cited in "This Matter of Religious Freedom" (1965d), 42. The image suggests perspectival shifts, as we will see in the consideration of the development of doctrine.

13. It is moved into central position, but Murray noted the ambiguity of the term, in that the first view also appealed to human dignity, and concluded to intolerance. At issue is what is meant by the term, what the basis of that dignity is. For the first view's understanding, 1964f, 7, 14.

14. The constitutional question is said to be "correlate" and inseparable (p. 22), that is, a civil right must be defined within the social reality of government. Murray preserves his independent individual and social starting points, as will be discussed further.

15. "The First View accuses the Second View of doctrinal errors—Liberalism and neo-Liberalism, subjectivism, relativism, indifferentism, Rousseauism, laicism, social and juridical modernism, humanistic personalism, existentialism, situation ethics, false irenicism."

16. This problem of the development of doctrine was, of course, a long-standing one in the Roman Church, at least since the beginnings of the Modernism controversy. Nor was the American Church immune to such controversies. Eugene Burke, in his "A Personal Memoir on the Origins of the CTSA" (Burke 1980), recalls his own problems with doctrinal development, as brought on by his 1949 CTSA paper, "The Scientific Teaching of Theology."

> Difficult as it is to recreate a session that took place almost thirty years ago, I yet remember that I missed the thrust of John Murray's formal and critical response to my paper as well as Bernard Lonergan's questions from the floor. I think it was at least a couple of years before I really caught their point, viz., that while I was using historical and positive sources I was not using them in a genuinely historical fashion; and secondly that my understanding of tradition was too inflexible because I read everything in the light of the contemporary magisterium. The first criticism I dealt with once I understood it.... The second criticism, however, took a long time for me to break through because of my own understanding of doctrinal development in the limited framework of implicit to explicit.

The "implicit to explicit" framework (the first in this citation) appears to have been common to much theological interpretation before Vatican II.

17. Murray adds: "At our distance, it is possible to deplore the fact that the Roman Church of the nineteenth century was not more solicitous to discern, beneath the surface of error, all that was reasonable, just, and humanly desirable in the great movement toward political and civil liberties that is a leading aspect of the 'Political Century,' as it has been called." We will see the ethical implications of this criticism in the next chapter.

18. Murray wrapped up his analysis with a suggestion of multiple perspectival shifts manifest in Vatican II: "And implicit in the significance [of *Dignitatis Humanae*] is perhaps the significance of the whole Council—its manifold testimony to the growth of the Church in historical consciousness, and in a human consciousness of the dignity of man, and in an ecumenical consciousness of her ministry of reconciliation, and above all in an evangelical consciousness of herself and of the word that has been divinely entrusted to her, which is not only the 'word of truth' (James 1:18) but also incidentally a word of freedom" (1967b, 147). I will examine these other shifts more closely in the next chapter.

19. This is mostly true of the religious freedom argument, as particularly conducted during the Council. There are indications in his 1964 systematic theology notes (1964a) and even his article "The Status of the Nicene Creed as Dogma" (1966f) that he was catching on to historical consciousness as a differentiation of human consciousness.

In his systematic theology notes he described "dialectics" as arising out of a situation in which "there are reasons for affirming and denying the same one proposition" (p. 7). The Nicene councils "infallibly sanctioned the ascent from the descriptive (*quoad nos*) to the definitive (*quoad se*) mode of thought." The point of these notes was to distinguish between dogmatic theology and systematic theology. Dogmatic theology is concerned with the affirmation of religious truth, thus is a form of judgment, whereas systematic theology is concerned with understanding that truth. The Nicene decrees did affect systematic theology, although they themselves were dogmatic, in that they did affirm another mode of understanding religious truth.

In one of his last religious liberty articles ("The Declaration on Religious Freedom" (1966a), Murray did more clearly distinguish between classicism and historical consciousness, but again remaining close to the Lonergan terminology.

> Classicism designates a view of truth which holds objective truth, precisely because it is objective, to exist "already out there now" (to use Bernard Lonergan's descriptive phrase)....In contrast, historical consciousness, while holding fast to the nature of truth as objective, is concerned with the possession of truth, with man's affirmations of truth, with the understanding contained in these affirmations, with the conditions—both circumstantial and subjective—of understanding and affirmation, and therefore with the historicity of truth and with progress in the grasp and penetration of what is true (p. 11).

But even here there are some problems:

> The pastoral concern of the Council is a doctrinal concern. However, it is illuminated by historical consciousness: that is, by concern for the truth

not simply as a proposition to be repeated but more importantly as a possession to be lived; by concern, therefore, for the subject to whom the truth is addressed; hence, also, by concern for the historical moment in which the truth is proclaimed to the living subject; and, consequently, by concern to seek that progress in the understanding of the truth demanded both by the historical moment and by the subject who must live in it (p. 12).

As noted in the text, Murray did slur over a distinction between the type of consciousness that was "affirmed" in Nicaea and the consciousness affirmed in *Dignitatis*. But the common element to both was church doctrine as affirmation or judgment. In Nicaea, a definitional mode of thought was approved. In Vatican II, first of all the two main "junctures" were judged to be correct, and then the complex principle of religious freedom itself. But beyond these, the Council affirmed a new way of viewing its own historical development, at least within the context of those values and behavior that are intimately related to the temporal, political order. There is, therefore, a move in Murray's own thought during this period toward "historical consciousness" as a differentiation of human consciousness which is most likely in line with Lonergan's own thought. Murray's problem was that he tried to include much more within the term than his dependence on Lonergan would allow.

20. Therefore the first part of the decree is based on reason; only in the second part, which is the minor part, are explicitly revelational premises appealed to (1965d, 41). Murray also claimed that the Council did not advance a primarily theological argument in the international forum because the secular order is not competent to judge the church's theological truth claims (1966h, 590–91).

21. Murray never did, for example, make much use of the notion of "subsidiarity" in his arguments, the notion that society cannot long endure without fairly autonomous engagement of moral energies and reflection at a grass-roots level of social organization. Such an argument has recently been pursued in Jay Mechling, ed., *Church, State, and Public Policy: The New Shape of the Church-State Debate* (Mechling 1978).

22. Pelotte let ride the claim that the decree could not be changed after the vote on the *textus re-emendatus*. The type of freedom which was affirmed was not changed, but as we shall see, the argument for that freedom was changed.

23. Murray's use of the term "autonomy" here, even with its individualistic overtones, is not dissimilar to its use when applied to secular society, as a corollary of the dualism principle.

24. The term "fundamental option" is uncharacteristic of Murray, but quite characteristically French (Louis Monden, *Sin, Liberty and Law* (New York: Sheed and Ward, 1965). This would suggest that Murray was mostly concerned with a French audience, the "French view," and French criticism in this article.

25. A normal Anglo-American, philosophical classification of rights claims divides rights (1) as immunities and as empowerments, and (2) according to the sectors of society against which those claims are made—usually against the state and the economic sectors. Again in common usage, rights as immunities are thought to be claims against primarily the state: the right not

to be coerced. And rights as empowerments are thought to be claims for a share of the goods and services generated by the economy. Joel Feinberg's *Social Philosophy* (Englewood Cliffs, New Jersey: Prentice-Hall, Inc., 1973) is an excellent presentation of that tradition.

Through my reading of that philosophical tradition, of the arguments that Murray advanced, and of the rights theory developed by David Hollenbach [*Claims in Conflict: Retrieving and Renewing the Catholic Human Rights Tradition* (New York: Paulist Press, 1979)], I have come to prefer a three-part general rights classification (which I believe is somewhat different from that suggested by Hollenbach). My classification, for want of better labels, is (1) rights as immunities, (2) participatory rights, and (3) rights of social construction. All three types of rights claims can be made against any sector of society: polity, economy, culture. In the political arena, a right of immunity would be the right not to have the state's coercive power turned on oneself or one's group; in the economic, it would be the right not to be starved to death or imbecility (or the right not to be separated from the means of production); in the cultural, the right not to be relegated, through coercion and/or socially dominant class caricatures, to the culturally inferior. Participatory rights would be, respectively, the rights to protection by the police powers that be, the right to gain access to the goods and services produced by the economy, and the right to an education. Rights of social construction are, again respectively, the right to help shape the very institutions which control social coercion, the distribution of goods, and cultural values.

Another way of characterizing this three-part classification would be in terms of who and what types of actions are called for by those claims. Immunity rights primarily reference the *inaction* or the refraining from *negative action* on the part of institutions and society. Participatory rights refer to *positive actions* to be taken by institutions and society. Social constructive rights, in contrast, lay claim to the *positive action* by individuals and subgroups *on or toward* institutions and socially held value commitments.

The differences between participatory rights and rights of social construction, I believe, are crucial and not often recognized. Participatory rights address the question of what the individual or subgroup can obtain from the whole, and as such can still connote a rather passive, nonsocial definition of the holder of those rights, and can remain fundamentally individualistic, as can rights as immunities. (But even those rights need not to be so understood, if read against the historical societies in which they developed.) Rights of social construction connote active ethical agency toward social institutions and socially held consensus contents, in the sense of active ethical agency as the term is used throughout this study. As such they suggest an intending of social reality as an intrinsic component, not as incidental, to the definition of these rights. And they also suggest a notion of social-ethical maturity which is generally lacking in many Anglo-American definitions of rights.

As discussed in the latter half of this chapter and through the remaining two chapters, Murray maintained a notion of rights as primarily immunities throughout much of his life. But then, after the council, he expanded that notion to included also the third classification of rights mentioned above, rights of social construction. He never did give much attention to participatory rights (again as used above).

In what follows, then, empowerment or rights of empowerment refers primarily to the ability to, and claim for, agency in actively shaping social institutions.

26. This theme of "responsibility" will increasingly pervade this and the remaining chapters. As will be argued in the conclusion to this chapter, responsibility on the part of the church was first of all a direct outcome of Murray's recognition that the church is a dialogic *partner* in the determination of moral values. The church is situated within a moral universe where insight and judgment can arise from multiple sources. In the next chapter we will see that "responsibility" is linked to Lonergan's four rational imperatives: be attentive, be intelligent, be rational, be responsible. And in the final chapter, where he finally is willing to bring religious discourse into the public forum, the theme of "responsibility" will primarily concern one's reaction to the God who acts in universal history. The church and civil need for creative responses to the various social forces situates an enabling notion of "freedom" in the center of Murray's ethical thought. Such a notion of freedom is, of course, a move well beyond freedom as immunity.

27. In this discussion, Republican Murray continues that he does not want to be understood as making a case against Johnson's "Great Society."

Chapter Five

1. The four main divisions of this chapter were suggested by distinct calls by Murray for equality as an initial condition for ethical and theological conversations. For each of these sets of calls (interchurch, Christian-atheism, learned-unlearned, and intrachurch), he first asserted the need for conversation or dialogue, then the need for a "footing of equality" or an attitude of "reciprocity" as a necessary condition for dialogue. Murray was shifting here from equality before the law as a requirement for democratic political organization to equality in conversation as a requirement at the more general level of cultural development. He was stepping beyond the singular juridical concern of the religious liberty argument to the problem of general cultural meaning, and finding there "reciprocity" or "equality" as a requirement at that level which is somewhat differently based than is "equality" at the juridical level. We will see this different basing in the fourth section of this chapter. For equality and reciprocity as requirements for ecumenism: 1966h, 592; for the Christian-atheist dialogue: 1969, 6, 16; for dialogue within the church: 1966i, 734. In this last call for reciprocity and equality in the church, Murray places that requirement as foundational for the "will to community," the latter becoming, as we shall see, his primary definition of the church.

2. "It may be asked at the outset, what is the use of this theological inquiry? Is it not useless, since from the catechism itself we already know and believe and are most certain that God is Father, Son, and Holy Spirit? ... The simplest answer—to be stated now and illustrated in all that follows—is to say that the same thing can be known in diverse ways. What is known from the catechism can be known more exactly from the Councils. And what is known from catechism and Councils can be further known from the Scriptures. In all three cases the same thing is known, but not in the same mode of knowledge." A more typically Lonergan presentation of the different "modes of knowing" can be found on pp. 6–8.

3. I am, of course, pushing Murray beyond a point where he would at this time want to go, or be capable of going—from cognitional to social pluralism. I have had occasions before to note Murray's monolithic notions of the Roman and Protestant churches (chap. 3). This growing notion of cognitional pluralism, however, within the recognition of the soteriological agency of the Protestant churches, would leave Murray's "Nicaea" article without any points of differentiation between the Roman and Protestant churches, save for some notion of institutional pluralism that was based on such cognitional pluralism. If "What think ye of *homoousion?*" is *the* ecumenical question, then cognitional pluralism is the basis of institutionalism.

4. The dating of this article presents some problems. "Le droit à l'incroyance" actually the first of eight Murray articles published in that volume of *Relations*. "Le droit" and the last article, "La liberté religieuse et la doctrine libérale [*Relations* 22 (Decembre 1962):333–34] have no apparent publication before 1962. However, the appearance of the intervening six articles ["I. La liberté de religion," pp. 118–20; "II. La perspective catholique," pp. 151–53; "III. La liberté et la loi," pp. 179–82; "IV. Le conscience," pp. 207–210; "V. Les devoirs de la conscience," pp. 234–38; and "VI. Les droits de la conscience," pp. 301–04] is a bit mysterious. They are for the most part a rewrite of Murray's *1946* "Ethical Problem," a line of argument from a rational psychological definition of conscience which he abandoned in 1947. This suggests that even the article studied here was written far earlier. But for our purposes, it is sufficient to highlight Murray's beginning attitudes toward social atheism. (These attitudes are certainly consistent with his notion of the religious component of natural law.) That these appeared in 1962 in the French Canadian publication suggests perhaps some appeal to Murray's earlier writings to counteract his later work.

5. At this point in his thought, Murray judged such a study would involve the recognition of the "social," nontheological causes of much of modern atheism, leading the way to a resolution of those social causes, from which point the problem of God could be discussed in its theological purity—without the obscuring social elements (1969, 17). But, as we shall see, when he did come to consider the problem in its theological purity, he found some theological causes or occasions for unbelief.

6. Or, keeping the Christian Trinitarian response parallel to the Hebraic, "We shall be there as who we are shall we be there" (p. 28).

7. Even here Murray, at this point I presume instinctively, distinguished the individual "fool" from a "foolish" people, individual and social atheism.

8. This movement was considered "inevitable" since it lies "in the essential dynamism of human intelligence" and because of the biblical "realism of the word of God," with the latter's insistence that what it speaks is true (1962b, 41).

9. In a 1967 address given at the University of Connecticut, Murray discussed the then current death of God movement in America. He argued that the death of God theologians argued from "an experience of the absence of God" or from an "absence of experience of God" to the conclusion that God is dead. For Murray this was in line with the nineteenth century attempt to argue from reason or action to the nonexistence of God, and therefore passé. They are the "soft radicals" who have been transcended by the contemporary "hard radicals" of Marxism and existentialist atheism (1967e).

10. Throughout much of this discussion I have used the terms "differentiation" and "pluralism" as near synonyms. This in part rests on my own conviction that, wherever there exists a difference in the meanings by which subgroups define themselves, there exists a social pluralism that can be a basis for war or for the generation of common understanding. That is, differentiations of any form within a social body translates readily to social pluralism, whether those differentiations are based on institutional, moral, religious, or even cognitional perspectives. This matter will be more fully discussed in the last chapter.

11. The following material was presented in a talk in Toledo, Ohio, in May, 1967. No copy of the talk is to my knowledge extant. The sections quoted here are taken from "Murray Says Church Was Too Sure," *The National Catholic Reporter* 3 (May 17, 1967):3, and a typewritten report in the Murray Archives, file number 544. The latter has been compiled from reports in *The Tablet*, May 20, 1967 and the *Advocate*, May 26, 1967. The typewritten report is entitled "Where the Church Went Too Far."

12. Murray was apparently trying to break what he understood to be the equation of authority with certainty within a classicist perspective, without, however, eliminating the notion of the magisterium as a forum for judgments of moral and religious truth.

13. One might speculate that his response to *Humanae Vitae* would have been at the very least somewhere in the neighborhood of the following. Certainly, he would have wondered if the Second Vatican Council, like Nicaea itself, had blessed, but did not immediately recognize that it had sanctioned, a new mode of understanding religious and moral truth. This concern might finally settle on the problem of magisterial authority which had in practice both affirmed (religious liberty) and denied (birth control) the historical differentiation of consciousness. As will become apparent in the remainder of this chapter, this last statement of the problem is not dissimilar to the direction in which Murray's conception of church authority did, in fact, move.

14. Murray insisted that the freedom of the press has not, and cannot, be given an individualistic foundational premise—again consistent with his religious liberty argument.

15. Recall that the best resolution he could find for this conflict was to claim that Pius XII delivered all the principles, but that he also recognized that institutionalizations must be left up to laymen—the closest Murray ever came to claiming that the church ought not evaluate particular social institutions.

16. Such a reading of this argument is not unlike his own reading of Leo XIII, with the latter's judgment concerning the immaturity of the People of God.

17. Murray was clearly dealing here with evangelical freedom as an empowerment, not simply as an immunity. This parallels his late treatment of even civil religious freedom as an empowerment, as spelled out in chapter 4.

18. Here Murray parallels a notion of "community consciousness" to the "political consciousness" of his religious liberty, civil society argument. With his newer primary definition of the church as "community," this Catholic "community consciousness" is placed within the church, becoming a social, historical reality that demands the church's ongoing concern and action. Socially held attitudes are no longer simply something outside the church with which she must be reconciled.

19. Corresponding to the three functions of authority, Murray suggested three functions of Christian freedom. The first is responsibility to exercise one's freedom, defined as "love, as the capacity for self-communication, as the spontaneous impulse to minister and not be ministered to, as the outgoing will to community with others." The second function is the "executive," a willingness to work with others for the sake of cooperative action. And the third function is that of "self-correction," the willingness not to be "a slave of the flesh." There is still the possibility in the second and third functions of freedom that "sacrifice" might be called for. The community still makes judgments, can and ought in certain situations be directive and coercive. He suggests that the latter two functions of freedom are for the sake of the first, but now that the first must be maximized before the last two can be properly utilized.

20. The term "languages" here reflects (1) Murray's long-standing insistence (in the first cooperation debate) on a common content along with volitional orientations for social action, and (2) my own suggestion that this needed common content can be carried by commonsensical, figurative, symbolic, etc., forms of communication, as will be discussed in the next chapter.

21. He adds: "This has not always been well understood in my beloved Church; it is only now beginning to be understood."

Also, cf. Lonergan 1957, 234f. In a section entitled "Reversal of the Longer Cycle," Lonergan writes: "There is such a thing as progress and its principle is liberty." Discussion of the cycles of progress and decline will be taken up in the next chapter.

22. I recall seeing Murray use the four imperatives "Be attentive..." in one of his last letters, but have not been able to relocate it. I suspect it was in correspondence with Potter concerning a U.S. governmental commission study of the military draft. Potter and Murray both supported the institution of a "selective conscientious objection" classification. Murray's problem came down to the question of whether or not American society was "wise" enough to support a just and true implementation of such a classification. It is in that context, I believe, that he appealed to the four imperatives. For Murray's thoughts on the subject: "Selective Conscientious Objection" (1967k).

23. In an attempt to ward off the suggestion that the church could, at a later date, deny the value of juridical religious freedom, Murray wrote: "Now ... we are in the *era of understanding*; these affirmations are made and the affirmations are true. It is not a question of how certain they are; what is true is true, and why don't we leave it at that at the moment and get on to something more important, which is to understand what has been said" (1966a, 584).

Chapter Six

1. "Timeless" in a conceptualist sense. With Murray's admission of the church's own sinfulness, he could later abandon this extensive defense of the church's past judgments without, however, abandoning his understanding of the possibility of true judgments of value, as will be discussed further.

2. See particularly pp. 251–52, where she appropriates as her own Carrillo di Albornoz's critique of Murray.

3. A "virtually unconditioned" judgment involves three subsidiary judgments: "A prospective judgment will be virtually unconditioned if (1) it is the conditioned, (2) its conditions are known, and (3) the conditions are fulfilled." The "conditioned" and the "conditions" are constantly open to the self-correcting processes of public discussion, as then are the judgments concerning the fulfillment of the conditions. Thus, for Lonergan and for Murray, the requirement of free public discourse in the social determination of value judgments.

4. It is also to recognize that we are essentially, not accidentally, social. Murray had insisted from the beginning that we are social beings, which of course meant that we must have social structures and institutions that support that sociality. Here he has moved on from the world of politics and economics to that of general culture, paralleling his shift from a classical preoccupation with institutions to the meanings by which we define ourselves.

5. The background for the following suggestions is Lonergan's treatment of the realms of meaning in *Method in Theology* (1972, 57–73). According to Lonergan, the world of immediacy that is typical of the infant is soon left behind for the many worlds that are mediated by meaning, including the intersubjective, artistic, symbolic, and literary. For Lonergan's notion of "common sense" meaning, I am reliant on *Insight* (1958, 173–81), although as will surface further on, I have problems with some of Lonergan's manner of describing common sense.

6. The difference between Lonergan's "common sense" and Murray's "prudential determination" is due to their different interpretations of the sources of America's practical orientation and concern for progress. Lonergan considers these characteristics intrinsic to the type of everyday reasoning that governs popular social construction; not so, as we shall see, for Murray.

A case could be made that Lonergan was far too limited in his description of the types of knowledge within which, and by which, modern everyday society is constituted. First of all, I would argue with Murray that propositional truth claims, which are totalistic and concern the long-term, have indeed entered the common sense modes of everyday discourse, although such propositions are dealt with in that arena as are any other propositions, by prudential methods. Second, however, I would argue that symbolic and emotional forms of meaning are also alive, if not entirely well, in contemporary society. And some figurative expressions can and do carry meanings which are totalistic, long-term, and even theistically transcendental. Murray's judgment concerning the causes of American fixations could be augmented by considerations concerning the similarity of propositional and symbolic knowledge, as discussed in section III. One might even argue that some scientistic and historicist slogans operate as figurative, rather than as conceptual, meanings.

7. The terms "post-scientific" and "post-historical" are used by Lonergan to designate general modes of social discourse, after the cognitional and social differentiations of scientific and historical thought have been developed and have interacted with common sense. He discusses these as variations of "undifferentiated consciousness in the later stages" in *Method*, pp. 97–99.

BIBLIOGRAPHY

The following bibliography is divided into two parts. The first is a listing of Murray's written works, grouped initially in chronological order, then, under each date, arranged with unpublished materials first, then books and articles. The second bibliography is made up of two different types of materials, (1) of works that deal directly with Murray's life and thought and (2) of works cited in the text.

I. Murray Bibliography

Donald Pelotte, in his *Theologian in Conflict*, has already compiled a fairly exhaustive Murray bibliography (1978, 191–98). The following relies heavily on his work, with some additions, subtractions, and corrections. Any materials referred to as "Murray Archives" can be found in the Special Collections Room, Joseph Mark Lauinger Library, Georgetown University, Washington, D.C. Since much of my own study revolves around the dating and reediting of Murray's articles, this bibliography has been arranged chronologically, and most of my annotations are concerned with the further publication and alteration of the initial articles. An asterisk (*) will designate those texts and versions that have been cited in my own text or notes.

Murray, John Courtney.
1933   "Crisis in the History of Trent." *Thought* 7 (December): 463–73.*
1938   "Taken from among Men." *Jesuit Seminary News* 12 (June): 3–5.*
1941   "Toward a Christian Humanism: Aspects of the Theology of Education." In *A Philosophical Symposium on American Catholic Education*, pp. 106–115. Ed. H. Guthrie and G. Walsh. New York: Fordham University Press.*
1942a "Book Reviews: New Periodicals." *Theological Studies (TS)* 3 (May): 290–93.
1942b "Current Theology: Christian Co-operation." *TS* 3 (September): 413–31.*
1942c Review of *The Layman's Call*, by William R. O'Connor (New York: P. Kenedy and Sons, 1942), *TS* 3 (December): 608–10.
1943a "Current Theology: Co-operation: Some Further Views." *TS* 4 (March): 100–11.*
1943b "Current Theology: Intercredal Co-operation: Its Theory and Its Organization." *TS* 4 (June): 267–86.*
1943c "Descriptive Notes." *TS* 4 (September): 466.
1943d "To the Editor." *TS* 4 (September): 472–74.
1943e "Principles of Peace." [A Review of *Principles of Peace: Selections from Papal Documents*, ed. Harry C. Koenig (Washington, D.C.: NCWC, 1943).] *TS* (December): 634–38.

1944a *The Pattern for Peace and the Papal Peace Program.* A pamphlet of the Catholic Association for International Peace. Washington, D.C.: Paulist Press.* Another version of this article, with some alterations, can be found as "Co-operation among All Men of Good Will" (Murray Archives, file 311). This latter was in turn translated and published as "La Cooperación Interconfessional Para la Paz." *Verbum* (Guatemala), January 9, 1945.

1944b "Toward a Theology for the Layman: The Problem of Its Finality." *TS* 5 (March): 43–75.*

1944c "Toward a Theology for the Layman: The Pedagogical Problem." *TS* 5 (September): 340–76.* This and the last article appeared in a condensed form in "Toward a Theology for the Layman," *Jesuit Educational Quarterly* 11 (March 1949): 221–28.

1944d "The Juridical Organization of the International Community." *The New York Law Journal* (October 9): 813–14.* Also published as: "World Order and Moral Law," *Thought* 19 (December 1944): 581–86.

1944e "Woodstock Wisdom." *Woodstock Letters* 75: 280–84.

1945a "On the Problem of Co-operation: Some Clarifications: Reply to Father P. H. Furfey." *The American Ecclesiastical Review* 112 (March): 194–214.*

1945b "Current Theology: Freedom of Religion." *TS* 6 (March): 85–113. *

1945c Memorandum and April 30, 1945 letter to Zacheus Maher (Jesuit American Superior) on the racial issue. Murray Archives, file 695.

1945d "Notes on the Theory of Religious Liberty." Memo to Archbishop Mooney, April. Murray Archives, file 326.*

1945e "Freedom of Religion, I: The Ethical Problem." *TS* 6 (June): 229–86.* This was much later translated and published in *Relations* (Montreal) 22 (Mai 1962): 118–20; (Juin 1962): 151–53; (Juillet 1962): 179–82; (Août 1962): 207–10; (Septembre 1962): 234 38; (Novembre 1962): 301–04; (Décembre 1962): 33–35.

1945f "The Real Woman Today." *America* 74 (November 3): 122–24.

1945g "God's Word and Its Realization." *America* 74, supplement (December 8): xix-xxi.

1946a "The Papal Allocution: Christmas." *America* 74 (January 5): 370–71.

1946b Review of *Religious Liberty: An Inquiry*, by M. Searle Bates (New York: International Missionary Council, 1945). *TS* 7 (March): 151–63.*

1946c "How Liberal Is Liberalism." *America* 75 (April 6): 6–7.*

1946d "Operation University." *America* 75 (April 13): 28–29.

1946e "Separation of Church and State." *America* 76 (December 7): 261–63.*

1947a "Admonition and Grace." Introduction and translation of *The Fathers of the Church: Writings of St. Augustine. II*, pp. 239–305 (New York: Cima).

1947b "Separation of Church and State: True and False Concepts." *America* 76 (February 15): 541–45.*

1947c "The Court Upholds Religious Freedom." *America* 76 (March 8): 628–30.*

1948a "Religious Liberty: The Concern of All." *America* 77 (February 7): 513–16.*

1948b "Dr. Morrison and the First Amendment." *America* 78 (March 6): 627–29; (March 20): 683–86.*

1948c "The Role of Faith in the Renovation of the World." *The Messenger of the Sacred Heart* 83 (March): 15–17.*

1948d "The Roman Catholic Church." *The Annals of the American Academy of Political and Social Science* 256 (March): 36–42. Also published as "What Does the Catholic Church Want?", *Catholic Digest* 12 (December 1948): 51–53; and "The Roman Catholic Church," *Catholic Mind* 46 (September 1954): 580–88.

1948e "The Root of Faith: The Doctrine of M. J. Scheeben." *TS* 9 (March): 20–46.* An excerpt from Murray's dissertation.

1948f "Government Repression of Heresy." *Proceedings* of the Third Annual Convention of the Catholic Theological Society of America, pp. 26–98.*

1948g "St. Robert Bellarmine on the Indirect Power." *TS* 9 (December): 491–535.*

1949a "On the Necessity for Not Believing: A Roman Catholic Interpretation." *The Yale Scientific Magazine* 23 (February): 11, 12, 22, 30, 32, 34.*

1949b "Reversing the Secularistic Drift." *Thought* 24 (March): 36–46.

1949c Review of *Free Speech in Its Relation to Self-Government*, by Alexander Meikeljohn (New York: Harper and Brothers, 1948). *Georgetown Law Journal* 37 (May): 654–62.*

1949d Review of *American Freedom and Catholic Power*, by Paul Blanshard (Boston: Beacon Press, 1949). *The Catholic Mind* 169 (June): 233–34.*

1949e "Contemporary Orientations of Catholic Thought on Church and State in the Light of History." *TS* 10 (June): 177–234.*

1949f "The Catholic Position: A Reply." *The American Mercury* 69 (September): 274–83; (November): 637–39.*

1949g "Current Theology: On Religious Freedom." *TS* 10 (September): 409–32.*

1949h "On the Idea of a College Religion Course." *Jesuit Educational Quarterly* (October): 79–86.

1949i "Law or Prepossessions." *Law and Contemporary Problems* 14 (Winter): 23–43.* Also published in *Essays in Constitutional Law*, pp. 316–42, ed. R. G. McCloskey (New York: Alfred Knopf, 1957).

1950a "The Natural Law." In *Great Expressions of Human Rights*, pp. 69–104. Ed. Robert M. MacIver. New York: Harper, 1950. Also published as "Natural Law and the Public Consensus," in *Natural Law and Modern Society*, pp. 48–81, ed. John Cogley (Cleveland: World Publishing, 1962). And formed the concluding chapter, "The Doctrine Lives: The Eternal Return of the Natural Law," of *We Hold These Truths* (*WHTT*), pp. 295–336,* with only slight revisions.

1950b "One Work of the One Church." *The Missionary Union of the Clergy Bulletin* 14 (March): 5–11. Also published in *Catholic Mind* 48 (June 1950): 358–64.

1951a "Toward a Christian Humanism: Aspects of the Theology of Education." In *A Philosophical Symposium on American Catholic Education*, pp. 106–55. Ed. H. Guthrie and G. G. Walsh. New York: Fordham Press.*

1951b "Paul Blanshard and the New Nativism." *The Month* New Series 5 (April): 214–25.*

1951c "The Problem of 'The Religion of the State.'" *The American Ecclesiastical Review* 124 (May): 327–52.* Also published as "The Problem of State Religion," *TS* 12 (June 1951): 155–78.

1951d "School and Christian Freedom." National Catholic Educational Association *Proceedings* 43 (August): 63–68.

1952a "For the Freedom and Transcendence of the Church." *The American Ecclesiastical Review* 126 (January): 28–48.*

1952b "The Church and Totalitarian Democracy." *TS* 13 (December): 525–63.*

1953a "Leo XIII on Church and State: The General Structure of the Controversy." *TS* 14 (March): 1–30.*

1953b "Christian Humanism in America." *Social Order* 3 (May-June): 233–44. Slightly edited and republished as chapter 8, "Is It Basket Weaving? The Question of Christian and Human Values" in *WHTT*, pp. 175–96.*

1953c "Leo XIII: Separation of Church and State." *TS* 14 (June): 145–214.*

1953d "The Problem of Free Speech." *Philippine Studies* 1 (September): 107–24.*

1953e "Leo XIII: Two Concepts of Government." *TS* 14 (December): 551–67.*

1954a Correspondence with Robert MacIver, dating from 1952 through 1954. Murray Archives, files 11, 15.* See MacIver entry for latter's correspondence.

    #3.   April 17, 1952: Murray to MacIver (Murray 1954a, #3): two-page letter and six-page comment on the Project's Communism critique.

    #5.   April 23, 1952: Murray to MacIver (Murray 1954a, #5).

    #7.   Updated: Murray to MacIver (Murray 1954a, #7): from internal data, a response to MacIver's August 26 letter (MacIver 1954, #6) and to further Project publications.

    #8.   February 4, 1954: Murray to MacIver (Murray 1954a, #8): sixteen pages of comments on the Project's "The Greater Mission of the University" and "The Denominational University," which became chapter 14 and appendix A of MacIver 1955.

    #10.   February 18, 1954: Murray to MacIver (Murray 1954a, #10).

    #12.   May 30, 1954: Murray to MacIver (Murray 1954a, #12).

1954b "On the Structure of the Church-State Problem." In *The Catholic Church in World Affairs*, pp. 11–32. Ed. Waldemar Gurian and M. A. Fitzsimons. Notre Dame, Indiana: University of Notre Dame Press.*

1954c "Leo XIII: Two Concepts of Government: Government and the Order of Culture." *TS* 15 (March): 1–33.*

1954d Notes to Murray's *Ci Riesce* talk at Catholic University, March 25. Murray Archives, file 456.*

1954e "The Problem of Pluralism in America." *Thought* 24 (Summer): 165–208. Also published in *Catholicism in American Culture* (College of New Rochelle, 1955) pp. 13–38.* Republished, with less positive affirmation of American society, in *The Catholic Mind* 57 (May-June 1959): 201–15, and as chapters 1 and 2, "E Pluribus Unum: The American Consensus" and "Civil Unity and Religious Integrity: the Articles of Peace," *WHTT*, pp. 27–78.*

1955a "Leo XIII and Pius XII: Government and the Order of Religion."
      Written for publication in 1955, but suppressed. Murray Archives, file
      397.*

1955b "Unity of Truth". *Commonweal* 63 (January 13, 1956): 381–82. Also
      published as "The Catholic University in a Pluralistic Society," *The
      Catholic Mind* 57 (May-June 1959): 253–60.* An address given at St.
      Louis University in 1955.

1955c "Special Catholic Challenges." *Life* 39–40 (December 26): 144–46. Also
      published as "Challenges Confronting the American Catholic," *The
      Catholic Mind* 57 (May-June 1959): 196–200.*

1955d "Catholics in America—a Creative Minority—Yes or No?" *Epistle* (New
      York) 21: 36–41. Also as "Catholics in America—a Creative Minor-
      ity?," *The Catholic Mind* 53 (October 1955): 590–97.*

1956a "St. Ignatius and the End of Modernity." In *The Ignatian Year at
      Georgetown*. Washington, D.C.: Georgetown University Press.

1956b "The School Problem in Mid-Twentieth Century." In *The Role of the
      Independent School in American Democracy*, pp. 1–16. Ed. William H. Conley.
      Milwaukee: Marquette University Press. Reprinted as "The Religious
      School in a Pluralistic Society," *The Catholic Mind* 54 (September 1956):
      502–11, and slightly reedited for chapter 6, "Is It Justice?: The School
      Question Today," *WHTT*, pp. 143–54.*

1956c "Kirche und Demokratie." *Dokumente* 12 (February): 9–16. This article
      attracted European attention, then Roman criticism.

1956d "The Quality of Reverence." *Journal of the Newman Club of the University of
      Minnesota*, June.

1956e "Questions of Striking a Right Balance: Literature and Censorship."
      Books on Trial 14 (June-July): 393–95. Reprinted as "Literature and
      Censorship," *The Catholic Mind* 54 (December 1956): 665–77; and
      slightly edited for chapter 7, "Should There Be a Law: The Question of
      Censorship," *WHTT*, pp. 155–74.* Translated and published as "Liter-
      atur und Zensur," *Frankfurther Hefte: Zeitschrift fuer Kultur und Politik* 17
      (December 1962): 824–33.

1956f "The Thesis Form as an Instrument of Theological Reflection."
      Proceedings of the Eleventh Annual Convention of the Catholic Theo-
      logical Society of America, Cleveland. Pp. 218–24.

1956g "Freedom, Responsibility and Law." *The Catholic Lawyer* 2 (July): 214–20,
      276. Reprinted in *The Catholic Mind* 56 (September-October 1958):
      436–47.*

1956h "Die Katholiken in der americanischen Gesellschaft." *Dokumente* 12
      (August): 10–14.

1956i "The Next Liberal Task for America." Talk given September 29, 1956
      at the "red Mass" in Boston. Murray Archives, file 454.*

1956j "The Bad Arguments Intelligent People Make." *America* 117 (Novem-
      ber 3): 120–23.*

1957a "The Christian Idea of Education." In *The Christian Idea of Education*, pp.
      152–63. Ed. Edmund Fuller. New Haven: Yale University Press.* Large
      portions are a rewrite of "The Catholic University in a Pluralistic
      Society" [1955b].

1957b "Church, State and Political Freedom." *Modern Age: A Conservative Review*
1 (Fall): 134–45. Also in *The Catholic Mind* 57 (May-June 1959): 216–29;
as "The Freedom of Man in the Freedom of the Church," in *Modern
Catholic Thinkers*, pp. 372–84, ed. A. Robert Caponigri (New York:
Harper, 1960); and as chapter 9, "Are There Two or One?: The
Question of the Future of Freedom," in *WHTT*, pp. 197–217.*

1958a "Church and State: The Structure of the Argument." Murray Archives, file 614.* Written in 1958. Publication not allowed by Rome.

1958b "America's Four Conspiracies." In *Religion in America*, pp. 12–41. Ed.
John Cogley. New York: Meridian Books. Reprinted in *The Catholic
Mind* 57 (May-June 1959): 230–41. Also appeared as "Introduction: The
Civilization of the Pluralistic Society," *WHTT*, pp. 5–24.*

1958c *Foreign Policy and the Free Society.* By Walter Millis and John Courtney
Murray. New York: Oceana Publications. This was a Fund for the
Republic sponsored exchange, with Murray's address, pp. 21–42, and
then a discussion between Millis, Murray, and other, pp. 53–116.
Excerpt published as "Confusion of U.S. Foreign Policy," *The Catholic
Mind* 57 (May-June 1959): 261–73. Also published as chapter 10,
"Doctrine and Policy in Communist Imperialism: The Problem of
Security and Risk," *WHTT*, pp. 221–247.*

1958d "Morality and Modern War." A Paper delivered before the Catholic
Association for International Peace, October 28, 1958. The Church
Peace Union, 1959. Reprinted as "The Morality of War," *Theological
Digest* 7 (Autumn, 1959): 131–37; as "God, Man and Nuclear War,"
Catholic Mind 57 (May-June 1959): 274–88; as "Remarks on the Moral
Problem of War," *TS* 20 (March 1959): 40–61; as "Theology and
Modern War," in *Morality and Modern Warfare*, pp. 69–91, ed. William
Nagle (Baltimore: Helicon Press, 1960). And slightly edited as chapter
11, "The Uses of a Doctrine on the Uses of Force: War as a Moral
Problem" in *WHTT*, pp. 249–273.*

1958e "The Making of a Pluralist Society." *Religious Education* 53 (November-
December): 521–28. Reprinted as "The University in a Pluralist
Society," in *Religion and the State University*, ed. Erich A. Walker (Ann
Arbor: University of Michigan Press, 1958). Reprinted as "State
University in a Pluralist Society," *Catholic Mind* 57 (May-June 1959):
242–52. Edited for chapter 5, "Creeds at War Intelligibly: Pluralism and
the University," in *WHTT*, pp. 125–52.*

1958f "How to Think (Theologically) about War and Peace." *Catholic Messenger*
76 (December): 7–8. Also as "U.S. Policy vis-à-vis the Soviet Union."
Catholic Association for International Peace *News* 19 (December 1958):
8–10.

1959a *"Unica Status Religio."* Murray Archives, file 611.* A religious liberty
article, submitted to Rome in 1959, the third for which publication
permission was denied.

1959b "The Liberal Arts College and the Contemporary Climate of Opinion."
Murray Archives, file 605. Talk given in November, at St. Joseph's
College.

1960a *We Hold These Truths: Catholic Reflections on the American Proposition.* New York: Sheed and Ward.* Made up of previously cited articles, but also including the new additions of: chapter 3, "Two Cases for the Public Consensus: Fact or Need," pp. 79–96; chapter 4, "The Origins and Authority of the Public Consensus: A Study of the Growing End," pp. 97–123, and a further article cited in the next two entries.

1960b "Morality and Foreign Policy, Part I." *America* 102 (March 26): 729–32.

1960c "Morality and Foreign Policy, Part II." *America* 102 (March 26): 764–67. This and the previous article appeared as chapter 12, "The Doctrine Is Dead: The Problem of the Moral Vacuum," *WHTT*, pp. 273–294.*

1960d "On Raising the Religious Issue." *America* 102 (September 24): 702.*

1961a "Hopes and Misgivings for Dialogue." *America* 104 (January 14): 456–60.* Also as part of a pamphlet published as *One Fold, One Shepherd* by America Press.

1961b "The American Proposition." *Commonweal* 73 (January 20): 433–35. Transcription of an interview on "The Catholic Hour."

1961c "What Can Unite a Religiously Divided Nation?" *Catholic Messenger* 79 (April 27): 1, 4; (May 4, 1961): 4. Republished as "The Return to Tribalism." *The Catholic Mind* 60 (January 1962): 5–12.*

1962a "Method in Theology." Course outline, bibliography, and hand-written notes for a Woodstock course, 1962. Murray Archives, file 486.*

1962b Letter to Archbishop L. J. Shehan, August, 1962. Murray Archives, file 847.*

1962c "Federal Aid to Church Related Schools." *Yale Political Review* 1: 16, 29–31.*

1962d "On the Structure of the Problem of God." *TS* 23 (March): 1–26. Republished with significant editing as *The Problem of God, Yesterday and Today* (New Haven: Yale University Press, 1964).*

1962e "Le droit a l'incroyance." *Relations* (Montreal) 22 (Avril): 91–92.*

1963a "The Schema on Religious Freedom: Critical Comments." Murray Archives, file 815.* Critique of Vatican II's first two religious liberty schemas.

1963b "Remarks on the Schema on Religious Liberty." Murray Archives, file 826.* Comments on the third (Murray's) schema.

1963c Foreword to *American Pluralism and the Catholic Conscience,* by Richard J. Regan, S.J. New York: Macmillan Press.

1963d Foreword to *Religious Liberty and the America Presidency: A Study in Church-State Relations,* by Patricia Barrett. New York: Herder.

1963e *The Elite and The Electorate: Is Government by the People Possible?,* pp. 7–8. An occasional paper on the role of political process in the free society. Published by the Center for the Study of Democratic Institutions, by the Fund for the Republic. Murray commented on an article by J. William Fulbright.

1963f "Things Old and New in '*Pacem in Terris.*'" *America* 107 (April 27): 612–14.* Also published in *American Catholic Horizons,* pp. 188–94, ed. Eugene K. Culhane (New York: Doubleday, 1966); and as a portion of

Key Themes in the Encyclical 'Pacem in Terris,' a pamphlet published by America Press, 1963, pp. 57–64.

1963g "Good Pope John: A Theologian's Tribute." *America* 108 (June 15): 854–55.*

1963h "Making the News Good News!" *Interracial Review* 36 (July): 34–35, 130–31.

1963i "The Church and the Council." *America* 104 (October 19): 451–53.

1963j "On Religious Liberty." *America* 109 (November): 704–06.* Also published in *American Catholic Horizons,* pp. 219–26, ed. Eugene K. Culhane (New York: Doubleday, 1966); and as "Religionsfreiheit als Konzilsthema," in *Das Konzil: Zweiter Bildund Textbericht,* pp. 138–40, ed. Mario von Galli, [Olten (Switzerland), 1964]; and as "Liberté religieuse: la position de l' épiscopat américain," *Choisir* (1964): 14–16.

1963k "Kirche und Staat in Nordamerika." *Dokumente* 19 (December): 423–33. Republished as "Das Verhaeltnis Von Kirche und Staat in Den USA," in *Das Verhaeltnis Von Kirche und Staat: Erwaegungen Zur Vielfalt Der Gerschichtlichen Entwicklung und Gegenwaertigen Situation,* pp. 51–71, Erchter-Verlag-Wuerzburg, 1965.* English original for this article in Murray Archives, file 883.

1964a "The Nature of Theology."* A brief paper used by Murray in the introduction to his systematic courses, 1964. Murray Archives, file 415.

1964b "Commentary on the Declaration." To Archbishop Koenig. Murray Archives, file 852.*

1964c "On the Future of Humanistic Education." In *Humanistic Education and Western Civilization,* pp. 231–47. Ed. Arthur A. Cohen in Honor of the 65th birthday of Robert M. Hutchins. New York: Holt, Rinehart, and Winston.* Excerpted in *The Critic* 22 (February-March 1964): 37–43.

1964d "The Social Function of the Press." *Journalistes Catholiques* 12 (Janvier-Avril): 8–12.* Expanded form of an address to the International Press Association, 1963.

1964e "Today and Tomorrow: Conversation at the Council: John Courtney Murray, Hans Kueng, Gustave Weigel, Godfrey Diekmann, and Vincent Yzermans." *American Benedictine Review* 15 (September): 341–51.* Also published in somewhat different form under the same title in *Ave Maria* 100 (1964): 10–11.*

1964f "The Problem of Religious Freedom." *TS* 25 (December): 503–75. Published as *The Problem of Religious Freedom,* Woodstock Papers, Number 7 (Westminster, Md.: The Newman Press, 1965)*; "De kwestie van de godsdienstvrijheld op het concilie." *Documentation Hollandaise du Concile* dossiers 9, Hilversum/ Antwerp, 1965, pp. 7–83; "Le problème de la liberté religieuse," in *La liberté religieuse: exigence spirituelle et problème politique,* Paris: Edition du Centurion, 195, pp. 9–112; and "Die Religioese Freiheit und Konzil II," *Wort und Warheit* 22 (1965): 409–30, 505–36.

1965a Memo to Cushing on Contraception Legislation. Undated. Murray Archives, file 148.*

264   J. Leon Hooper, S.J.

1965b Foreword to *Freedom and Man*, pp. 11–16. Ed. John Courtney Murray. New York: P. J. Kenedy.

1965c "Religious Freedom." In *Freedom and Man*, pp. 131–40. Ed. John Courtney Murray. New York: P. J. Kenedy.*

1965d "This Matter of Religious Freedom." *America* 112 (January 9): 40–43.*

1965e Address at the reception of the Thomas Jefferson Award, March 22. Murray included atheists as legitimate conversation partners in social determination.

1965f "Osservazione sulla dichiarazione della libertà religiosa." *La Civiltà Cattolica* 116 (18 Dicembre): 536–54. Also published as "The Issue of Development of Doctrine," *Documentation Hollandaise du Concile* 206, Rome, n.d., pp. 1–7*; "La declaration sur la liberté religieuse," *Nouvelle Revue Théologique* 88 (January 1966): 41–67.

1966a "The Declaration on Religious Freedom." In *Vatican II: An Interfaith Appraisal*, article, pp. 565–76, and discussion, pp. 577–85. Ed. John H. Miller. Notre Dame: Association Press.*

1966b "The Declaration on Religious Freedom." In *War, Poverty, Freedom: The Christian Response*, pp. 3–16. Concilium, 15. New York: Paulist Press.*

1966c "The Declaration on Religious Freedom: A Moment in Its Legislative History." In *Religious Liberty: An End and a Beginning*, pp. 15–42. Ed. John Courtney Murray. New York: Macmillan and Company.*

1966d "Religious Freedom." In *The Documents of Vatican II*, introduction, pp. 673–74, and text with commentary, pp. 674–98. Ed. Walter M. Abbot and Joseph Gallagher. New York: An Angelus Book, America Press.*

1966e "The Vatican Declaration on Religious Freedom." In *The University in the American Experience*, pp. 1–10. New York: Fordham University Press.*

1966f "The Status of the Nicene Creed as Dogma." *Chicago Studies: An Archdiocesan Review* 5 (Spring): 65–80.* Delivered as a talk on ecumenism in a Lutheran-Catholic Dialogue, Baltimore, July 1965.

1966g "The Declaration on Religious Freedom: Its Deeper Significance." *America* 114 (April 23): 592–93.*

1966h "The Issue of Church and State at Vatican II." *TS* 27 (December): 580–606.*

1966i "Freedom, Authority, Community." *America* 115 (December 3): 734–41.*

1966j "On the Most Blessed Trinity." Murray Archives, file number 493.* Introductory notes to a 1966 Murray course.

1967a "Declaration on Religious Freedom." In *American Participation at the Second Vatican Council*, pp. 668–76. Ed. Vincent A. Yzermans. New York: Sheed and Ward.

1967b "Vers une intelligence du développement de la doctrine de l'Eglise sur la liberté religeuse." In *Vatican II: La Liberté Religieuse*, pp. 111–47. Ed. J. Hamer and Y. Congar. Paris: Les Editions du Cerf.* Also published as "Zum Verstaendis der Entwicklung der Lehre der Kirche ueber die Religionsfreiheit," in *Ueber die Religionsfreiheit: Lateinischer und Deutscher Text*, pp. 125–65 (Paderborn: Bonifacius Druckerei, 1967). English original for these in Murray Archives, file 880.

1967c "A Will to Community." In *Theological Freedom and Social Responsibility*, pp. 111–16. Ed. Stephen F. Bayne, Jr. New York: Seabury Press.* Also published as "We Held These Truths," *The National Catholic Reporter* 3 (August 23, 1967): 3.

1967d Review of *Academic Freedom and the Catholic University*, by Edward Manier and John W. Houch (South Bend, Ind.: Fides Publishers, 1967). *AAUP Bulletin* 53: 339–42.

1967e "The Death of God." Address at the University of Connecticut, January 10. Murray Archives, file 529.*

1967f "Religious Liberty and Development of Doctrine." *The Catholic World* 204 (February): 277–83.*

1967g "Our Response to the Ecumenical Revolution." *Religious Education* 42 (March-April): 91–92.*

1967h Review of *The Garden and the Wilderness: Religion and Government in American Constitutional History*, by M. D. Howe (Chicago: University of Chicago Press, 1965), *Yale Law Review* 76 (April): 1030–35.

1967i "Murray Says Church Was Too Sure." *The National Catholic Reporter* 3 (May 17): 3.* Report of Murray's Toledo address, May 5, 1967, supporting the majority report on birth control.

1967j "Where the Church Went Too Far." Murray Archives, file number 544.* A typewritten compilation of reports from *The Tablet*, May 20, 1967, and the *Advocate*, May 26, 1967.

1967k *Selective Conscientious Objection.* Published in pamphlet form by Our Sunday Visitor.* The text of an address at Western Maryland College, June 4, 1967.

1967l "Freedom in the Age of Renewal." *American Benedictine Review* 18 (September): 319–24.

1967m "The Danger of the Vows: An Encounter with Earth, Woman and the Spirit." *Woodstock Letters* 116 (Fall): 421–27.

1968 "De argumentis pro iure hominis ad libertatem religiosam," in *Acta Congressus Internationalis de Theologia Concilii Vaticani II*, ed. A. Schoenmetzer (Rom, 26 Sept.—1 Okt, 1966) (Rom, Vatikan), pp. 562–573.* From a conference in Sept. 1966.

1969 "The Unbelief of the Christian." In *The Presence and Absence of God*, pp. 69–83. New York: Fordham University Press.*

1970 "La libertà religiosa e l'ateo." *L'ateismo contemporaneo* 4: 109–117. English original in Murray Archives, file 325.*

II. Works on Murray and Works Cited

Adler, Mortimer.
    1941 "The Order of Learning." *Catholic School Journal* 41: 334–36.
Barker, Sir Ernest.
    1948 *Traditions of Civility: Eight Essays.* Cambridge: Cambridge University Press.
Bates, M. Searle.
    1945 *Religious Liberty: An Inquiry.* New York: International Missionary Council.

Baum, Gregory.
    1966 "Declaration on Religious Freedom—Development of Its Doctrinal Basis." *The Ecumenist* 4 (September-October): 121–26.
    1975 *Religion and Alienation: A Theological Reading of Sociology.* New York: Paulist Press.
Berle, Adolf A.
    1959 *Power Without Property.* New York: Harcourt, Brace.
Bévenot, Maurice.
    1942 "No Common Christian Basis?" *Clergy Review* 22 (June): 266–69.
    1954 "Thesis and Hypothesis." *TS* 15 (September): 440–46.
Bowie, W. Russell.
    1949 "The Catholic Position." *The American Mercury* 69 (September): 261–73; (November): 637.
Burgess, Faith E. R.
    1971 *Ecclesia et Status: The Relationship Between Church and State According to John Courtney Murray, S.J.* Duesseldorf: Stehle.
Burghardt, Walter J.
    1967 "A Eulogy." *Woodstock Letters* 96: 416–20.
    1969 "From Certainty to Understanding." *Catholic Mind* 67 (June): 13–27.
    1976 *Religious Freedom: 1965–1975.* New York: Paulist Press.
    1985 "Who Chilled the Beaujolais?" *America* 153 (November 30): 360–63.
Burke, Eugene.
    1980 "A Personal Memoir on the Origins of the CTSA." *Proceedings* of the Thirty-Fifth Convention of the Catholic Theological Society of America, June 11–14, 1980, San Francisco. Vol. 35, pp. 337–45.
Butterfield, William.
    1942 "Co-operation with Non-Catholics." *Clergy Review* 22 (April): 160–65.
Canavan, Francis J.
    1982 "Murray on Vatican II's Declaration on Religious Freedom." *Communio* 9 (Winter): 404–5.
Carrillo De Albornoz, A. F.
    1959 *Roman Catholicism and Religious Liberty.* Geneva: World Council of Churches.
    1963 *The Basis of Religious Liberty.* New York: Association Press.
    1965 "Religious Freedom: Intrinsic or Fortuitous?" *Christian Century* 82 (September 15): 1122–26.
    1967 *Religious Liberty.* Trans. John Drury. New York: Sheed and Ward.
Cogley, John.
    1956 "In Praise of Father Murray." *Commonweal* 65 (December 7): 253.
Coleman, John A.
    1976 "Vision and Praxis in American Theology: Orestes Brownson, John A. Ryan, and John Courtney Murray." *TS* 37 (March): 3–40.
    1979 "A Possible Role for Biblical Religion in Public Life," *TS* 37 (December): 705.
Connell, Francis J.
    1941 "Catholics and Interfaith Groups." *The American Ecclesiastical Review* 105 (November): 336–53.

Cuddihy, John Murray.
  1979 *No Offense: Civil Religion and Protestant Taste*, pp. 64–100. New York: Seabury Press.
Curran, Charles E.
  1982 "John Courtney Murray." In *American Catholic Social Ethics: Twentieth-Century Approaches*, pp. 172–232. Notre Dame: University of Notre Dame Press.
Dawson, Christopher.
  1933 *Enquiries into Religion and Culture*. New York: Sheed and Ward.
  1938 *Beyond Politics*. New York: Sheed and Ward.
  1942 *The Judgment of Nations*. New York: Sheed and Ward.
  1950 *Religion and the Rise of Western Culture*. New York: Sheed and Ward.
  1960 *America and the Secularization of Modern Culture*. Houston: University of St. Thomas.
Deedy, John.
  1978 *Seven American Catholics*, pp. 125–53. Chicago: Thomas More Press.
Finn, James.
  1984 "Pacifism, Just War, and the Bishops' Muddle." *This World* 7 (Winter): 31–42.
Fischer, John.
  1956 "Editor's Easy Chair." *Harper's* 213 (October): 14, 16–18, 20.
Flaherty, Daniel L.
  1966 "Christian Marxist Dialogue." *America* 115 (December 17): 805.
Friedrich, Carl Joachim.
  1954 *From the Declaration of Independence to the Constitution: The Roots of American Constitutionalism*. New York: The Liberal Press.
Furfey, Paul Hanley.
  1942 *History of Social Thought*. New York: The Macmillan Co.
  1943 "To the Editors." *TS* 4 (September): 474.
Goerner, Edward A.
  1965 *Peter and Caesar: Political Authority and the Catholic Church*. New York: Herder and Herder.
Greene, Theodore M.
  1953 "The Middle of the Road: A Liberal Protestant Interpretation." *The Yale Scientific Magazine* 23 (February): 9, 10, 20, 26, 28.
Gustafson, James M.
  1975 *Can Ethics Be Christian*. Chicago: University of Chicago Press.
  1978 *Protestant and Roman Catholic Ethics: Prospects for Rapprochement*. Chicago: University of Chicago Press.
Hales, E.E.Y.
  1958 *The Catholic Church in the Modern World*. London: Burns and Oates.
Hehir, J. Bryan.
  1976 "Issues in Church and State: A Catholic Perspective." In *Issues in Church and State: Proceedings of a Dialogue between Catholics and Baptists*, pp. 81–95. Ed. Claude U. Broach. Winston-Salem, N.C.: Ecumenical Institute.
  1985 "The Unfinished Agenda." *America* 153 (November 30):386–87, 392.

Herberg, Will.
  1955 *Catholic, Protestant, Jew.* New York: Doubleday and Company.
Higgins, George G.
  1985 "Some Personal Recollections." *America* 153 (November 30): 380-86.
Hock, Raymond Anthony.
  1964 "The Pluralism of John Courtney Murray, S.J., and Its Relationship
         to Education." Dissertation, Stanford University.
Hofstadter, Richard, and Walter Metzger.
  1955 *The Development of Academic Freedom in the United States.* New York:
         Columbia University Press, 1955.
Hollenbach, David.
  1976 "Public Theology in America: Some Questions for Catholicism after
         John Courtney Murray." *TS* 37 (June): 290-303.
  1985 "The Growing End of an Argument." *America* 153 (November 30):
         362-66.
Hollenbach, David, Robin W. Lovin, John A. Coleman, J. Bryan Hehir.
  1979 "Theology and Philosophy in Public: A Symposium on John Courtney
         Murray's Unfinished Agenda." *TS* 40 (December): 700-15.
Johnson, E. Ernest.
  1944 *Religion and the World Order.* New York: Harper and Brothers.
Kossel, Glifford George.
  1984 "Religious Freedom and the Church: J. C. Murray." *Communio* 11
         (Spring): 60-74.
Krause, Edward C.
  1975 "Democratic Process in the Thought of John Courtney Murray and
         Reinhold Niebuhr." Dissertation, Boston University.
Lawler, Peter Augustine.
  1982 "Natural Law and the American Regime: Murray's *We Hold These
         Truths.*" *Communio* 9 (Winter): 368-88.
Lindbeck, George A.
  1961 "John Courtney Murray, S.J.: An Evaluation." *Christianity and Crisis* 21
         (November 27): 213-16.
Lippmann, Walter.
  1922 *Public Opinion.* New York: Hartcourt Brace and Company.
  1955 *Essays in Public Philosophy.* Boston: Little, Brown.
Lonergan, Bernard.
  1941 "St. Thomas' Thought on *Gratia Operans*," *TS*, 2 (1941): 289-324; 3
         (1942): 69-88, 375-402, 533-574.
  1958 *Insight.* New York: Philosophical Library.
  1972 *Method in Theology.* New York: Herder and Herder.
  1974 *A Second Collection.* Ed. William Ryan and Bernard Tyrrell. Philadelphia:
         The Westminster Press.
Love, Thomas T.
  1965a *John Courtney Murray: Contemporary Church-State Theory.* New York:
         Doubleday.
  1965b "John Courtney Murray: Liberal Roman Catholic Church-State
         Theory." *Journal of Religion* 45 (July): 211-24.
  1965c "The Problem of Religious Freedom." *Journal of Church and State* 8
         (Autumn): 475-77.

1967 "John Courtney Murray." In *Modern Theologians: Christians and Jews*, pp. 18–39. Ed. T. E. Bird. Notre Dame: University of Notre Dame Press.

Lovin, Robin W.

1978 "The Constitution as Covenant: The Moral Foundations of Democracy and the Practice of Desegregation." Dissertation, Harvard University.

MacIver, Robert M.

1954 Correspondence with Murray. See Murray 1954a listing for the latter's responses.

#1. October 19, 1951: MacIver to Murray (MacIver 1954, #1): introduction.

#2. March 31, 1952: MacIver to Murray (MacIver 1954, #2): comments on Murray's critique of a first statement on religious liberty, neither of which is on file.

#4. April 22, 1952: MacIver to Murray (MacIver 1954, #4): brief comment on Murray's April 17 letter.

#6. August 26, 1952: MacIver to Murray (MacIver 1954, #6): MacIver's case for scientific starting point.

#9. February 11, 1954: MacIver to Murray (MacIver 1954, #9): MacIver states that Murray was the only one who substantially objected to the Project's finished product.

#11. May 5, 1954: MacIver to Murray (MacIver 1954, #11).

1955 *Academic Freedom in Our Time*. New York: Columbia University Press.

McEnroy, Rayman Owen.

1973 *John Courtney Murray's Thought on Religious Liberty in Its Final Phase*. Rome: Pontifical Lateran University.

McManus, William E.

1895 "Memories of Murray." *America* 153 (November 30): 366–68.

McNearney, Clayton Leroy.

1970 "The Roman Catholic Response to the Writings of Paul Blanshard." Dissertation, University of Iowa.

Maritain, Jacques.

1930 *The Things That Are Not Caesar's*. Trans. J. F. Scanlan. New York: Charles Scribner's Sons.

1943a *Education at the Crossroads*. New Haven: Yale University Press.

1943b *The Rights of Man and Natural Law*. Trans. Doric C. Anson. New York: Scribners.

1947a *Christianity and Democracy*. Trans. Doris C. Anson. New York: Charles Scribner's Sons.

1947b *The Person and the Common Good*. Trans. John J. Fitzgerald. New York: Charles Scribner's Sons.

1951 *Man and the State*. Chicago: University of Chicago Press.

Marsden, George M.

1980 *Fundamentalism and American Culture: The Shaping of Twentieth-Century Evangelism: 1870–1925*. New York, Oxford: Oxford University Press.

May, Joseph R.

1958 *The State and the Law of Christ*. Rome: Ponta Grossa.

Mechling, Jay (Ed.).
   1978   *Church, State, and Public Policy: The New Shape of the Church-State Debate.* Washington, D.C.: American Enterprise Institute for Public Policy Research.

Moody, Joseph N.
   1961   "Leo XIII and the Social Crisis." In *Leo XIII and the Modern World.* Ed. Edward T. Gargan. New York: Sheed and Ward.

Morrison, Charles Clayton.
   1947a "Reply to a Taunt." *Christian Century* 64 (November 19): 1391-93.

   1947b "The Meaning of 'Separation.'" *Christian Century* 64 (November 26): 1447-48.

   1947c "Getting Down to Cases." *Christian Century* 64 (December 10): 1512-14.

Niebuhr, H. Richard.
   1951   *Christ and Culture.* New York: Harper and Row,

   1957   *The Social Sources of Denominationalism.* New York and Cleveland: Meridian Books.

   1959   *The Kingdom of God in America.* New York: Harper Torchbooks.

   1963   *The Responsible Self.* New York: Harper and Row.

   1970   *Radical Monotheism and Western Culture.* New York: Harper Torchbooks, [1943].

Niebuhr, Reinhold.
   1932   *Moral Man and Immoral Society.* New York: Charles Scribner's Sons.

   1965   *Man's Nature and His Communities.* New York: Charles Scribner's Sons.

Novak, Michael.
   1966   "Moral Society and Immoral Man." In *Church-State Relations in Ecumenical Perspective,* pp. 92-112. Ed. Elwyn A. Smith. Pittsburgh: Duquesne University Press.

O'Collins, Gerald S.
   1984   "Murray and Ottaviani." *America* 151 (November):287-88.

Ottaviani, Alfredo Cardinal.
   1953   "Church and State: Some Present Problems in Light of the Teachings of Pope Pius XII." *The American Ecclesiastical Review* 128 (May): 321-34.

Palmer, T. Vail.
   1965   "Eschatology and Foreign Policy in the Thought of Reinhold Niebuhr, William Ernest Hocking, and John Courtney Murray." Dissertation, University of Chicago Divinity School.

Pavan, Pietro.
   1966   "The Right to Religious Freedom in the Conciliar Declaration." In *Religious Freedom,* pp. 37-52. Concilium 18. New York: Paulist Press.

   1959   "Declaration on Religious Freedom." In *Commentary on the Documents of Vatican II,* IV, pp. 49-86. Ed. Herbert Vorgrimler. New York: Herder and Herder.

Pelotte, Donald E.
   1976   *John Courtney Murray: Theologian in Conflict.* New York: Paulist Press.

Pribilla, Max.
   1949   "Dogmatische Intoleranz und burgerliche Tolerranz." *Stimmen der Zeit* (April): 27-40.

Protestants and Other Americans United.

1948 "Separation of Church and State: A Manifesto by 'Protestants and Other Americans United.'" *The Christian Century* 65 (January 21): 79–82.

Regan, Richard.

1967 *Conflict and Consensus.* New York: Macmillan Company.

Rielly, J. E.

1961 "Contemporary Catholic Thought on Church and State: An Analysis of the Work of Jacques Maritain and John Courtney Murray." Dissertation, Harvard University.

Rohr, John A.

1966 "Murray and the Critiques." *Continuum* 4 (Spring 1966): 734–42.

1978 "John Courtney Murray's Theology of Our Founding Fathers' 'Faith': Freedom." In *Christian Spirituality in the United States: Independence and Interdependence,* pp. 1–30. Ed. Francis A. Eigo. Villanova, Penna.: Villanova University Press.

1985 "John Courtney Murray and the Pastoral Letter." *America* 153 (November 30): 373–79.

Rommen, Heinrich.

1945 *The State in Catholic Thought: A Treatise on Political Philosophy.* St. Louis: B. Herder Book Company.

1947 *The Natural Law: A Study in Legal and Social History and Philosophy.* Trans. Thomas R. Hanly. St. Louis: B. Herder.

1950 "Church and State." *The Review of Politics* 12: 321–40.

1954 "The Church and Human Rights." In *The Catholic Church in World Affairs,* pp. 115–53. Ed. Waldemar Gurian and M. A. Fitzsimmons. South Bend, Indiana: University of Notre Dame Press.

Rossiter, Clinton.

1953 *Seedtime of the Republic.* New York: Harcourt, Brace and Company.

Ryan, John A., and Francis J. Boland.

1940 *Catholic Principles of Politics.* New York: The Macmillan Company.

Sanders, Thomas G.

1965 *Protestant Concepts of Church and State.* Garden City, New York: Doubleday and Company.

Sebott, Reinhold.

1977 *Religionsfreiheit und Verhaeltnis von Kirche und Staat: Der Beitrag John Courtney Murrays zu einer modernen Frage.* Rome: Università Gregoriana Editrice.

Shea, George W.

1950 "Catholic Doctrine and 'The Religion of the State'." *The American Ecclesiastical Review* 123 (September): 161–74.

Smith, Elwyn A.

1972 *Religious Liberty in the United States: The Development of Church-State Thought Since the Revolutionary Era.* Philadelphia: Fortress Press.

Smith, Homer W.

1949 "Objectives and Objectivity in Science: A Naturalist Interpretation." *The Yale Scientific Magazine* 23 (February): 7, 8, 16, 18, 28.

Sturzo, Luigi.
  1939 *Church and State.* New York: Longmans, Green and Company.
  1946 *Nationalism and Internationalism.* New York: Roy.
Tinnelly, J. T.
  1961 "The Challenge of John Courtney Murray: Can an American Public Philosophy be Stated." *Catholic Lawyer* 7: 270–96.
Whelan, Charles M.
  1985 "The Enduring Problems of Religious Liberty." *America* 153 (November 30): 368–72.
"The Wisconsin Bus Bill"
  1946 "The Wisconsin Bus Bill." *The Christian Century* 63 (October 30): 1302–3.

INDEX

Academic community: civil, 70, 85–87, 99, 102–3; theological, 187–88, 190–92. *See also* Education, American; Theology

American Catholic Right: 60–62 *passim*, 88, 104–5, 109

Arius: 138, 163, 170

Atheism: rejection of, 25, 41, 45, 46–47, 165–68; Continental, 60, 66–67, 165, 167, 227; scientist, 93, 113–14, 165; dialogue with, 159–60, 168–75, 212, 251. *See also* Existentialism; Marxism; Scientism; Secularism

Attentiveness: *see* Cognitional operations; *and under* Responsibility

Authority, civil: state's, 35–40 *passim*, 68, 72, 230–31; people's, *see* Authorization principle

Authority, ecclesiastical: 10; control over lay action, 17–18, 22, 28–29; as spiritual, 42, 53–58; giving principles, 16–17, 74, 237; requiring humility, 147, 160; classicist, 179, 253; analogically understood, 181–83; serving freedom, 183–90; judgment function of, 191–93. *See also* Church, mission of

Authorization principle: definitions and specifications, 68–69, 74–75, 80, 95–96; in American debates, 82–92 *passim*, 105–8, 114–15; linked to consensus theory, 97–100; as constructive ethical agency, 96–97, 157ff, 182–83; and relativism, 115–20; in Murray's later arguments, 121, 155, 181, 188–89

Autonomy, moral: violation of, 20, 63, 169; absolute, 36f, 64, 66, 102. *See also under* Intermediate groups; Laymen; Temporal order; Theology

Bates, M. Searle: 83–84, 228, 229

Bea, Augustin Cardinal: 123

Belief and unbelief: 170–75, 188

Beliefs: indifferentistic, 13, 20, 226; natural, 24–25, 40, 228; as social perspectives, 89–90, 109–10. *See also* Faith, Perspectives

Bellarmine, Robert: 53–55, 72, 233

Benedict XV: 227

Berle, Adolf: 97

Bias: of arguments, 5–7, 14, 127, 149, 246; of groups, 213–16, 219, 220–21, 224

Birth control: 88, 90–91, 179–80, 253

Bishops: in '40s arguments, 12–18 *passim*, 27f; in '60s arguments, 158, 183f, 187, 191–92. *See also* Magisterium

Blanshard, Paul: 102

Bowie, W. Russell: 101f

Burgess, Faith: 202, 254

Catholic education: *see under* Education, American

Censorship: 86–89, 104–5, 116, 241, 243, 244

Church, mission of: toward common good, 11–20 *passim*, 44–45, 77ff, 80, 109–10, 126, 129, 135–36, 226; preserve integrity, 13–14,

273

Group bias: *see under* Bias
Gustafson, James: 197

Harmony: between philosophy and
theology, 32, 45, 228; goal of
social action, 38–45 *passim*, 64,
68, 73–74. *See also* Peace
Herberg, Will: 86
Heresy: defined according to
content, 20, 58, 85; contains
truth, 179; according to
intentionality, 188, 193, 237
Historical Consciousness: vs.
classicism, 137–39, 161, 248–49;
as church perspectival shift,
137–38, 142, 154–55, 176–80
passim, 191, 247. *See also*
Doctrine, development of
Historical method: 30, 51–52,
229
Historicism: 84, 115–17, 202–3,
213, 255. *See also* Relativism
Historicity: 8, 115–17, 139, 161,
189–90, 194, 195–96, 201–2,
243. *See also* Contingency;
Emergence; *and under*
Consensus; Rights
History, dualism of: 172–73,
210
Hollenbach, David: 250
Holy Spirit: 21, 110, 172, 174f,
216
Human Dignity: individualistically
understood, 35, 144, 146, 232,
247; socially understood, 129,
132–37 *passim*, 149–53, 173, 179,
217; basing ethical obligations,
4, 151–53, 182, 185, 199, 220

Ideal specifications: 14, 31,
42–43, 60, 72–74 *passim*, 126–27,
138; Murray's argument
against, 62, 71f, 236
Ideological critique: 195–97;
examples of 6–7, 10, 49, 199,
205, 208–9, 212–13, 219, 226.
See also Bias; Dialectics

Indifferentism: 13–27 *passim*,
226
Indirect powers: *see* Powers,
church's
Individualism: philosophical,
36–37, 52, 97, 144–45, 147–48,
199, 241; Murray's, 47–49,
76–80 *passim*, 198, 230, 238;
theological, 106-7, 146–47, 238,
244
Institutions: need for, 15–16,
42–43, 73, 228. *See* Necessary
institutions, *and under* Common
good; Contingency; Grace
Intentionality: *see*
Questions; *and under* Love;
Principles, types; Reason
Intercredal cooperation:
structural goals of, 11–17 *passim*,
217, 228; forms of, 12;
authoritative appeals for, 12–17
passim; "spiritual" goals of, 15,
23–25; collapse of Murray's
argument, 26–29; benefits for
Murray's thought, 29–30,
49–50; in theological matters,
161–65. *See also* Bishops;
Indifferentism; Laymen; Priests.
Intermediate groups: 39, 61,
60–70, 151f, 186–87, 231, 249;
autonomy of, 47–48, 69, 80,
245. *See under* Common good,
agents of; Rights, holders of
Intolerance: 46–47, 64, 70ff,
141; as ideal 72–74 *passim*,
126–27, 236. *See also*
Establishment
Irrationalism: 92, 109–14
passim

Jacobinism: 66f, 74, 238
John of Paris: 55–56, 72
John of Salisbury: 114
John XXIII: on the state, 130; on
human dignity, 132, 141, 150,
153; on social freedom, 135,
152; call for dialogue, 158, 174;
on Marxism, 167–68

intermediate groups, 39, 69ff,
85, 100, 220, 231, 244; non-
Catholics, 41, 46–47, 239;
individuals, 40–42, 68; state,
40–41, 58, 69f, 72, 147;
members within the church,
181–82, 186–90
Rommen, Heinrich: 240

Sanders, Thomas G.: 239, 244
Scholasticism: *see under*
Theology
Scientism: 86, 92–95 *passim*,
102f, 111–14 *passim*, 171–72,
177f, 214, 255
Secularism: as enemy, 30, 67,
143, 165, 167, 205; in American
debates, 84–85, 101–5 *passim*,
239, 244
Self-interest: 99, 106–7
Separation, interpretations of:
Murray's, 44, 64, 72–75 *passim*;
Third Republic's, 66–67, 71f;
Protestant, 83–84, 100, 239, 244
Shea, George W.: 61f
Sin: 159–60, 166, 175, 186, 188,
212, 215
Smith, Homer W.: 93
Social consciousness:
gnosis/agnosis, 170–72, 210–11,
223. *See* Consensus, contents of
Social discourse: 2; to evoke
moral maturity, 8, 204, 222;
necessity of, 50, 88–89, 105,
112–13, 157–58, 163, 181,
186–87; as self-correcting, 4,
202–3, 208f, 219, 254, 255;
dispositional determinants of, 6,
104, 111, *see also* Bias, group. *See
under* Equality; Protestantism
Social dualism: theologically
based, 40–43, 54f, 78, 114, 121,
128, 168, 237f; defining powers,
53–58; used to critique
opponents, 63–64, 72–74, 102,
145–46, 172; used to interpret
history, 130–33, 141–42,

167–69, 237. *See also* Primacy of
spiritual; Temporal order,
autonomy of; Gelasian; *and under*
Church, mission;
Differentiations; Rights, based
Social ethics: 2–7, 37f, 89–90,
216–24. *See also* Social discourse,
and under Consensus;
Experience; Maturity
Social ontology: 77, 127, 150–52,
238. *See also* Realism
Society: definitions of, 52, 54,
61–62, 76–80. *See also* People;
Authorization, *and under*
Differentiations
Spellman, Francis Cardinal: 123
Spiritual means: *See* Power,
church's
Spiritual order: vs. temporal,
15, 77–80. *See also* Primacy of
spiritual; Spirituality; *and under*
Intercredal cooperation;
Transcendence
Spiritual power: *See*
Empowerment; Freedom; Grace;
Authorization; Power, church's;
God's; Moral agency
Spirituality: Catholic lay,
19–22; natural law, 24–29
passim, 62–63; *See also* God,
encountered
State, definitions of:
essentialistic, paternalistic,
personified, classical, ethical,
36–47 *passim*, 63, 70, 80, 130–32;
autonomous, 40, 55–58 *passim*,
66, 68; mature/immature, 54–59
passim, 79; empowering, 69–70,
151ff; juridical, *see* Law, civil:
limits of; constitutional, *see*
Constitutionalism. *See also*
Totalitarianism; Democracy; *and
under* Authority, civil; Common
good, agents; Power; Rights,
holders
Studium: *see* Academic
community